HISTORY O
NORWAY

JOHN A. YILEK

Wasteland Press

www.wastelandpress.net
Shelbyville, KY USA

History of Norway
by John A. Yilek

Revised Edition – August 2018
ISBN: 978-1-68111-024-0
Library of Congress Control Number: 2015935290

Printed in the U.S.A.

0   1   2   3   4

Also by this author – *Stories of Norway*, 2018

The author thanks the Skott and Sagmo families for their generous
hospitality on his visits to Norway. *Tusen takk!*

CONTENTS

AUTHOR'S NOTE 1

CHAPTER ONE: *The First Norwegians — and the Sami* 3
The Ice Age and the Stone Age in Norway / The Sami / Rock art / Proto-Norse society before AD 700 / Age of Migration / Longhouses

CHAPTER TWO: *The Vikings of Norway* 17
The Vikings attack England and Scotland / Ireland / France / Spain and the Mediterranean / Areas of Viking expansion / The meaning of "Vikings" / Reasons for the Viking expansion / Viking ships and navigation / The Vikings at home / Marketplaces / Ottar's voyages / Norwegian Viking settlements / Normandy / Iceland / Greenland / North America

CHAPTER THREE: *Unification, Civil Wars, and the Age of Greatness* 45
Harald Fairhair / From Håkon the Good to Danish rule / Olav Tryggvason / St. Olav / Harald Hardråde / Stamford Bridge / Civil wars / Sverre and the Birkebeinere / The Age of Greatness / The northern border regions and the Sami / Changes in the countryside, along the coast, and in the cities and towns

CHAPTER FOUR: *Norway's Decline* 79
The Black Death / The Hanseatic merchants / Pietro Querini / Queen Margrete / The Reformation / Swedish wars / Mining and society in Røros / Norway in 1700 / Changes in Sami life and customs

CHAPTER FIVE: *Norway in 1814* 107
Challenges, protests, and rebellions / The Danish king and his court / The Napoleonic Wars / High society / The Continental System, war, and blockade / Changes in Sweden affecting Norway / Swedish diplomacy / Napoleon's invasion of Russia / Christian Frederik to Norway / From Leipzig to Kiel / Norwegian reaction to Kiel / The first Eidsvoll meetings and the proclamation / The Eidsvoll assembly /

Provisions of the Eidsvoll Constitution / The reaction of the Great Powers and Sweden / The Swedish invasion and the Moss Convention / The first Storting and the union with Sweden / The economy after the war / Constitutional issues / Foreign relations and the Bodø affair / Syttende mai

CHAPTER SIX: *From Nationalism to Independence* 153
Edvard Grieg / The new Norwegian language / The great upheaval / Nybrottsmannen – the man who clears the land / On to northern Norway and the cities / Emigration from Norway to America / Parliamentary democracy / Norwegianization of the Sami / Polar explorers / Independence in 1905 / New royal family / After 1905 / The Great War / The Labor Party

CHAPTER SEVEN: *World War II in Norway* 191
Neutrality and disarmament in the interwar years / Prelude to war in Norway / Invasion / German advances throughout Norway / German and NS administration of Norway / Police state / Norway's government-in-exile / Norwegian military resistance / Austvågøy / Telavåg / Heavy water sabotage / The Oslo Gang / Scorched earth / White buses / Liberation

CHAPTER EIGHT: *To the Present Day* 241
Norway's economy / Immigration / Sami rights / Foreign and defense policy

BIBLIOGRAPHY 251

LIST OF ILLUSTRATIONS 259

INDEX 261

AUTHOR'S NOTE

This book is the first comprehensive history of Norway by an author from an English-speaking country in several decades. Apart from the occasional book or article about the Vikings, emigration from Norway to America, or World War II, the vast majority of publications about Norway's past were written in Norwegian and are not accessible to almost all English speakers outside of Scandinavia. And yet Norway has a unique, rich and varied history that should be of interest to readers of nonfiction, tourists, diplomats, business people, teachers, professors, researchers, students, and the millions of people of Scandinavian descent in the United States, Canada, Great Britain, and the rest of the world.

Therefore, I have written this book to provide a clear, informative and up-to-date history of Norway in the English language, based largely on both old and new sources from Norway. In order to present a concise, engaging narrative, I have focused on the most significant people and events in Norwegian history, and I have included many fascinating stories. My main objective is to give the reader a fundamental understanding of Norway's history in just a few hours of reading time.

Throughout the book, I have generally used Norwegian spelling of names, places, and various other terms related to Norway. In describing people and events before totally-accurate historical records were kept (that is, before about AD 1300), I have tried to separate fact from fiction in providing an interesting, readable account rather than a scholarly debate.

I hope that you, the reader, will enjoy my story of Norway.

CHAPTER ONE:

The First Norwegians — and the Sami

This introductory chapter discusses where the Norwegians and the Sami came from, and how the society and culture of the Norwegians developed over thousands of years before the age of the Vikings.

The Ice Age and the Stone Age in Norway

Much of Europe and all of Scandinavia were covered by glaciers, ice, and snow in the final Ice Age, which lasted until about 10,000 BC. In some places the ice sheet was almost ten thousand feet deep. So it was virtually impossible for man or beast to survive in such a climate, except perhaps for polar bears and other Arctic and sea creatures that could withstand the frigid, barren conditions. Therefore, during the last Ice Age, the early Europeans lived primarily in the south near the Mediterranean Sea where the land was ice-free.

As temperatures rose near the end of the Ice Age, the ice began to recede, and over hundreds of years new forests and grasslands gradually spread to northern Europe, including the coastlines of Scandinavia. At the same time, reindeer, moose, and fur-bearing animals started to trek northward. They were pursued by human hunters and their families, who became the first inhabitants of Norway after the Ice Age.

While some of these early people in Norway came from the south through what is now Denmark and Sweden, others came from the east through Russia and Finland. Still others approached Norway from a lost land mass called Doggerland that was located between Norway and Britain in the North Sea. It was a hazardous journey across land, ice, and sea to the relatively inhospitable land in the Far North.

Most of the early settlers lived along the coast of Norway, but some ventured inland to the valleys and even the mountains, where traces of ancient human activity have been found. The oldest evidence of humans in Norway consists of bones and flint from about 10,500 BC at a place called Blomvåg near Bergen.

The period of time after the Ice Age is commonly called the Stone Age because the people used stone implements before the introduction of bronze and iron. The tools and weapons were made of quartz and flint, but also bone, antlers, and tusks. The people were so-called hunter-gatherers. That is, they lived by hunting and trapping wild animals such as reindeer, moose, boar, seal, bear, and squirrel, by catching cod and other fish, and by gathering berries, nuts, and roots from the forests and meadows. They hunted with bow and arrow, axes, and knives. This was long before the introduction of livestock and crop farming in Norway. By 8000 BC there was a rapid withdrawal of the ice, and almost the entire coastline of Norway was sparsely settled.

Archeologists have identified various groups of the early settlers, and they refer to those groups as cultures. The Komsa culture lived in Troms and Finnmark in northern Norway beginning in about 10,000 BC. They were hunter-gatherers who used quartz weapons and tools. They were also skillful boat builders in a primarily maritime society along the coast, so the tradition of Norwegian seafaring started already in the early Stone Age. Some of the early settlers were even artists as evidenced by the petroglyphs or rock carvings that they left behind. The Komsa culture seems to have had cultural ties to a later group of people called the Sami, the indigenous people of northern Scandinavia and Russia, who were most likely their descendants.

Traces of an ancient culture called Fosna, possibly related to Komsa, have been found farther south along the west and south coasts of Norway. This group of people may have come from Doggerland in the North Sea. The land mass called Doggerland gradually became smaller as the ice melted and the oceans rose, and it was fully submerged in about 6000 BC after a massive undersea landslide and tsunami called the Storegga Slide. In contrast to the Komsa culture that made tools and weapons out of quartz, the people of the Fosna culture used flint in their tools, axes, and arrowheads.

The next significant Stone Age group in Norway was the Nøstvet culture, which lived along the coast between Oslo and Trondheim from about 6200 to 3200 BC. Whereas the earlier cultures were essentially nomadic in that they moved from place to place, in the Nøstvet culture we find evidence of stationary settlements that grew over time. The Nøstvet people were still hunter-gatherers. However, there is also evidence of very basic livestock and crop farming by another group of people called the Funnel Beaker culture near the Oslofjord beginning in about 4000 BC. The first farmers grew crops by use of the slash and burn method. That is, they cut down and burned part of the forest to fertilize the soil with ash, and then they raised crops on the land until the soil was exhausted after a few years, at which point they started the process over again in another part of the forest.

The people of the Battle Axe culture arrived in southern Norway from Sweden in about 2800 BC, and their culture and society developed throughout the Bronze Age and the Iron Age over the next 3,500 years. They might be considered the first true Norwegians, a comparatively tall and mostly blond-haired people who spoke an Indo-European language that eventually became known as Germanic. Today the Germanic family of languages includes Norwegian, Swedish, Danish, Icelandic, German, Dutch, and English. These early people are called the Battle Axe culture because they produced elegant, polished axes made of colored stone. They were also responsible for introducing bronze technology in Norway so that tools and weapons could be made of metal. They even had a bronze musical instrument called a *lur* that sounded like a modern brass instrument. Since bronze is an alloy of tin and copper, these people must have traded products with people in other lands because tin is not available in Norway. In fact, they also imported jewelry, tools, and weapons from other parts of Europe.

These earliest Norwegians were engaged in more systematic, permanent livestock and crop farming, and their agricultural methods eventually spread to the rest of Norway. They herded domesticated pigs, cattle, sheep, and goats, and they raised barley, oats, and wheat, much like their descendants in Norway over the following thousands of years. Their culture also included religious practices and ceremonies, as shown by their burial mounds that can be found in southern Norway. The burial mounds were apparently reserved for the leading members of society, so there was already a class system in place that differentiated between the wealthiest and most powerful upper class and the rest of the people.

The first written description of Norway and the Norwegians was provided by Pytheas, a Greek geographer and explorer from Marseilles in the south of France. He made a historic voyage to Britain and northern Europe in about 325 BC. Sailing for six days north of Britain to a place called Thule near the frozen sea, he described a land of the midnight sun where the sun did not set in the summer. Pytheas spent the summer in this place, which was probably somewhere along the west coast of Norway north of present-day Trondheim. He described people who lived on oats, vegetables, wild fruit, and roots, and who brewed a drink of grain and honey that was apparently an early Norwegian version of mead or beer.

The Sami

While the earliest Norwegians were developing their culture and society mostly in southern and central Norway, another important group of people migrated to northern Norway. They probably originated on the west side of the Ural Mountains of Russia and made their way to northern Scandinavia. Once they finally reached their destination, they intermixed with the existing descendants of the Komsa culture. The result was the Sami, the indigenous people of northern Norway and adjacent areas. There is evidence of Sami culture in Norway dating back to at least 1000 BC and perhaps as early as 2000 BC.

The Sami speak several dialects of their own distinctive Finno-Ugric language, which is related to Finnish, Estonian, and Hungarian but not to the Germanic languages. At first, they were hunter-gatherers, and many of them engaged in seasonal migration, following herds of wild reindeer between the coast and the mountains. The Sami made boats to fish and to hunt seal, walrus, and even whales. At an early stage, they had contact with the Norwegians whose settlements gradually spread northward up the west coast. It was the Norwegians who apparently taught agriculture to the Sami, although most of the Sami seemed to be content as hunters, trappers, and fishermen.

Like the other ancient cultures, the earliest Sami first used stone, bone, tusks, and antlers to make their tools and weapons. However, by 700 BC the Sami were importing iron technology from Russia, long before iron was made by the Norwegians farther south.

The earliest written description of the Sami was by a Roman historian named Cornelius Tacitus in his book entitled *Germania* in AD 98. He called them Fenni and said that they were proficient hunters who ate wild plants and wore clothes of animal skins and wool. He also mentioned that the Sami women joined the men in the hunt for wild animals. Other ancient descriptions of the Sami described them as hunters who traveled on skis that were pointed upwards at both ends.

Today the Sami make up the largest minority group of people in Norway. They also live in Finland, Sweden, and the Kola Peninsula of Russia. The Sami refer to the entire region where they live as Sápmi. Some people have unknowingly called them Lapps, but that is a derogatory term that means uncivilized people on the periphery or poor people that wear patched clothing. It is appropriate instead to call them the Sami, which is the term they use to describe themselves.

Rock art

The early cultures left behind many amazing collections of rock carvings that can be found in various parts of Norway. The largest site of rock art in the world is the UNESCO World Heritage Site at Alta in Finnmark in northern Norway. This area contains approximately six thousand rock carvings that date from about 5200 to 200 BC. The impressive carvings were made by descendants of the Komsa culture and are similar to examples of rock art found in Russia and Finland.

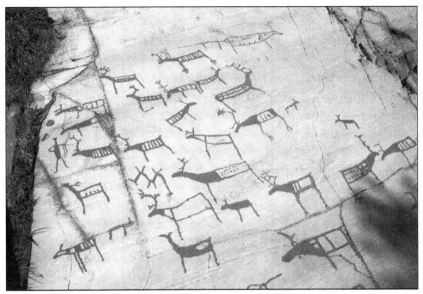

1.1 Reindeer rock art in Alta

Some archeologists claim that the rock artists were both inland hunters and coastal fishermen who made the carvings at ceremonial gatherings. The drawings were carved into hard sandstone by quartz chisels and hammers, and some of the carvings are painted to highlight the scenes. These rock carvings provide a rare glimpse at the lives, activities, and customs of the ancient inhabitants of the Far North. They include scenes of hunting, fishing, trapping, and gathering food, and boats and boat building, as well as ceremonies with shamans, drums, dancing, and processions. Some of the boats that are pictured hold as many as thirty people. Later carvings also depict agricultural activities.

The rock designs show many animals, including bears that were apparently considered sacred objects of worship. There are also reindeer, moose, birds, wolves, dogs, foxes, rabbits, ducks, geese, swans, halibut, salmon, and whales. The hunters are shown using spears and bow and arrow, and the people are moving on skis and snowshoes. Many of the rock carvings seem to reflect the Sami culture and way of life as it developed over time.

Proto-Norse society before AD 700

During the last five hundred years BC, until they were conquered by the Romans, the Celts made up the dominant society in most of central and western Europe south of Scandinavia. The Celts were the ones who developed iron technology in much of Europe. However, while some Celtic iron weapons and tools were imported by the Norwegians during this period, the widespread production of iron in Norway did not begin until later when Norwegian farmers started to produce their own iron tools and weapons made of bog iron from lakes and swamps. The iron was smelted by the use of charcoal from the forests.

The new iron technology was significant in that it allowed the Norwegians to produce strong knives, tools, sickles, plows, and axes. They used these iron implements to clear much more land for agriculture. In the period from AD 1 to 500, the population grew substantially, and many new farms were established away from the coastlines in the interior valleys of southern, central and even northern Norway. In fact, many present-day place names in Norway date from this period.

Ever since the last few hundred years BC, the Norwegians had developed an agriculture-based society in which the family farm, led by the free landowning farmer called the *bonde*, was the principal economic, social and cultural unit. The Norwegians' Germanic cousins in Denmark built clusters of farms containing several families. However, in the more sparsely populated Norway, it was common for a single family of one or two generations to build and occupy an isolated farm. Except for the occasional grandparent, the family usually did not consist of more than two generations because the normal lifespan at that time was only thirty to forty years.

The bonde who led the farm was the oldest man in the family who was still strong and healthy enough to actively work on the farm and run the operation. Apart from the bonde and his immediate family, there might also be laborers, servants, slaves, and even tenant farmers who worked on the farm. They would grow some grains and vegetables, but they were primarily engaged in livestock farming by raising cattle, sheep, goats, and pigs to produce meat, wool, hides, milk, butter, and cheese. The farm was largely self-sufficient, providing all of the residents' food, shelter, and clothing. The people ate meat, porridge, bread, butter, cheese, and berries, as well as fish caught in nearby lakes and streams. They drank water, milk, beer, and mead, and they sometimes even imported wines. They also made their own clothing from wool and hides.

There was already a primitive form of land ownership, and the bonde sometimes marked the boundaries of his inner farm with fences or rocks, although different farmers often shared common pasture land, forests, and streams outside their immediate farms. Many farms included a *seter*, which was a summer pasture located in the mountains. The bonde and his family would take their livestock up to the seter for the summer. Rules of inheritance were also developed. Under the so-called alodial system of inheritance, the ownership of the farm and seter was transferred to the bonde's oldest male heir, who became the next bonde and had to provide some form of compensation to his siblings. Members of the family also had the right to reacquire the farm if it was sold outside the family. These types of farms, along with the forms of ownership and inheritance, were all in existence before the Viking age, and they survived in modified form until modern times.

Over time, some of the wealthiest farmers took leadership positions in various regions of Norway. That is, they became chieftains who served as administrative, military and religious leaders. Farmers paid tribute to their chieftain in the form of farm produce or other goods, and in return the chieftain was responsible for protecting the farmers in his area from other chieftains and tribes. For added protection, the chieftain often formed his own band of professional warriors called the *hird*. Some chieftains became very wealthy and influential as indicated by their burial mounds containing valuable jewelry and weapons.

When a few chieftains became even more powerful and expanded their areas of influence, they became known as petty kings or jarls (earls). In AD 550 the Gothic historian Jordanes could already identify groups of people in different regions of Norway that were ruled by one or more petty kings, jarls, or chieftains. Those regions included Romerike, Telemark, Agder, Rogaland, Hordaland, Romsdal, and Hålogaland.

The Norwegians in each region formed their own legislative and judicial assembly that was called the *ting*. A ting was a periodic gathering of all of the freemen in an area, with the petty king, jarl, or chieftain acting as the presiding official. At the ting, the freemen made rules, settled disputes, and tried and sentenced criminals. The sentences ranged all the way from small fines to banishment from the region.

In the years before AD 1, the Scandinavians developed their own North Germanic language called Proto-Norse. From the period between AD 180 and 500, there is evidence of writing in Proto-Norse in the form of runes. The original runic alphabet, called Elder Futhark, was made up of twenty-four different characters or letters that were based on the Latin alphabet and symbols from parts of Italy. Later the runic alphabet was reduced to sixteen characters. Most of the runic inscriptions that survive to this day are short passages written on stones, weapons, or jewelry.

The runestones were often dedicated to living or deceased family members or leaders. A good example of a runestone written in Proto-Norse by the use of Elder Futhark is the Tune runestone, which dates from about AD 400. It was found near Sarpsborg, Norway, and is now located at the University Museum of Cultural History in Oslo. The stone appears to have been raised by a man or woman and three daughters to honor their chieftain.

By about AD 700 Proto-Norse had evolved into Old Norse, the language of the Vikings, which in turn was divided into Old West Norse in Norway and Old East Norse in Denmark and Sweden. So at that time there were already differences in the languages spoken in various parts of Scandinavia. The Scandinavians continued to carve runestones and other runic inscriptions in Old Norse throughout the Viking age.

Age of Migration

As mentioned above, a chieftain typically had his own professional army or *hird* to protect himself and the farmers in his region. They needed protection not only from neighboring chieftains and tribes, but also from other Germanic tribes that migrated to Norway from faraway lands.

The period from AD 400 to 600 in western Europe, including Scandinavia, is called the Age of Migration. Under pressure from the dreaded Huns who attacked from Asia, the Slavs from central and eastern Europe, and various Germanic tribes, many of the people in Europe were on the move during this period that began with the demise and fall of the Roman Empire. The migrating people were looking for new places to live that were safer or more spacious or prosperous.

Perhaps the best known example of this migration involved the Angles, Saxons, and Jutes who originally lived in northern Germany, southern Denmark, and Frisia. In the period from AD 400 to 500, there was a mass migration of these people across the English Channel to Britain, where they came to dominate the Celtic Britons and eventually established Anglo-Saxon England.

Similarly, Norway experienced an influx of Germanic tribes. The *horder* came to Norway from the Harz Mountains of central Germany and established themselves in the region of Hordaland in Norway. The *ryger* left the Baltic coast of northern Germany and settled in Rogaland in Norway. The *trøndere* came from Sweden and invaded and took over the area around the Trondheimsfjord. There were also smaller groups of people who moved to Norway during or shortly after the Age of Migration, including members of the wealthy Yngling family who left Old Uppsala in Sweden to establish petty kingdoms in Vestfold on the west side of the Oslofjord. The Ynglings would later become one of the leading families of Norway in Viking times.

These foreign Germanic tribes essentially invaded various parts of Norway and conquered the existing people in those areas. There is archeological evidence of hill fortifications, defense works around settlements, and several battles, as the original Norwegians sought to protect themselves and their property from the onrushing tide of migration. It was during this period that a relatively peaceful land turned into a militaristic society in which warriors wielded weapons such as spears, swords, axes, lances, and shields. The aggressive nature of some of the invading tribes, such as those that settled in Hordaland and Rogaland and along the Oslofjord, would continue into the Viking age, when they began to attack people in other lands. However, by then the invaders had been at least somewhat assimilated into the existing population of Norway and had become Norwegians.

In addition to migration, after AD 500 there was increased trade and other interaction between Norwegians and people in other lands. That was especially true of commerce with Britain and Frisia. Part of the impetus for these expanded contacts was that the production of iron tools and nails enabled the Norwegians to build stronger boats that could travel longer distances to market towns such as Dorestad near the mouth of the Rhine River. Chieftains became more involved in shipbuilding and trade, importing jewelry, glass, pottery, gold, silver, wine, and weapons in exchange for furs, hides, dried fish, and walrus ivory from various parts of Norway.

However, until shortly before the Viking age, the ships of the Norwegians were still propelled by rowing rather than sails, and they generally stayed within sight of land, so they normally did not cover long distances over the seas. For example, the *Kvalsund* ship from the late seventh century was discovered in a swamp in western Norway in 1920. It was beautifully constructed for a crew of twenty-one men and had many of the features of later Viking ships. But the ship most likely did not have a mast or a sail, and it only had a rudimentary keel, so it probably would not have been sailed across the ocean.

Longhouses

Beginning in about 500 BC and continuing for more than 1,500 years through the Viking age, the Norwegians' principal form of dwelling was the longhouse. This rectangular structure was the home of the bonde or chieftain and his family. A typical longhouse was anywhere from forty to two hundred feet long and sixteen to twenty-five feet wide. The structure was supported by large timbers at the corners, which were dug into the ground (a technique that unfortunately caused them to rot over time) or more preferably were wedged onto a stone foundation. The walls were made of wood or stone, or alternatively of sod in places where other materials were not readily available. A longhouse roof was usually constructed with wooden planks covered by birch bark and turf or even wooden shingles. The floor was flattened earth. There were no windows, and there was typically only one door on the south side to avoid the cold north wind.

In the main room of the longhouse, there were wide wooden platforms along the walls that were used for sitting, eating, working, and sleeping. An open stone hearth or one or more fire pits for cooking and heating were in the middle of the room. There were no chimneys, so there was a hole in the ceiling to let the smoke escape. Light was provided by the fire and by oil lamps. There might also be separate rooms for sleeping, storage, or working, and some of the rooms could even contain wood paneling. In many early longhouses, during the winter the livestock also lived in a large room in the same longhouse, although Norwegians later came to realize that it was better to keep their horses, cattle, pigs, sheep, and goats in a separate building.

In addition to the longhouse, there were often other buildings on the farm, all grouped in a cluster around a courtyard. Those other buildings might include living quarters for laborers, servants, and slaves, a smithy, barns, storehouses, and various other work buildings.

Some petty kings, jarls, and chieftains built huge longhouses that also served as halls for ceremonies and feasts. At these events, the leader would sit on his high seat above the others, with his wife and other favorites at his side. A reconstruction of a wealthy and powerful chieftain's longhouse and farm is located at Borg on the island of Vestvågøy in Lofoten. There the longhouse was originally built in about AD 550 and was gradually expanded and reconstructed over time until it was 272 feet long, almost the size of a football field. The building served as the chieftain's residence and also as a guild hall for religious ceremonies and feasts.

1.2 Reconstructed chieftain's longhouse and guild hall at Borg, Lofoten

It appears that the chieftain at Borg was part of an alliance of several chieftains all along the coast of northern Norway, which was called Hålogaland. Together these chieftains maintained the peace in their coastal shipping and trade routes. The Borg chieftain was trading goods with other parts of Norway and Europe. His farm included many buildings, pastures, and several boathouses along the shore of a nice harbor.

The chieftain's longhouse at Borg was finally abandoned toward the end of the tenth century after the initial unification of Norway and the introduction of Christianity. One of the last chieftains at Borg was Olav Tvennumbruni, a pagan who moved to Iceland along with many other wealthy chieftains and farmers who wanted to preserve their independence and Norse religion in the Viking age.

CHAPTER TWO:

The Vikings of Norway

The Vikings were ruthless warriors, pirates, and raiders, but they were also merchants and traders, craftsmen, settlers, farmers, and explorers. This chapter explores the mysteries surrounding the Vikings, including where they came from and how and why they attacked, traded, and settled throughout Europe and the North Atlantic, with special emphasis on the Vikings from Norway.

The Vikings attack England and Scotland

Near Portland on the south coast of England in AD 789, some farmers looked to the horizon and saw three fast ships sailing towards them from across the sea. It was an ominous sight, as the vessels looked like dragons or sea serpents and they were filled with men. Someone sent word to the local town, where the king's reeve (administrator) and his men mounted their horses and rode to the shore. When they got there, a group of tall, burly men had already beached their ships and were walking towards them.

The reeve thought they were merchants who had landed at the wrong place. He approached the strangers, and in a harsh, arrogant manner he upbraided them and instructed them to follow him and his men to the king's manor and marketplace. The strangers were foreigners who could barely understand the reeve, and they definitely did not appreciate his tone or his haughty attitude. An exchange of words led to a confrontation, and the foreigners suddenly drew their swords and other weapons and murdered the reeve and all of his men. Then they got back in their ships, rowed away from shore, set sail, and vanished as quickly as they had come.

The strangers were Vikings from Hordaland in Norway, and this was the first Viking attack ever recorded. Over the next few years, other Viking ships and men appeared along the coast of southern England, and the king of Mercia started to set up defenses against the seaborne foreigners.

In 793 the Vikings struck again, this time farther north at a place called Lindisfarne, a tranquil island off the northeast coast of England. At Lindisfarne there was a village, a church, a school, and a monastery that had been founded in the previous century to convert the pagan Anglo-Saxons to Christianity. Lindisfarne was the oldest monastery in Northumbria and the seat of the bishop. It was well known throughout England and the rest of Christian Europe as a center of learning and scholarship. The monks at Lindisfarne diligently studied and carefully copied texts. For example, they produced the Lindisfarne Gospels, beautifully scripted and illustrated reproductions of the first four books of the New Testament.

On June 8, without warning, a band of Vikings stormed ashore from their small fleet of ships, and they were greeted by a number of monks. Instead of returning the greetings, the Vikings slaughtered the monks and ransacked the defenseless village and monastery and especially the church, where they hauled off valuable chalices, crosses, relics, and other items of gold and silver, while unmercifully killing anyone who got in their way. They grabbed several monks to be kept or sold as slaves and then went back to their ships, where they packed up their booty and captives and sailed away, leaving behind a trail of chaos and destruction.

The sack of Lindisfarne was the most famous (or infamous) Viking raid of all time, and some historians consider it to be the start of the Viking age. Word of the bloody assault spread throughout England and Europe, where rulers and churchmen alike were shocked and outraged that ruthless heathens could somehow sail across the sea, appearing out of the blue to mount a brutal attack on innocent, peaceloving men of the cloth and their sacred church and shrine. Bishops and priests attributed the bloody attack to the wrath of God, who was punishing his people for the sins of the world. The Vikings returned to attack Lindisfarne so many times that in 875 the monks finally dug up their patron saint's coffin and took it and the Lindisfarne Gospels with them as they abandoned the place. They wandered around Britain for seven years before finding a place of refuge that was safe from the fury of the dreaded Vikings.

Viking attacks on towns, churches, and monasteries throughout Britain increased in number and intensity. In 794 the Vikings raided the monastery at Jarrow, after which many Vikings were killed when part of their fleet was destroyed in a storm, an event that the Christians felt was God's rightful vengeance for the evil deeds of the heathens. From there the Vikings moved north, where in 795 they sacked St. Columba's monastery at Iona, the principal seat of the Scottish Church. In 802 they returned to Iona and burned the place down, and in repeated attacks in 806 and 807 they killed scores of people, making off with valuable treasures. In all of these instances, the Vikings and a few ships appeared suddenly out of nowhere, plundered, killed, and vanished back to sea in lightning attacks against defenseless towns and churches. As rumors reached Norway of the successful attacks and the enormous riches that were readily available for the taking, more and more Vikings sailed to England and Scotland to join the rampage.

Ireland

The next stop was Ireland, a land that was already experiencing violent conflicts between competing Irish clans. The Vikings from Norway stepped into the fray and conducted repeated raids on towns, churches, and monasteries along the coasts and rivers of Ireland. These attacks began in 795 and continued for much of the ninth century. As in Britain, they killed townspeople, bishops, priests, and monks, while taking slaves and stealing expensive items. The bands of Vikings became larger and larger until 837, when a massive fleet of 120 ships appeared with a huge army that invaded the interior of Ireland and met strong resistance.

Beginning in the 830s, the notorious leader of the Norwegian Vikings in Ireland was Turgeis (also called Thorgils). Among other things, he attacked Ireland's religious capital of Armagh, held the abbot for ransom, installed himself as the new abbot, converted the abbey and many churches into pagan temples, and forced the Irish to worship the Norse gods. He was finally captured, sewn into a sack, and drowned in a lake by the king of Tara in 845.

In 851 the Danish Vikings showed up to challenge the authority of the Norwegian Vikings in Ireland. In an alliance with various Irish clans, the Danes expelled the Norwegians, who soon returned to Ireland with a vengeance to reestablish their prominence under the leadership of Olav the White, who was probably a member of the influential Yngling family from Vestfold on the west side of the Oslofjord.

For the first few decades in Ireland, the Vikings only engaged in hit-and-run raids, sailing back to Norway or the North Atlantic islands for the winter months. However, in 840 they began to overwinter in Ireland. They built fortresses called longports to protect their ships in the harbors and rivers. Over time the longports became towns and trading centers, including Dublin, Limerick, Waterford, Wexford, and Cork. Thus, many of the cities in Ireland were originally founded by the Vikings. In the ninth century, Dublin became a major Viking market town where the slave trade flourished and where Vikings even began to mint coins to be used in their trading activities. Olav the White became the king of Dublin in 852, and he used the town as a base to launch several attacks on Scotland until he returned to Norway and was killed there in battle in 871.

Many Norwegians settled in Ireland, where they were eventually assimilated into the Irish population. In addition, the Norwegian Vikings established settlements in other places around the Irish Sea, including England, Wales, and the Isle of Man, as well as Scotland and the nearby islands such as Orkney, Shetland, the Hebrides, and the Faeroes.

France

Norwegian Vikings also set their sights on France, which was part of the empire of the great Charlemagne. The attacks began in 799 when they plundered the monastery on the island of Noirmoutier at the mouth of the Loire River. They followed up with many more attacks on the same monastery, as well as other places along the French coasts and rivers. This caused Charlemagne to strengthen his defenses, which temporarily deterred and reduced the number of Viking attacks. But after Charlemagne died in 814, his empire was divided and the defenses gradually weakened. Thereafter, both Norwegian and Danish Vikings, together and separately, resumed their attacks with even greater ferocity. Norwegian Vikings from the Oslofjord overwintered in France for the first time in 836, selecting Noirmoutier as their base for constant attacks along the coasts and rivers. In 841 a fleet of Viking ships sailed up the Seine River, where the raiders plundered and burned the city of Rouen and extracted large ransoms before they would go away.

Based on their experience in Ireland, the Vikings learned that it was most lucrative to launch attacks on Christian holy days when the towns and markets were crowded with people and valuable goods. On the feast day of John the Baptist in June 843, sixty-seven Viking ships from Ireland attacked and plundered the city of Nantes. They killed the bishop during the mass, murdered many priests and townspeople, and pillaged the city. After this brutal attack, Nantes literally became a deserted ghost town for years.

To top it off, on Easter Sunday, March 28, 845, the Vikings overran and looted Paris, and the Frankish king Charles the Bald was forced to pay them a ransom of seven thousand pounds of silver to get them to leave. The leader of that expedition was Ragnar Lodbrok, who then attacked the coast of Britain, where he was shipwrecked and captured. He was killed when the king of Northumbria had him thrown into a pit of poisonous snakes.

The Viking raids in France continued for several decades, and entire towns and even regions of the country were depopulated as many people were killed and others fled the exposed and undefended coastlines and rivers. In about 860 a monk named Ermentarius from Noirmoutier described a constant stream of countless ships carrying hordes of Vikings that plundered and burned cities and towns and massacred Christians throughout the country.

The Vikings returned to Paris in 885. They besieged the city for months and finally made off with another huge ransom. Over time the Franks eventually learned how to improve their defenses, such as by constructing low, fortified bridges to impede the movement of Viking ships upriver and by fortifying their towns and abbeys. However, the Vikings remained a serious threat to France into the tenth century.

Spain and the Mediterranean

The Vikings on Noirmoutier heard rumors of great riches to the south of France, and it did not take them long to find their way down the coast and commence attacks on the Iberian Peninsula of Spain and Portugal. However, unfortunately for them, the Vikings had not bargained for the violent reception they would receive from a formidable new foe – the Spanish Moors.

In 844 fifty-four Viking ships sailed to the coast of Moorish Spain, took the city of Seville, and killed many townspeople. In response, the Moors formed an army in Cordoba and then attacked and defeated the Vikings in Seville. The Moors employed catapults to fling huge balls of fire that destroyed thirty Viking ships. Apart from the lucky ones who fled the scene, over one thousand Vikings were killed. About four hundred were captured and had to convert to Islam to save their own skins. They weren't in France anymore, and they definitely had met their match.

However, the Vikings apparently had short memories and were not easily daunted. In 859 two brothers named Hasting and Bjørn Ironside assembled a sizeable Viking army and left the Norwegian base at Noirmoutier with a fleet of sixty-two ships on an epic three-year voyage to Iberia and the Mediterranean Sea. First they tried to attack Spain, but once again they were defeated by the Moors. So the Vikings turned their attention to Portugal, looted the city of Lisbon, and then sailed through the Straits of Gibraltar. They moved on to North Africa, where they raided the coastline and captured a number of black people who they called blue men. The Vikings kept them in captivity to be sold later at the Dublin slave market. The Viking fleet moved across the Mediterranean to the Rhone Valley in the south of France, sacked Pisa in Italy, and then approached the city called Luna not far away.

The Vikings were very impressed by the beautiful, stately architecture of the city of Luna, and they were convinced that it was Rome, which was intended to be their ultimate destination. They wanted nothing better than to plunder the great center of western Christianity. So they attacked Luna, but the city's defenses held and the Vikings could not breach the walls of the city. At that point, they decided to fool the enemy by using a variation of the ancient Trojan Horse trick.

Hasting sent word to the bishop of Luna that he was deathly ill and that he wanted to be baptized as a Christian before he died. The bishop agreed, and the city gates were opened to allow just a few Vikings to carry a prostrate Hasting to the cathedral. While the

Viking chieftain pretended to be near death and his comrades were on their best behavior, he was baptized and then promptly escorted with his men out of the city. Shortly thereafter, the Vikings again contacted the bishop with the sad news that Hasting had met his maker. They requested a Christian funeral for their leader in the cathedral, and once again the bishop relented. This time a larger contingent of Vikings carried Hasting in his coffin through the city walls and into the cathedral. During the funeral service, the bishop leaned over Hasting's body to pray for his soul. Hasting then jumped up and slew the bishop with a thrust of his hidden sword. Pandemonium broke loose, as the Vikings attacked everyone in the church, plundered the city, and left with as many treasures as they could carry back to their ships.

The Vikings later found out that the city was not Rome, and they never did make it to the holy city, but they proceeded to Greece and perhaps all the way to Egypt. Then they sailed back to Spain, where they lost many ships and men in a storm and were again defeated, this time by a Moorish fleet. Nevertheless, they sacked Pamplona before returning to Noirmoutier with their twenty remaining ships and a fair amount of their booty and slaves.

Areas of Viking expansion

The Norwegians were not the only Vikings. There were others who were Danes and Swedes, and they also raided and traded in various parts of Europe and beyond. As explained above, the Norwegian Viking activity took place primarily in the British Isles, the North Atlantic islands, France, Spain, and the Mediterranean.

The Danes were active in Ireland and France, and they also repeatedly attacked Frisia, Germany, and the Baltic region. For example, they raided the market town of Dorestad near the mouth of the Rhine River and moved up the Rhine, the Elbe, and other rivers to attack German towns, churches, and monasteries.

In addition, after the Norwegians' initial hit-and-run attacks along the coast of England, beginning in 865 the Danes made a more concerted and prolonged effort to invade, occupy, and establish settlements in the northeastern half of England in the ninth and tenth centuries. Their seat of power in England was the city of York, which the Vikings called Jorvik. They actually intended to conquer all of England, but by 886 their advance was halted by the West Saxon king Alfred the Great of England and his army, navy, and defense works. Alfred and the Danes then entered into a treaty that recognized Danish dominance and rule in their half of England, an area that was called the Danelaw.

Later in the tenth century, the Norwegians joined the Danes in ruling Jorvik and the Danelaw from time to time, but in 954 the Viking rulers were expelled and England became a more unified country that included the Danish settlers as well as Englishmen, all under the rule of English kings and nobles. However, the Vikings resumed their attacks on England later in the tenth century, and in the early eleventh century Danish kings such as Knut the Great ruled all of England for a few decades.

The Swedish Vikings also attacked the Baltic coast, but their primary sphere of influence was Russia. They established the kingdom of Gardarike based in the cities of Novgorod and Kiev, where they ruled the Slavic population for centuries, continuing even after they were assimilated into Slavic society. They also established trade routes along the Russian rivers all the way to the Black Sea and even the Caliphate of Baghdad in what is now Iraq. They were called the *Rus*, which originally may have meant the men who row boats, and that designation was the origin of the name of Russia. The Swedes unsuccessfully attacked Constantinople (which they called Myklegard) several times, including massive assaults on the city by huge fleets in 860 and 907. Having failed to conquer the city, the Vikings switched sides. Some of them joined the Byzantine army, and others formed the Varangian Guard – the personal bodyguards of the Byzantine emperor. From time to time, there were also Norwegians who joined the Swedish Vikings in their exploits in Russia and the Byzantine Empire.

The meaning of "Vikings"

The term "Vikings" was most likely derived from Viken, which was the area around the Oslofjord, including Vestfold on the west side and Østfold on the east. So it referred to men from the Oslofjord. However, at an early stage the term took on the connotation of ruthless seaborne raiders or pirates from any part of Scandinavia. In more recent times the term is broadly used to describe all the people of Scandinavia and their immediate descendants during the period from the late eighth century to 1066.

In the age of the Vikings, the people of Europe and Asia had other names for the raiders and traders from the Far North. The English also called them Danes, whether they came from Denmark or some other Scandinavian land. To the Irish they were *Gaill* or foreigners. In France they were known as the Northmen, and in areas in and around Russia they were called the Rus. The Greeks of the Byzantine Empire referred to them as *væringer*, a term that gave rise to the name of the emperor's Varangian Guard.

The Arabs had their own special designation for the Vikings, calling them *al Magus*, which meant pagan fire worshippers. This name may have resulted from the occasional Viking practice of cremating their dead on a burning ship or a funeral pyre.

Reasons for the Viking expansion

So why did these Norwegians, Danes, and Swedes, who had largely kept to themselves, suddenly burst onto the scene to plunder, trade, and settle in other lands throughout the European Continent and adjoining areas? In addition to their own motivations, there were various circumstances that created the opportunities for Viking expansion in the eighth through eleventh centuries.

The Vikings' primary motivation for launching attacks against people and places in other lands was undoubtedly pure greed – to enrich themselves – and a thirst for power and glory. They came from a relatively poor agricultural society in the Far North. When they discovered that gold, silver, and other treasures and goods were available for the taking in undefended places, they helped themselves to as many riches as they could carry away.

Most of the Viking leaders from Norway were chieftains and their sons who lived along the coast. The chieftains wanted to increase their wealth, power, and influence. They already had hirds of armed professional warriors who could carry out the raids, and the chieftains needed to preserve the loyalty of the warriors and farmers in their respective areas. So they stole from others in order to become wealthier and to compensate and buy the loyalty of their followers. Other Viking leaders were sons of chieftains, especially younger sons who were not going to inherit their fathers' positions and property. There were also plenty of other ambitious warriors. They were all motivated to seek fame and fortune by enriching themselves and their men and thereby staking a claim to be considered chieftains in their own right.

The Viking attacks were violent because they lived in a tough, militaristic society where chieftains and their followers regularly battled against each other, and boys were taught how to fight and use weapons at an early age. The Vikings had excellent weapons that they made or imported, including swords, battle axes, spears, and bow and arrow. For protection they wore chain mail or heavy leather coats, as well as helmets (without horns), and they carried lightweight round wooden shields. It is also important to note that, apart from the Viking attacks, in the same era there were other frequent battles and wars, plunder, and killing that were commonplace all over Europe, and warriors like the Magyars, Slavs, and Moors could be every bit as ruthless and violent as the Vikings.

The violence was also part of the Norse religion and society that glorified battles, courage, weapons, and booty. It was the ultimate honor for a Viking to die fighting in battle because he believed that maidens called Valkyries would then take him to Valhalla, Odin's hall of the slain, where he and his comrades would feast all day and fight all night in preparation for the final battle called *Ragnarok* between the gods and the giants. So the Vikings were a formidable fighting force, and the collapse of Charlemagne's empire, as well as weak or nonexistent defenses throughout Europe, gave them the opportunity to kill, burn, pillage, and steal without much opposition.

2.1 Viking helmet from Gjermundbu, Ringerike

So what the Vikings do with all of their booty? Clearly they kept some of the treasures and goods and shared some with their families and followers. In many cases they traded some of their booty in exchange for food and other goods that they consumed or used in their daily lives. But amazingly they also buried much of their silver and gold as hoards that have been discovered all over Scandinavia, Britain, Russia, and other parts of Europe.

It is still a mystery why the Vikings buried many of their most priceless possessions. One explanation is that they buried the goods for safekeeping so they would not be found by their enemies or others, and then they died before they could retrieve the goods. That may account for some of the booty, but why would so many Vikings negligently leave behind such riches instead of using them or at least giving them away to their families or followers? Perhaps a better explanation is that in many cases the buried goods were sacrifices to the Norse gods, or that the Vikings believed they would be able to take possession of the buried goods once again in the afterlife after they died. That would also explain the treasures found in burial mounds in Scandinavia.

The Viking expansion involved not only brutal attacks and lucrative trading but also settlement and colonization in places such as the North Atlantic islands. Since arable land was scarce in parts of western Norway, some Vikings decided to move to other, more spacious lands where they could own and operate larger farms and where the ground was more fertile for crop and livestock farming. That was particularly true of younger sons who were not going to inherit their fathers' lands in Norway. Other Viking colonists moved away from Norway to gain or preserve their independence from kings, jarls, or chieftains at home.

Some Vikings left Norway both to plunder and to engage in farming. One example was Svein Åsleivsson, who lived in the Orkney Islands and combined the roles of Viking chieftain and farmer. In a typical year, he would plant his crops in the spring, then conduct Viking raids in Ireland and other places in the summer, and finally return home to harvest his crops in the fall. After the harvest was safely in, he and his men might set off on another raiding expedition until the harsh winter weather brought them back home to rest until the following spring.

Viking ships and navigation

The Vikings never would have been able to raid, trade, and settle in other lands if they did not have excellent ships and navigational skills. The Viking ships were far superior to any other ships in Europe, with the possible exception of the Moorish navies. In fact, at the time, except for a few misguided monks who occasionally tried to cross the ocean in unseaworthy craft, the Vikings were the only Europeans who dared to sail across the open seas far from the nearest landfall. That made their attacks and other activities over a wide area even more surprising and effective.

Over hundreds of years before the initial Viking attacks on the British Isles, the Scandinavians had gradually improved and perfected their shipbuilding methods and innovations. For example, they did not use masts and sails until the eighth century, even though such equipment was already in use by other Europeans. But they were quick learners, and by the time of the attack on Lindisfarne in 793, the Viking ships contained the best sails, masts, and rigging in all of Europe.

The Viking ships were flexible, light, strong, maneuverable, and very seaworthy. Some of them were fast enough to make over twelve knots. The ships were clinker-built, meaning that the planks of the hull were overlapping for added strength. Those planks were naturally curved oak selected by the master shipbuilder based on the length and shape of the ship, and they were attached with iron nails and rivets and firm supports and crossbeams. There was a high bow and stern, sometimes decorated to look like a ferocious dragon or serpent, and a large removable rudder oar near the back of the right (or starboard) side of the ship.

The Vikings came up with several innovations that were not found on other ships at the time. First, the tall mast and the large square sail could be raised and lowered, depending on the wind conditions and the proximity to land. Second, a Viking ship sat high in the water with a low draft, so it could be beached on the shore or even rowed up shallow lakes and rivers. Third, the ships were remarkably light so they could be transferred by portage from one stream to another, usually by rolling or dragging the ship on logs. Finally, the Viking ships were the first to have a well-developed, strong keel, which was a large plank at the bottom of the ship. The keel provided strength and stability even in heavy seas, and it was essential in enabling the Vikings to be the first Europeans to successfully sail across the seas and oceans.

There were many different designs of Viking ships over the years, but the two basic types were the longship and the *knarr*. The longship was a fast, sleek, long and narrow warship with a large sail and many pairs of oars. The oarsmen often placed their shields on the sides of the ship for protection. However, the longships were used primarily to transport the warriors. The Vikings usually fought on land and not at sea, in part because no one other than King Alfred the Great of England, the Moors, and other Scandinavians had fleets that would dare to challenge the Vikings and their longships. The knarr was a cargo and passenger ship that was shorter and wider. In addition to the crew, it could hold passengers, goods, and even farm animals. The knarr was used by many Norwegians to move their families and possessions to their new settlements on the North Atlantic islands, but it was also used by merchants to carry their wares to and from the market towns.

2.2 *Oseberg* ship, Viking Ship Museum in Oslo

The Viking Ship Museum at Bygdøy in Oslo contains two beautifully preserved Viking ships called the *Gokstad* and *Oseberg* ships. Both were excavated from burial mounds in southern Norway. The *Oseberg* ship dates from the ninth century and was built for a crew of thirty-five. It was buried with a noblewoman and her female slave. The noblewoman may have been the Yngling queen Åse, grandmother of King Harald Fairhair. There are magnificent wood carvings on the ship, which also contained a ceremonial cart, sleds, furniture, farm equipment, clothing, looms, kitchen utensils, other implements, and even dead horses and dogs, all of which were intended to accompany the deceased passengers into the afterlife.

The Vikings were expert navigators who used a system of dead reckoning to determine their current position based on their previous position and their estimated course and speed. They also fixed their position and course by using a primitive astrolabe to establish their latitude, by observing the sun and stars, and by using their knowledge of sea routes, landmarks, islands, ocean currents, the wind, and other factors. They probably used a sun compass, and a sunstone to locate the sun even in overcast conditions. In addition, they observed whales and birds and used a plumb line (that is, a line with an attached weight at the end) to estimate the depth of the sea and their proximity to land.

The Vikings at home

While there were Viking raiders and traders on the coast of Norway, most Norwegians continued to be farmers who tended their crops and livestock, much as their ancestors had done for over a thousand years. Their diet still consisted of meat, fish, porridge, bread, butter, cheese, milk, water, beer, and mead. They ate on plates with their knives, spoons, and fingers, but no forks. Farmers also hunted and fished in the areas surrounding their farms. Their clothing was made by spinning and weaving wool, and their outer garments were made of hides and fur, while they had shoes made of animal skins. Each farm was largely self-sufficient.

Viking women wore long woolen dresses that were fastened with oval brooches at the shoulders. The women were described by Arab observers as beautiful, clean, and well-groomed, wearing eye makeup and jewelry of gold and silver. They were also known for their independence, and they had the right to inherit and own property and divorce their husbands. The farmer's or chieftain's wife was the person in charge of the farm and the home when her husband was away.

Marketplaces

The Vikings were active traders, merchants, and craftsmen who imported and exported booty and other products at both seasonal and year-round marketplaces that they built near their homes and along their trade routes. The most prominent Viking market towns outside of Norway were Hedeby in Denmark, Birka near present-day Stockholm in Sweden, Staraja Ladoga near Lake Ladoga in northwest Russia, Jorvik, and Dublin.

In Norway, various chieftains established seasonal trading centers in places along the coast including Tjøtta in Hålogaland (northern Norway), Lade at present-day Trondheim, and Sandnes in southern Norway. The chieftains built, protected, and supported these trading centers near their homes as sources of income. It was also primarily the chieftains and their master shipbuilders who built the ships that were used to transport merchants and goods to and from the trading centers.

The leading Viking trading center in all of Norway was Kaupang (meaning marketplace) near present-day Larvik in Vestfold. This was the first year-round town in Norway, established in about 800 by the Yngling family on the shoreline just below one of their farms and ceremonial halls called Skiringssal. About five hundred people lived in the town, which featured timber-paved streets, piers, wells, and many buildings including houses and workshops. Some of the residents were Viking craftsmen such as bead makers, blacksmiths, metal workers, comb makers, carpenters, weavers, shoemakers, leather workers, and shipbuilders. They all produced goods that were traded in the town.

The list of items traded at Kaupang is impressive. They included beads and other jewelry, drinking glasses and jugs, pottery, amber, swords, spears, axes, arrows, helmets, clothing, horse harnesses, scales, coins, and various other handicrafts. Some of these goods were imported from Britain, Ireland, France, and the Baltic region, and other items originated as far away as the Black Sea and Asia. They were exchanged for products of Norway including skins, hides, furs, tusks, antlers, soapstone, dried fish, whetstone, iron, and handicrafts of various kinds. The townspeople and traders at Kaupang ate pork, fish, bread, porridge, cabbage, butter, and cheese, and drank water, milk, mead, and imported wine.

The flourishing trade at Kaupang continued throughout the ninth century, but by the early tenth century the town had become just a summer marketplace. Kaupang disappeared around 970, possibly because the Yngling chieftains had lost their power and influence when the Danish kings became dominant in that part of Norway.

Ottar's voyages

In about 890 a Norwegian chieftain named Ottar from Hålogaland visited the court of King Alfred the Great of England. He described his country, his farm, and his various voyages. The members of the king's court were so impressed that they recorded his story in an Anglo-Saxon translation of a Latin history of the world. It was the first written reference to the country called Norway.

Ottar said that he lived the farthest north of any Norwegian, probably near modern-day Tromsø. He was most likely one of the chieftains along the coast of northern Norway who formed an alliance to maintain the peace in their trade routes. His geographical description of Norway is strikingly similar to modern Norway, except that he describes the east side of the Oslofjord as part of Denmark.

Ottar was considered a very wealthy chieftain, and his livestock farm included six hundred reindeer, twenty cows, twenty sheep, twenty pigs, and some horses. He also grew a few crops on his small plot of arable land. But most of his wealth actually came from taxes that he collected from the Sami, who paid him with furs, feathers, whalebones, and ropes. Ottar also described his various voyages, including a walrus hunting expedition to the White Sea of northern Russia and a trading voyage to Skiringssal in southern Norway and Hedeby in Denmark.

Norwegian Viking settlements

Many Norwegian Vikings moved to other lands where they established farms and settlements. As mentioned earlier, in the ninth and tenth centuries the Norwegians settled in England, Scotland, Wales, and Ireland, as well as on nearby islands such as Orkney, Shetland, the Faeroes, the Hebrides, and the Isle of Man. In fact, the Norwegian settlements on some of those islands may have been established before the year 800.

If the islands or other areas were already inhabited by the local Celts, Picts, or Englishmen, the Vikings forcibly took over most or all of the land. However, in some places such as the Isle of Man and the Hebrides, the Vikings peacefully coexisted with the native population for hundreds of years. In addition, the Norwegian Vikings established settlements in more faraway places such as Normandy, Iceland, Greenland, and even North America.

Normandy

By the late ninth century, the jarl of Møre had become one of the most powerful men in all of Norway, and he was a friend and an ally of King Harald Fairhair. The jarl ruled the region of western Norway that is located around the present-day city of Ålesund. He had several sons, including a younger son named Rolf who was born on the island of Giske. Rolf grew up to be a Viking warrior, and he was commonly called Rolf the Walker (*Ganger Hrolf*) because he was so big that no horse could carry him. The Franks later called him Rollo.

As a young Viking, Rollo and his band of ruffians raided the Baltic coast, and then they started raids along the coast of Norway. Rollo's attacks on fellow Norwegians infuriated King Harald

Fairhair, who was trying to maintain the peace along the lucrative trade routes of western Norway. Even though Rollo was the son of his friend and ally, Harald banished Rollo from all of Norway. At that point, Rollo and his men left Norway and conducted raids in the Hebrides, Ireland, and France. More Vikings joined them, and Rollo became the leader of a large Viking army of Norwegians and Danes.

Since the 840s the Vikings had constantly attacked and plundered Normandy in northwest France. Rollo and his men arrived on the scene in about 900 and took over the city of Rouen. Another group of Norwegians settled farther west on the Cotentin Peninsula of Normandy. After so many Viking attacks, the Franks had abandoned much of the land, so the Vikings established settlements in various parts of Normandy.

2.3 Statue of Rollo the Viking in Ålesund

In about 910 Rollo and his army moved inland and unsuccessfully attacked Paris and Chartres, and they remained a threat to the population in the valley of the Seine. After decades of assaults by the Vikings, King Charles the Simple, the king of the Western Franks, finally had enough. He negotiated an agreement with Rollo called the Treaty of Saint Clair-sur-Epte in 911 or 912.

Under the treaty, Rollo was formally granted the city of Rouen and the surrounding area (that is, part of eastern Normandy), which he and his men already occupied. Charles also gave Rollo his daughter Gisla to be his new wife. In return, Rollo agreed to convert to Christianity, to stop attacking the Franks, and to protect the Seine River Valley from further Viking attacks. This was not the first time that European rulers had enlisted Viking leaders to protect them from other Vikings, and the plan worked because Paris and the Seine Valley were thereafter free from Viking raids.

At a ceremony at the Rouen Cathedral, Rollo was baptized as a Christian. The bishop suggested that Rollo kiss Charles' foot as a sign of submission. Rollo refused, but he selected another Viking to do so. However, instead of kneeling down to kiss the king's foot, the burly Viking lifted Charles' foot, which caused the king to fall backwards and hit his head, much to the amusement of the Vikings in attendance.

Rollo shared the lands in and around Rouen with his men, and he established an efficient administration characterized by strict law and order and feudalism. That is, the Vikings became French feudal lords who ruled over the local population. They also became Christians and were assimilated into French culture and society. Within a couple of generations, they spoke French and not Old Norse as their primary language. But they preserved their militaristic ways and their Viking ships, and they conducted a profitable slave trade on the streets of Rouen.

After Charles died, Rollo began to attack adjacent regions of France, and he and his descendants gradually spread their control to the rest of Normandy. In 1006 their region was recognized as the duchy of Normandy and Rollo's descendants became the dukes of Normandy.

Finally, in 1066 Rollo's great-great-great grandson, then known as William the Bastard (and later as William the Conqueror), took his army across the English Channel, won the Battle of Hastings, and became the king of England. Thereafter the Normans and their progeny continued to rule England for centuries, while other Norman kingdoms were established in southern Italy and Sicily. Various Norman descendants subsequently led armies in the Crusades, including King Richard the Lionheart of England.

Iceland

Nadd-Odd was a Norwegian outlaw who was banished from Norway. He intended to move to the Faeroe Islands, and in 860 he sailed from Norway. But he was blown off course all the way to Iceland. At that time, Iceland was an island without any inhabitants except for a few Irish monks who quickly departed when the Vikings arrived. After Nadd-Odd's initial journey, other Norwegian Vikings explored Iceland. They found the island to be a place with a somewhat desolate landscape that included rocks, geysers, and volcanoes, but there was also land that could be farmed and fjords like in Norway. There were even some forests of birch and other scrub trees until they were cut down or otherwise destroyed by the agricultural practices of the new settlers.

The first successful settlement in Iceland was led by Ingolf Arnarson, a Norwegian chieftain from Sunnfjord in western Norway. In about 874 he sailed to Iceland and brought with him all of his family, followers, slaves, weapons, livestock, and other possessions. As he approached the island, he threw wooden pillars from his chieftain's high seat overboard, and he vowed to settle in the place where they came ashore. Unfortunately, he and his men lost sight of the pillars, and they had to search for them until the following year. The pillars were finally found at a small inlet covered by a vapor cloud from a geyser. Arnarson and his followers settled in that place, which they called Reykjavik (meaning Smoky Bay), the future capital of Iceland.

During the period from 870 to 930, as many as twenty thousand people settled in Iceland. They were Vikings and their families, followers, and slaves from Norway, Ireland, Scotland, and other North Atlantic islands. The Norwegians were mostly chieftains and other wealthy farmers who left Norway in search of better farmland or to escape the rule of King Harald Fairhair and his allies in Norway. In fact, so many people left western Norway for Iceland that the king imposed a tax on emigrants to try to stem the tide. But his efforts were futile. Iceland was a relatively easy five- to seven-day journey across the sea from Norway, and there was ample land on which to establish new farms.

Some of the settlers were women, and the most prominent of them was Aud the Deep Minded. She was the daughter of a Norwegian chieftain and the widow of the Viking king Olav the White of Dublin. After Olav was killed, she moved her family and household to western Iceland, where she established a large farm and became a chieftain in her own right. She gave some of her land to her followers, including freed slaves, and she enjoyed the same rights as the other chieftains. However, when the *Allting* was established in Iceland in 930, women no longer had the right to vote at the ting.

In Iceland the settlers established a somewhat egalitarian society of free farmers. In contrast to Norway, they did not have kings or jarls. But the wealthiest chieftains on the largest farms became the political and religious leaders in Iceland. In fact, the Allting was essentially a national assembly of the chieftains and their advisers.

Greenland

Thorvald Asvaldsson was a Norwegian from Jæren in Rogaland who was outlawed and banished for some murders. He and his son Eirik the Red moved to Iceland, where Eirik established a farm in about 950. He was called Eirik the Red because of his flame colored hair and beard, and he also had a fiery personality.

Trouble began when Eirik's slaves caused a landslide that destroyed a neighboring farm, and the neighbor killed the slaves. This enraged Eirik, who killed the neighbor and another person, and these acts resulted in the banishment of Eirik from that part of Iceland. At his new farm in another region of Iceland, Eirik once again started quarreling with his neighbor and killed two of his neighbor's sons. The Icelanders then had their fill of Eirik, and they banished him from the entire island for three years.

Eirik had heard of another land west of Iceland that had been sighted by a Norwegian named Gunnbjørn Ulfsson in about 900. So Eirik sailed to the new land in search of a place to live and farm. First he explored the east coast which he found to be an uninhabitable place covered with glaciers and ice that reached right to the shoreline. So he moved on to the west coast, which contained lush meadows with wildflowers, berries, and birch trees along the banks of long, crystal blue fjords. The climate was relatively mild for the Arctic because the coastline was warmed by the Gulf Stream and the northern regions were going through a warm spell. There were also no people in the places that he explored, and he decided to stay there for three years.

During that time he also decided to essentially become a real estate developer in the new land, which he called Greenland to make it sound appealing. At the end of the three years, Eirik returned to Iceland, where he made a successful pitch to potential settlers. In about 985 he, his wife Thjodhild, their family, and a fleet of twenty-five ships containing many other families left Iceland on their way to the west coast of Greenland. Only fourteen ships made it there, and the others had to turn back or were lost at sea. Eirik and his family settled at a prime location called Brattahlid on the Eiriksfjord. The ruins of his farm can still be seen there today, including a small church that Eirik built for his Christian wife.

Greenland was eventually settled by as many as four thousand people in two different settlement areas called the Eastern and Western Settlements, both on the west coast. The settlers built about six hundred homesteads and made a living of livestock farming, hunting, and fishing. They even had their own ting, nineteen churches, a monastery, a nunnery, and a bishop. Since lumber for building houses and ships was not found in Greenland, the Norse probably made periodic expeditions to Labrador in North America to find supplies of timber.

Unfortunately the Norse settlements in Greenland vanished sometime before 1500, and there was no further contact between Greenland and either Iceland or Europe for centuries. The last recorded event of the Norse population in Greenland was a wedding at the Hvalsey Church in the Eastern Settlement in 1408. No one knows what happened to the last Norse inhabitants of Greenland. The weather turned much colder in the fourteenth and fifteenth centuries, and it might have become too difficult to live there, causing the Norse to die out or move away. With the onset of the colder weather, the Inuit people who lived in the far northern regions of Greenland started moving into the areas occupied by the Norse. Although there were peaceful contacts between the two peoples, there were also some conflicts which may have killed the Norse or forced them to leave. There is also an Inuit legend that European pirates came to Greenland, where they attacked and killed many Norse settlers and looted and burned their farms, and at that point most of the Norse packed up and departed Greenland while the rest of them went to live with the Inuit.

North America

As shown by Eirik's exploration of Greenland, the Vikings were brave and capable explorers. But some of their voyages of exploration were accidental rather than intentional.

In about 985 a Norwegian merchant ship captain named Bjarne Herjolfsson decided to visit his parents in Iceland. When he arrived at their farm, he learned that they had moved to Greenland with Eirik the Red. So Bjarne and his crew sailed for Greenland, but they lost their way and ended up far to the west, where they saw a new land with hills and forests and with mountains farther north. Bjarne's men wanted to land and explore this place, but he turned the ship around and sailed for Greenland. He and his men had unknowingly discovered North America, although they never set foot on the land.

Eirik the Red's son Leiv Eiriksson heard about the sighting of land to the west, and he purchased Bjarne's ship and assembled a crew. They sailed from Greenland to North America in about the year 1000. First they came to a forbidding place of glaciers and flat rocks in the north that they called Helluland. It was probably the southern coast of Baffin Island in modern-day Canada. Heading south, they reached a land of beaches and forests, and they called the place Markland. It was most likely present-day Labrador. Finally they sailed farther south to the northeastern tip of Newfoundland, where they found a grassy meadow and a small brook along a cove on the coastline. In this place, they built a camp consisting of longhouses and other buildings.

After a lengthy stay, Leiv and his men returned to Greenland, where other Norsemen then sailed to and explored Newfoundland and the areas around the Gulf of St. Lawrence. The Norse called this place Vinland (wineland) because they found grapes growing somewhere south of Newfoundland. They also encountered indigenous people, and there were violent clashes between the Norse and the native population. The Norsemen decided they could not live in such a hostile environment, so they abandoned Leiv's camp and returned to Greenland.

In 1960 and 1961, Norwegian writer and explorer Helge Ingstad and his wife, archeologist Anne Stine Ingstad, discovered the location of Leiv Eiriksson's camp on the shore of Newfoundland near a small fishing village called L'Anse aux Meadows. Archeological excavations of the site have revealed eight buildings including longhouses, smaller dwellings, a smithy, and a furnace hut, and even a dry dock for repairing ships. The buildings were apparently used year-round and were constructed with thick sod walls, roofs over wood frames, living areas for as many as ninety people, kitchens, saunas, fire pits, workshops, and storage rooms. The Norse items that were uncovered at the site include a bronze ring pin, iron rivets, a stone lamp, a spinning whorl, a jewelry loop, a bone needle for knitting, a glass bead, a whetstone, knives, and scissors.

It appears that Leiv Eiriksson's camp was a working settlement for men, women, and slaves, and that it was abandoned in an orderly manner over a thousand years ago after the Norwegians and their immediate descendants had become the first Europeans to discover America approximately five hundred years before the voyage of Christopher Columbus.

CHAPTER THREE:

Unification, Civil Wars, and the Age of Greatness

During the Middle Ages, Norway became a unified country, experienced more than a century of civil wars, and emerged as one of the leading kingdoms of Europe. This chapter focuses on the kings and others who were responsible for those events, and also describes the growth of towns and cities and changes in the countryside.

Harald Fairhair

In the ninth century, Norwegian Vikings on the coast raided and traded in other lands, while farmers in the interior of Norway tended their fields and livestock. Norway was not yet a unified country. On the contrary, Norway was divided into many different regions, and each region was ruled by a petty king, a jarl, or a chieftain. Those leaders and their armies (called hirds) often fought against one another to increase their power and expand their areas of rule. The person who would begin the process of unifying the country was a petty king named Harald, who was called Harald Fairhair or Harald Luva.

He was born in about 860 as the son of a petty king who was a member of the Yngling family. That family ruled the area known as Vestfold on the west side of the Oslofjord. After his father died, Harald was raised by his mother's family in Sogn in western Norway, where his maternal grandfather was also a petty king. By the time he came of age and became a petty king in his own right, Harald was an ambitious person who wanted to unify a large part of Norway under his rule.

The Icelandic saga called *Heimskringla* states that Harald fought to unify the country in order to impress and win the hand of a beautiful maiden. He supposedly refused to cut his long blond hair until he accomplished his goals of ruling the country and marrying the maiden. The story of the maiden is probably pure fiction. It does appear that Harald unified the country by entering into an alliance with various powerful jarls and chieftains primarily in order to pacify and protect the trade routes along the west coast of Norway as their main source of income.

In this effort, one of Harald's principal allies was Håkon Grjotgardsson of Hålogaland, a chieftain who moved his home and hird from northern Norway to Lade at present-day Trondheim and became the jarl of Lade. Another important ally was Ragnvald, the jarl of Møre, who ruled part of the west coast of Norway near present-day Ålesund. Those jarls and various chieftains agreed to submit to Harald as king of Norway with the understanding that they would retain independent rule over their own regions. So instead of a tight union, Norway became unified only in the sense that it was now a loose confederation of Harald Fairhair and various regional leaders who recognized him as the king. Their areas of control were primarily along the coast of Norway, and most of the inland areas did not become part of Harald's kingdom.

However, there were other chieftains, especially in Rogaland and Hordaland in southwest Norway, who opposed the alliance and refused to submit to Harald as king. Harald and his allies fought long and bloody wars against the rebel chieftains. Those wars culminated in the naval Battle of Hafrsfjord that took place sometime before the year 900 in a fjord south of modern-day Stavanger.

In the Middle Ages, sea battles in Scandinavia were fought in a manner that was much different than modern naval engagements. Their ships did not have cannons, explosives, or gunpowder, so individual ships could not maneuver for position, open fire, and destroy the ships of the enemy. Rather, a naval battle was fought like a land battle, but the warriors faced the added risk of falling into the sea and drowning. At the beginning of the battle, each side would often tie its ships together in one or more large rectangles, each called a fighting platform. The fighting platforms would then approach each other, and archers on each side would shoot hundreds of arrows at the other side in an attempt to kill or wound as many of the enemy as possible. When the fighting platforms collided, the men from one side or the other would charge and board the enemy's ships. Using their swords, axes, spears, and shields, the two sides would engage in fierce hand-to-hand combat, like in a land battle, until one side or the other prevailed.

At Hafrsfjord, Harald Fairhair and his allies won a decisive victory over the rebels. Thereafter, the king's alliance was in control of the trade routes along the coasts of Norway. Harald confiscated the lands of his defeated opponents, and he increased his income further by setting tolls on ships sailing in the trade routes and by imposing taxes on his subjects. He had a large band of warriors in his hird, and they all lived extravagantly at his court at Avaldsnes north of

Stavanger. Some of the other chieftains and farmers did not appreciate Harald's taxes, tolls, and other rules, and many left Norway to settle in Iceland and on other North Atlantic islands.

Harald also attempted to improve the relations between Norway and other lands, which had deteriorated due to frequent Viking attacks throughout Europe. For example, Harald sent his younger son Håkon to England to be raised and educated at the court of King Athelstan. In England, Håkon was baptized as a Christian even though his father back in Norway remained loyal to the Norse gods. In honor of the new relationship, Harald gave the English king a Viking ship with a gilded bow and a purple sail, and in return he received an English sword decorated in gold. More importantly, Harald agreed not to support any more Viking attacks on England. Harald died in about 932, leaving at least twenty sons by several wives as his heirs.

From Håkon the Good to Danish rule

Harald Fairhair's chosen successor was his eldest son Eirik, a ruthless tyrant who promptly tried to eliminate his competition by killing most of his brothers. That earned him the name Eirik Bloodaxe. King Eirik was feared and despised by most of the chieftains and farmers, and he was forced to flee Norway after only a couple years of rule. He ended up in England where he became the last Viking king of Northumbria until he was killed in 954.

After Eirik fled the country, the new king of Norway was Harald's younger son Håkon, the Christian who had been raised and educated by the king of England. Håkon ruled from 934 to 961, and he was so popular in Norway that he was called Håkon the Good. He is known for two innovations in governing the country. First, he formed or expanded the *lagting*s, which were regional legislatures and courts that made rules and decisions for larger areas than the local tings. Second, Håkon started the *leidang*, which was a naval force that supported the king and defended the country. At the king's request, the freemen in each local district of Norway were required to provide a ship, a crew, weapons, equipment, and provisions for up to two months each year. During that period, the ships were under the command of the king, who would call out the leidang by a series of bonfires in the mountains.

Unfortunately, like his father, Håkon did not control the entire country. He was opposed by the sons of Eirik Bloodaxe, and they were supported by King Harald Bluetooth of Denmark. They attacked the Norwegian king and his hird, and Håkon was wounded in battle in Hordaland and died shortly thereafter in 961. But in 970 the Danish king betrayed the sons of Eirik Bloodaxe and struck a new deal with Jarl Håkon of Lade.

Norway was then ruled by the king of Denmark in cooperation with the jarl of Lade. The jarl maintained control over the coastlines of western and northern Norway, while the Danish king and various petty kings ruled Viken around the Oslofjord. The jarl and the petty kings acknowledged the king of Denmark as their overlord. However, after a few years the jarl and the new king Svein Forkbeard had a falling out, and in 986 the Danish fleet was defeated by the jarl and the Norwegian leidang in a sea battle at Sunnmøre in western Norway, Nevertheless, the Danish kings continued to claim to be the rightful rulers of part or all of Norway for many years thereafter.

Olav Tryggvason

The onset of Danish rule in Norway meant the end of the predominance of the Yngling family and the heirs of Harald Fairhair. However, there were others who tried to assert their right to rule Norway by claiming to be descendants of the Fairhair dynasty, and one of them was Olav Tryggvason.

He was the son of a petty king in Viken who was killed before Olav was born. When Olav was very young, the hird of the sons of Eirik Bloodaxe tried to kill him and his mother, but mother and son hid in Norway and then escaped to Sweden. They intended to seek refuge in Russia. However, as they crossed the Baltic Sea, their ship was intercepted by pirates, and young Olav was sold into slavery in exchange for a goat. He spent his boyhood years as a farmhand in Estonia until he was discovered and freed by his uncle who took him to the Viking kingdom of Gardarike in Russia.

Olav became a Viking raider at the early age of twelve. He participated in raids in the Baltic, the Netherlands, Scotland, and Ireland, and he gradually assumed the position of a powerful Viking leader. In 991 Olav assembled a fleet of ninety-three Viking ships, raided the coast of England near Folkestone and Sandwich, and defeated the English army at the Battle of Maldon. He demanded and received from the English a payment of ten thousand pounds of gold and silver. His raids in England continued for three more years, during which he besieged London along with the Danish king Svein Forkbeard and extracted an even larger payment of sixteen thousand pounds.

By 994 Olav was a rich man. He had also become a Christian, and he entered into an agreement with King Aethelred the Unready of England. As part of the deal, Olav was confirmed in the cathedral at Andover with Aethelred as his sponsor, he received expensive gifts from the king, and he promised never to attack England again. He could make this promise because now his sights were set on Norway.

In 995 many chieftains and farmers in Trøndelag around the Trondheimsfjord were in open revolt against the harsh rule of Jarl Håkon of Lade. The rebels were victorious in their uprising against the forces of the jarl, and he tried to hide from the rebels in a pigsty. But there he was killed by his own slave named Kark.

At about the same time, Olav Tryggvason arrived in Norway with a large fleet and army, and he was proclaimed king of Norway at the *Øreting* in Trøndelag. In return, Olav promised to uphold the law, allow the Norwegians to practice their Norse religion, and not interfere with the power and authority of the local chieftains. He and the Trøndelag chieftains combined their armies and took control of Viken around the Oslofjord and Hålogaland in northern Norway. In addition, Olav formed an alliance with Erling Skjalgsson, the most powerful chieftain in western Norway. With

Olav and his allies in control of most of Norway, the sons of the deceased jarl of Lade fled to Sweden, and the rule of the Danish kings in Viken was suspended.

So at first Olav Tryggvason was a popular leader who had restored the independence of Norway under a Norwegian king. He was handsome, brave and strong, and he was so athletic that he could dance on the oars of his ship. Olav is credited with founding the city of Nidaros (now called Trondheim) in 997, although there was probably a small village in that location before that date. He also minted the first Norwegian coins in Norway, and he spread Christianity to the Faeroe Islands, Iceland, and Greenland.

But Olav broke all the promises he had made when he became king. He forced Norwegians to convert to Christianity at the point of a sword. He prohibited the Norse religion, destroyed heathen temples, murdered many people who refused to convert, and tried to reduce the power of the chieftains. These actions brought Olav into conflict with chieftains and farmers alike, especially in the heathen heartlands of Trøndelag and Hålogaland. In fact, Olav became very unpopular in most of the country.

In the meantime, Eirik, the son of the deceased jarl of Lade, was in the court of the king of Sweden, where he conspired with the rulers of Sweden and Denmark to attack Olav Tryggvason and take back control of Norway. Olav heard about their plans and decided to attack first. He called out the leidang, but no one responded. The chieftains and farmers refused to provide Olav with any ships or other support.

Nevertheless, in the year 1000 Olav left Norway with a small fleet of only eleven longships, and set sail for the Baltic Sea where he had made an alliance with a Polish duke who agreed to support him with additional ships and men. The Battle of Svolder was a sea battle in the Baltic Sea, and Olav's fleet was totally outnumbered and overwhelmed by the combined fleets of the Swedish and Danish kings and Eirik of Lade. The Polish duke's forces did not fight on Olav's side because their commander was paid off by the king of Denmark. The battle was no contest, and

Olav was surrounded on his flagship called *The Long Serpent*. Not wanting to be taken captive, he jumped overboard, put his shield over his face, and drowned.

The victors divided up Norway. Sweden took the region of Ranrike. Svein Forkbeard, the king of Denmark, became the king of Norway and assumed control of Viken. Eirik and Svein, the sons of the jarl of Lade, were named the regents of the Danish king in Trøndelag, Hålogaland, and western Norway. King Svein and the jarls were supported by many Norwegian chieftains who were promised a degree of independence and the right to practice their heathen religion. But Norway's status as an independent kingdom was over for the time being.

St. Olav

Olav Haraldsson, later called St. Olav, was the next Norwegian to become king of Norway, and he eventually became the patron saint of the country. In many respects, his life and career were strikingly similar to Olav Tryggvason. He was born in 995 as the son of a petty king in Viken, and he claimed to be a descendant of Harald Fairhair. He was already a Viking warrior at age twelve. Later he attacked England, amassed a fortune of great wealth, switched sides and became a Christian, became king of Norway, brutally forced conversion of the people to Christianity, and was overthrown and killed. However, there were some differences between the two Olavs. Olav Haraldsson was not nearly as handsome or athletic as his predecessor, and for most of his life he was called Olav Digre, meaning Fat Olav. But he was strong-willed and ambitious, and he succeeded (where Olav Tryggvason failed) in making Norway a more unified, Christian country.

As a young Viking, Olav participated in raids in the Baltic region and the Netherlands. When he became a Viking leader, he and his men attacked England and killed the archbishop of Canterbury in 1011. After collecting a ransom of forty-eight thousand pounds from the English in 1012, the largest Viking ransom ever paid, he formed an alliance with the English king

Aethelred the Unready and fought against the Danish invaders of England. In 1013 he and the English king fled to Normandy, where Olav served in the army of the duke of Normandy and was baptized as a Christian in Rouen. While in Normandy, he observed the efficient administration and feudal system of the Normans that would become a model for his subsequent rule in Norway.

Returning to fight in England, in 1014 Olav saved the city of London from Danish control by destroying London Bridge. That event was the origin of the nursery rhyme "London Bridge is falling down". However, the Danes were on the verge of winning the war in England, and Olav decided to return to Norway.

In 1015 Olav Haraldsson, his Viking army of only about 120 men, and a few English bishops sailed on two merchant ships to Norway. The Danish king and the jarl of Lade were still busy fighting in England, and their absence gave Olav an opportunity to try to become the king of Norway. But at first Olav was not successful in taking over the country, as he faced strong, armed opposition in Trøndelag. However, he used his family connections and his great wealth to obtain the loyalty of some Norwegian chieftains and prominent farmers in the inland areas around Gudbrandsdalen and eastern Norway, and he and his allies defeated several petty kings who did not support him. His fate was decided on Palm Sunday in 1016, when Olav and his fleet won a decisive victory over the fleet of the jarl of Lade at the Battle of Nesjar at the mouth of the Oslofjord. Olav was proclaimed king of Norway, and Danish rule of the country was interrupted once again.

Thereafter, Olav united the country, including the coastline and the inland regions, under an efficient central administration. He appointed *lendmenn* (lords) and *årmenn* (king's representatives or stewards) to administer the local districts and the royal lands on his behalf. The lendmenn became wealthy because they were permitted to receive income from the king's lands, fines, and taxes in their districts. Olav wanted to make sure that his lendmenn were loyal, so in some cases he appointed lesser chieftains or even leading farmers, and that raised the resentment of various powerful chieftains who were not appointed and thus did not share in the largesse. While the lendmenn were intended to be feudal lords like their counterparts in Normandy, Olav was never really successful in his efforts to make Norway a feudal society. This was because most of the farmers in Norway were independent landowning freemen and not poor peasants, and they were not about to be dominated and ruled by the king's lendmenn.

Olav's other main accomplishment was to make Norway a Christian country. Like Olav Tryggvason, Olav Haraldsson forcibly required Norwegians to become Christians, he murdered heathens who did not convert, and he destroyed pagan temples. But Olav Haraldsson was much more successful than his predecessor in that he formed a new and lasting national church organization.

In 1024 King Olav and his leading Christian adviser, Bishop Grimkell of England, convened a national assembly at Moster that established the Church of Norway led by the king. The assembly also set moral and religious rules for all Norwegians. Those rules required all of the people to be baptized, proclaimed marriage to one wife as a sacrament, and provided for rites of Christian burial. The rules prohibited all other religions, as well as various heathen customs such as the practice of leaving unwanted babies out in the forest to die. Slavery was also discouraged if not prohibited. However, in order to keep everyone happy, Olav had to preserve certain pagan practices, such as the popular beer fests that were allowed as long as the beer was first blessed and toasts were made to Christ and the Virgin Mary.

In addition, it became the responsibility of each local community in Norway to build and support a local church and to hire and pay a local priest. Within the next two hundred years, hundreds of stone and wooden churches were built throughout Norway, including the unique wooden stave churches, some of which still dot the countryside or are found in outdoor museums in Norway.

3.1 Hopperstad stave church in Vik, built in 1130

During King Olav's reign, Norway experienced several years of peace and independence. But Olav ruled with an iron hand and did not tolerate dissent, and from time to time he arrested or killed his opponents and confiscated their lands. Over time the resentment of some of the leading chieftains reached a breaking point as they experienced a loss of their independence, power, and heathen religion. Moreover, the king of Denmark and England, Knut the Great, continued to assert his claim over Norway.

Some of the chieftains and their hirds started a rebellion against Olav. Things came to a head in 1027 when the powerful chieftain Erling Skjalgsson was murdered by Olav's men after he surrendered in a sea battle. News of that event spread quickly, and Olav lost the support of chieftains and farmers throughout the country. Many joined an alliance with Knut the Great, including some who were bribed by the Danish king to do so. Knut's army and navy invaded Norway in 1028. Olav fled to Sweden and then to Gardarike in Russia where he stayed with his brother-in-law Prince Jaroslav. Back home in Norway, Knut the Great was proclaimed king. Knut appointed Jarl Håkon of Lade as his regent in Norway, but the jarl was lost at sea in 1029. When Olav heard the news of Håkon's demise, he decided to make his way back to Norway to try to reclaim his throne.

In 1030, after two years in exile, Olav returned to Norway with a small army of Swedes, Icelanders, and Norwegians. They crossed the mountains from Sweden to Trøndelag, where they ran into a much larger opposing force of chieftains and farmers at a place called Stiklestad north of Nidaros. At the Battle of Stiklestad on July 29, 1030, Olav was killed and his army was soundly defeated. His attempt to regain the throne of Norway ended in failure.

Two of Olav's followers secretly removed his body from the battlefield, and later he was buried in the sands along the Nid River at Nidaros. Shortly thereafter there were stories of miraculous cures and other mysterious events related to Olav, his name, and his gravesite. A year after his burial, his body was exhumed and he appeared to still be alive with a ruddy complexion and hair and nails that had continued to grow. So he was declared a saint by Bishop Grimkell, and his sainthood was later confirmed by the pope. Christians began to make pilgrimages to St. Olav's shrine at Nidaros, and several churches in Europe were named after him.

Over time St. Olav became a uniting symbol of Norway. The date of his death, July 29, is called *Olsok* and is an annual Christian day of celebration in Norway. His lasting legacy is the Church of Norway, which continues in modified form to this day. St. Olav's body is still buried at an unknown location on the grounds of Nidaros Cathedral in Trondheim, which was built in his honor. Due in large part to Olav's efforts and reputation, and in order to give the papacy more control and influence over the Norwegian Church, the pope gave Norway its own archdiocese based in Nidaros in 1152.

In 1029 Knut the Great appointed his young son Svein as the new regent in Norway, and Svein ruled the country along with his English mother named Alfiva. They instituted a harsh and arbitrary rule characterized by heavy fines and taxation. The king of Denmark took control over Norwegian imports and exports, held hostages to discourage any revolt, and even prohibited anyone from leaving

Norway without his permission. The problems were compounded by a famine in Norway during the regency period. The king and his regent also tried to reduce the powers and rights of the chieftains, who felt betrayed and came to despise the king and Danish rule.

After St. Olav was killed, his young son Magnus was taken to safety in Gardarike. In 1034 two Norwegian chieftains, who had been enemies of St. Olav at the time of the Battle of Stiklestad, traveled to Russia. The following year they brought Magnus home to Norway where he was proclaimed king of Norway. The Danish regent Svein and his mother fled the country without a fight, and Norway was again an independent kingdom ruled by a Norwegian king. In fact, the Danish empire fell apart after Knut the Great's death in 1035, although his successors continued to claim the thrones of England and Norway for a time.

In 1037 young King Magnus was taken to a meeting with young King Hardeknut of Denmark, the son of Knut the Great, at a place along the Göta River in what is now Sweden. At this meeting, they entered into a peace treaty, agreeing that each king would be the heir of the other king. So the survivor of the two kings would become the king of both Norway and Denmark. Hardeknut later became the king of England. When he died in a drinking binge at a party in 1042, Magnus was elected king of Denmark to add to his rule in Norway, but the English crown was given to an Englishman of royal lineage named Edward the Confessor. Even though the Danes no longer ruled England, as a result of the agreement on the Göta River the Norwegian kings continued to lay claim to the English throne.

Harald Hardråde

St. Olav's younger half brother, and the future king of Norway, was Harald Hardråde (meaning the hard ruler). Harald was a lifelong soldier who obtained his surname because of his harsh treatment of his opponents. He was an intimidating figure, well over six feet tall, with a large beard, moustache, and eyebrows, and he was very brave and strong.

He was also the last Viking king of Norway, and the end of his reign in 1066 is said to mark the conclusion of the Viking age, although there were occasional Viking attacks thereafter. Like so many Vikings before him, Harald Hardråde was primarily motivated to seek power, fame, and fortune.

When he was only fifteen, Harald led an army from central Norway to join Olav's army at Stiklestad. Harald was wounded in the battle, but he was taken to safety in the forest and then over the mountains to Sweden. He wound up in Gardarike, where he joined the army of Prince Jaroslav and fought in Poland, Estonia, and Russia. He also had a crush on the prince's daughter Ellisiv, and he proposed to her. But, despite his royal connections, she could not accept the proposal of someone who was not a wealthy man.

So Harald moved on, leading an army of five hundred men to Constantinople, where he became a colonel in the Byzantine army. He commanded a Viking fleet against pirates in the Mediterranean and fought with distinction in Asia Minor, Italy, Sicily, and Palestine. He also brutally suppressed a rebellion against the Byzantine emperor and burned the homes of rebels in Bulgaria. Harald was so successful that he became an official of the emperor's court and the commander of the Varangian Guard.

Harald had already become a very wealthy man, but his thirst for more riches eventually got him into trouble. He was imprisoned for misappropriating money from the emperor's treasury, and he was fortunate to be freed from prison in a palace rebellion in 1042. Realizing that he had outstayed his welcome in Constantinople, he slipped back into Russia, and by then he was sufficiently wealthy and powerful to marry Ellisiv in 1045.

After his return to Russia, Harald finally learned that his nephew Magnus had become the king of Norway, so he decided to return to his home country and assert what he felt was his rightful claim to be the king. He and Ellisiv sailed back to Scandinavia, where Harald began to conspire with Knut the Great's nephew, Svein of Denmark, to invade Norway and oust Magnus from the thrones of both Norway and Denmark. But in 1046 Harald received a better offer from Magnus and switched sides. Magnus promised Harald half the kingdom of Norway if Harald would share his fortune with Magnus. Harald accepted this proposal only to find out later that Magnus and the royal treasury of Norway were bankrupt. Nevertheless, Magnus and Harald served as co-kings of Norway in an uneasy relationship that ended when Magnus died in 1047. Harald Hardråde had achieved his goal to be the sole king of Norway.

Harald also wanted to succeed Magnus as king of Denmark, but that position was given to Svein. An irate Harald then repeatedly attacked the coast of Denmark over the next several years. He even burned the market town of Hedeby in Denmark in 1049. However, by 1064 his funds were running low, so he entered into a truce with Svein and abandoned his claim to the Danish throne.

Not everyone in Norway was enthused about the return of Harald Hardråde and his accession to the throne. That included several petty kings and chieftains who still wielded power in various parts of the country. In particular, a powerful chieftain named Einar Tambarskjelve kept his own army and fleet and challenged the authority of Harald in Trøndelag. Harald dealt with him by inviting him to a meeting and then having him and his son killed on the spot. Harald then brutally crushed a rebellion of farmers in eastern and central Norway after they objected to his high taxes and fines. Over the course of several years, Harald and his army destroyed the power of the petty kings and chieftains once and for all, and opposition to his rule disappeared. In those years he clearly earned his name as the hard ruler.

Harald was successful in achieving the goal of St. Olav to establish a truly all-powerful central and local administration controlled by the king, his hird, and his appointed lendmenn and årmenn throughout Norway. There were still wealthy ex-chieftains and free farmers, but from now on the aristocracy of Norway would be selected by the king.

Harald Hardråde was considered the founder of Oslo, the new town at the head of the Oslofjord, and he also established a Norwegian currency. Like Olav Tryggvason and St. Olav, Harald minted Norwegian coins, but he went one step further in replacing all foreign coins with Norwegian coins as the acceptable currency in Norway.

Stamford Bridge

As a result of Magnus' prior agreement with Hardeknut at the Göta River, Harald Hardråde claimed to be the rightful king of England. In January 1066 King Edward the Confessor of England died without leaving any heirs. The leading contenders to be the next king of England were King Harald Hardråde of Norway, Duke William of Normandy, King Svein of Denmark, and an English nobleman named Harold Godwinson. William claimed that Edward the Confessor had promised him the throne, but some statements by Edward on his deathbed indicated that he really wanted Godwinson, the powerful earl of Wessex, to be his successor. Svein was considered the least likely candidate, and he was not currently in the mood to invade England and assert his claim after enduring so many years of war against Norway.

Another claimant was Earl Tostig, the brother of Harold Godwinson and the former earl of Northumbria. He had lost his earldom after he murdered a number of nobles and otherwise abused his office. Tostig actually had little or no support in England. When the English nobility promptly elected Harold Godwinson as king of England in January 1066, Tostig was resentful and jealous of his brother. He became a pirate and conducted raids along the coast of England until he decided on a plan to overthrow his brother by striking a deal with one of the other contenders to the throne.

First Tostig approached Duke William and later Svein of Denmark without success. So then he made contact with Harald Hardråde and promised him extensive popular and military support in England if Harald invaded England to take the throne and share his power with Tostig.

It did not take long for Harald Hardråde to accept Tostig's proposal, but he made it clear that he alone must be the next king of England. After his experience as co-king with Magnus in Norway, he was not going to share the crown with anyone. Tostig agreed, and Harald assembled a large army and fleet in Norway. But he also had bad premonitions. In a dream, St. Olav warned him not to invade England.

Harald overcame his misgivings, and his considerable Viking fleet sailed from Norway to Shetland and Orkney, where he picked up additional ships and men. Tostig had also promised him a large fleet, but when Harald arrived off the northeast coast of England in early September, Tostig showed up with only twelve ships manned by a few of his own followers and some Flemish pirates. However, by then Harald's forces included three hundred ships and over ten thousand men.

Harald and Tostig then raided the English coast, sailed upriver, and attacked the city of York. The city was defended by two English earls and their armies, but they were far outnumbered by Harald's army, and they sent an appeal for assistance to King Harold Godwinson.

Godwinson had assembled a large English army in southern England, where he expected an invasion by William of Normandy. By the time he found out about Harald Hardråde's invasion of Northumbria, his supplies were running low and his troops had begun to disperse. So Godwinson had to recall and re-form his army. Sensing that the threat from Norway was of more immediate concern, Godwinson led his army of several thousand men north on a forced march covering over two hundred miles in just nine days. It was a magnificent achievement, and now Godwinson and his army were in position to face off against the Norwegian invaders near the city of York.

On September 20 Harald Hardråde's army scored a decisive victory over the northern earls, and the city of York appeared to be defenseless. The city fathers and Harald agreed on September 24 to a surrender of the city to the Norwegians, and they arranged a meeting to finalize the surrender and deliver hostages at a place called Stamford Bridge on the following day.

The morning of September 25, 1066, dawned brightly as a clear, warm day. Expecting no opposition, the Vikings left their chain mail, some of their weapons, and a third of their army back at the ships and strolled toward Stamford Bridge, located on a small river near York. As the main force of Norwegians was relaxing and sunning themselves on the east side of the bridge, Harald Hardråde looked west and saw in the distance the glint of iron and a huge force of men. The surprised Norwegian king asked Tostig who they were, and they finally concluded that it was the entire English army. Suddenly the Viking army was itself outnumbered.

The English attacked and killed several Norwegians who were foraging for food on the west side of the river. Then they tried to storm across the bridge, but they were stopped in their tracks by several Norwegians who were defending the narrow crossing. In particular, there was one giant Viking who stood in the middle of the bridge, swung his battle axe, and killed countless Englishmen. He literally held off the advance of the English army for over an hour. But he was finally killed by an English soldier who floated in a boat under the bridge and speared him through the planks of the bridge.

The English army crossed over the bridge to the east side of the river and prepared to attack the main force of Norwegians. A brave Viking like Harald Hardråde was not about to withdraw, so he assembled his troops and prepared to meet the English onslaught, while also sending for reinforcements from his ships.

Just before the final battle was about to begin, twenty English horsemen approached Harald and Tostig. Their leader asked Tostig to switch sides and offered him one-third of the English kingdom. Tostig asked what was in it for the king of Norway, and the Englishman replied that they could only offer him a large burial plot on English soil. Needless to say, the offer was rejected, the horsemen rode away, and Harald asked Tostig to identify the impressive leader of the horsemen. Tostig replied that it was his brother, King Harold Godwinson. Harald Hardråde was enraged that Tostig had not told him earlier, because then his men could have cut down the English king and ended the battle right then and there.

The final battle ensued, and the outnumbered Vikings were routed over the course of several hours. Harald Hardråde fought bravely and furiously at the front of his troops, but he was soon killed by an arrow to the throat. Tostig tried to rally the defenders, and he was also killed. The Norwegian reinforcements from the ships ran long and hard to the battlefield to the point of exhaustion, and they were also slaughtered. At the end of the day, it was a total English victory over the Norwegians, 90 percent of whom had died on the battlefield. Harold Godwinson permitted Harald Hardråde's son Olav to leave with his remaining men and only twenty-four ships, but first Olav had to agree to return to Norway and not attack England again. He also had to deliver to the English all of the gold that Harald Hardråde had brought with him to England. Olav and the small fleet left for Norway, and Olav became the king of Norway as Olav Kyrre (the Peacemaker). The Viking age was over.

Harold Godwinson then led his army on another forced march, this time back to southern England. William of Normandy and his army came across the English Channel and invaded England. On October 14, 1066, the Normans defeated the English at the Battle of Hastings. Harold Godwinson was killed, and William, a descendant of the Vikings, became the king of England.

Civil wars

Norway was ravaged by a series of civil wars during the period from 1134 to 1240. The problem was that, when a king of Norway died, the Norwegian rule of royal succession did not designate one successor to be the new king. Rather, upon the death of the king, any legitimate or illegitimate male descendant of either that king or any previous king of Norway could claim the throne if he descended through the male line. Therefore, there could be many different contenders who all had an equal right to the throne, and then it was up to various local or regional tings to elect the next king from that group of contenders. So Norway was both a hereditary and an elective monarchy.

Unfortunately, different tings in different parts of Norway would sometimes elect different people to be the next king. If more than one person was elected, all the elected contenders might then try to agree among themselves who would be king or co-kings. If they did not agree, they would fight it out until one contender and his army prevailed and the victorious contender became the king. During the period of the civil wars, a long list of contenders and their followers were constantly battling against each other. Even if one contender won the battles, there were always new contenders who would surface, make their claims, and start the wars all over again. Ironically, it was an Irishman, not a Norwegian, who first caused the civil wars.

In the 1120s an Irishman who called himself Harald Gilchrist (or Harald Gille) showed up at the court of King Sigurd the Crusader of Norway. Sigurd was known as the Crusader because he had led one of the Crusades to the Holy Land, conquered the city of Sidon for the Christians, and even lived to tell about it, returning home to Norway to reclaim his crown. The strange visitor named Gilchrist looked like an Irishman with dark hair and dark eyes. He also dressed like an Irishman and talked like an Irishman. The members of the king's court were amused at his bad, broken Norwegian. Furthermore, his reputation as a drunken womanizer had preceded him. He was all of those things, but he was also slick, friendly and persuasive. Even his chosen name of Gilchrist, meaning servant of Christ, was meant to curry favor with the influential leaders of the Norwegian Church.

Gilchrist came up with an amazing story about how he was the long lost son of King Magnus Barefoot and the half brother of King Sigurd. He explained that he was in Norway to claim his rightful position as heir to the Norwegian throne. Sigurd politely listened to his story and then asked his own advisers what he should do with the stranger. They told the king that he would have to make up his own mind, although they were undoubtedly more than skeptical of the claims of this unusual and unwelcome interloper.

Sigurd was a fair person, so he told Gilchrist that he would be permitted to prove the truth of his story in a trial by ordeal, but only if Gilchrist first agreed not to claim the throne during the lifetimes of Sigurd and his son Magnus. Gilchrist sensed his opening and readily agreed. In the trial by ordeal, he walked on bare feet over nine red-hot plowshares, and then his feet were bandaged. Three days later a priest removed the bandages and declared that Gilchrist's feet were healed so he must be telling the truth. In the face of this persuasive evidence, Sigurd accepted Gilchrist into his court as a member of the royal family.

When Sigurd died in 1130 and Magnus was ready to become the next king, Gilchrist suddenly reneged on his previous agreement and claimed half the throne, arguing that his agreement had been obtained by duress. In contrast to Gilchrist, Magnus was an arrogant, disagreeable person who was not well liked, and he felt compelled to share the throne with the more popular Gilchrist, who had raised his own army and enjoyed the support of many lendmenn. But Magnus insisted upon retaining all of the royal powers and privileges. Over the next four years, the co-kings experienced a stormy relationship, and in 1134 Magnus and his army attacked Harald and his forces. Gilchrist was defeated and fled to Denmark, where he was supported by the king of Denmark.

Believing that he was rid of the Irishman for good, Magnus disregarded the advice of his officials and permitted his army to go home, while he and his fleet retired to Bergen. Early in 1135 Gilchrist and his new fleet attacked. Magnus and his fleet were totally surprised and bottled up in the harbor, where they were defeated. Magnus was captured, and Gilchrist handed him over to his own slaves with instructions to make sure that Magnus could never be a king again. The slaves blinded Magnus, cut off one of his feet, and also castrated him to prevent any future heirs. Magnus was sent off to a monastery in the Trondheimsfjord. At that point, Magnus decided that his days as king were over, so he started a course of study to become a monk. Gilchrist became the king of Norway.

Less than two years later, in 1136, another pretender named Sigurd Slembe arrived on the scene. At the king's court, he made his claim as rightful heir to the throne, and Gilchrist responded by trying to have him killed. Slembe narrowly escaped and he returned to catch Gilchrist by surprise in the bedchamber of his mistress. Slembe murdered Gilchrist and released Magnus the Blind, which was somewhat unfortunate because the latter had almost completed his course of study to become a monk. Nevertheless, Slembe and Magnus proclaimed themselves as the new co-kings, but they had little support and they were opposed by supporters of the sons of Gilchrist, including Inge the Hunchback and Sigurd the Mouth. There followed a long series of civil wars in which they were all killed and others emerged to make their claims to be the rightful king of Norway.

Sverre and the Birkebeinere

In about 1176 a young priest arrived in Norway on a ship from the Faeroe Islands, literally the backwater of the Norwegian kingdom. Later he would say that God sent to Norway a little low man from the outer skerries. His name was Sverre, and he would turn out to be one of the most significant and mysterious personalities in the history of Norway. He was back in Norway, the land of his birth, to fulfill his destiny. First he needed to find out who held the real power in a country still racked by civil wars.

Sverre was the son of a woman named Gunnhild who had married a comb maker named Unas. As a young man, Sverre studied under Unas' brother Roe, who was the bishop of the Faeroes, and Sverre was ordained as a priest. He apparently had a wife and children in the Faeroes, and there were rumors that Bishop Roe had used his influence to extract the young priest from some criminal allegations regarding an assault. In any event, Sverre wanted to leave all of that behind him and start a new life in Norway. He spent the next year traveling around the country.

At that time, a leading aristocrat named Erling Skakke was the most powerful person in Norway. He was called Skakke, meaning crooked or tilted, because his neck had been wounded in battle and he could not hold his head up straight. Nevertheless, Skakke was influential enough to have made a deal with the church and the aristocracy to change the Norwegian rule of royal succession and elect his son Magnus as the king of Norway. Under the old rule of succession, Magnus would not have qualified to be king because he was the grandson of King Sigurd the Crusader through the maternal line; that is, his mother was Sigurd's daughter. But the new law of succession provided that the oldest legitimate male descendant of any deceased king would be the new king, whether he descended on the paternal side or the maternal side of the family. The law was written to specify just one person to be king and hopefully to avoid any more civil wars. Thanks to some creative drafting of the new law by Skakke, his son Magnus just happened to be the one person who qualified to be king. Skakke was cold and calculating enough to even kill his stepson in order to eliminate a rival to Magnus.

Skakke got the church to agree to the new law by giving the church more rights including the right to receive increased fines for violations of church laws, and by agreeing that the bishops and their appointees would dominate the committee that would determine the identity of each new king. In addition, Magnus pledged his loyalty to the pope and his obedience to the church, and in 1163 he was crowned as the new king by the archbishop in the presence of a papal legate from Rome. It was the first royal coronation in Scandinavia. However, the civil wars continued because there were still other contenders to the throne who rejected Magnus and the new law of succession. Nonetheless, Magnus was in a very strong position in that he commanded the largest army and navy and he had the firm support of the church and the aristocracy.

After traveling around Norway for several months, Sverre showed up at the castle of Birger Brosa, the powerful earl of Götaland in Sweden who was married to Brigida, the sister of the former king Sigurd the Mouth (the son of Gilchrist). The young priest came up with his own incredible story about how his mother took a pilgrimage to Rome, where she confessed that her son Sverre was really the illegitimate son of King Sigurd the Mouth, and the pope instructed her to disclose this secret information to her son. So Gunnhild finally told Sverre the truth, and now Sverre wanted to become the king of Norway as a rightful heir under the old rule of royal succession. Birger Brosa was suspicious of Sverre and his story and refused to help him. In fact, most modern historians seem to agree that Sverre's tale was just a figment of his vivid imagination and that there is no way he could have been the son of Sigurd the Mouth.

Undaunted by his temporary setback, Sverre moved on to visit Sigurd the Mouth's daughter Cecilia in Värmland. She listened to his story and gave him a friendly reception, but no real support.

At this point, perhaps at the urging of Birger Brosa, Sverre ended up in a Swedish forest in the middle of the frozen winter early in 1177. There he found a ragtag band of about seventy soldiers who were hiding and cowering in the woods. They were a bunch of lowlifes from Norway, including former criminals and unemployed farm hands, who were the remnants of an army that had fought for a young pretender to the Norwegian throne named Øystein Møyla. He was called Møyla, meaning Little Miss, because of his childlike appearance. In January 1177 they had been badly defeated by Magnus' army at the Battle of Re, and Møyla had been killed shortly after the battle when he sought refuge in the farmhouse of one of Magnus' supporters. Now they were just trying to flee from Magnus' forces and somehow survive the winter.

Magnus and his followers made fun of this lower class outfit by calling them the *Birkebeinere* (meaning the Birchlegs) because they were so poor that they had to wrap birch bark around their legs when their pants wore out. But the Birkebeinere used this name of derision as a badge of honor, and they were actually proud to call themselves the Birchlegs. Since they had nothing better to do, they patiently listened as Sverre retold his story. Despite his claims, he certainly did not look like a Norwegian king because he was short and stocky. But Little Miss was dead and they had nowhere else to go, so they decided to elect Sverre as their new leader and pretender to the throne. That decision at least would give them some reason to carry on and fight another day. At first Sverre turned them down. But then the Birchlegs threatened to kill him unless he accepted, so Sverre reluctantly became their leader.

For someone without any military experience, the young priest turned out to be an excellent general. From day one he motivated the troops with his inspirational speeches. More importantly, he realized that his small band would be no match for Magnus' large army in a face-to-face battle, so he taught the Birkebeinere to be experts at intelligence, deception, and guerilla warfare. They learned how to spy on the enemy and then use mobile forces to attack in surprise, hit-and-run raids that wore down the opposing forces over time. As they began to have success, they made their way over the mountains and picked up many new recruits on their way to Nidaros.

In the summer of 1177, the Birkebeinere attacked and defeated Magnus' lendmenn and their forces at Nidaros at a time when Magnus' main army and navy were not present. Sverre was proclaimed king by the *Øreting* in Trøndelag. However, King Magnus and Erling Skakke were still in control of the rest of the country.

The turning point of the war came in June 1179. Magnus, Skakke, and their large fleet landed at Nidaros, and the Birkebeinere appeared to withdraw far to the south of town. But after a few days Sverre re-grouped his forces near Nidaros and delivered an impassioned speech. He told them that total victory was now within their grasp, and he promised that, if anyone killed a lendmann or some other high official, then that person would be appointed to the same position by Sverre. In the meantime, Magnus' men were convinced that the Birchlegs had been effectively defeated and dispersed. They let their guard down, had a huge party, got rip-roaring drunk, and went to sleep.

In the early morning hours of June 19, the Birkebeinere launched a surprise attack on the drunken, sleepy soldiers and routed them completely in the Battle of Kalvskinnet. Skakke was killed, and Magnus barely escaped with a small part of his army and just a few of his ships.

At this point, Sverre became recognized as king in more parts of the country, while Magnus controlled other areas and was supported by the church and the king of Denmark. Sverre built up his army and navy, and he constructed fortresses in the towns that he controlled. He built ships with tall sides that made them difficult for the enemy to board and that allowed his troops to shoot and throw weapons downward at their opponents. The war continued, but Sverre and the Birkebeinere won most of the battles as they often outwitted the enemy.

The two kings and their respective armies were quite different. Magnus had a regal appearance – tall, handsome and strong. In battle he fought bravely next to his standard (flag) on the front line, at great risk to his personal safety. But apart from his hird of professional soldiers, his men were relatively untrained farmer conscripts commanded by their lendmenn as officers.

In contrast, Sverre was not particularly impressive looking, but he was a shrewd tactician, a master of deception, and an effective leader. In a land battle, Sverre stayed safely behind the front lines, mounted on his horse, where he could view the entire battlefield and direct all units of his army throughout the battle. By 1180 his Birchlegs had become a large, formidable, professional fighting force.

In that year, the two armies fought a major battle at Ilevollene along the Trondhemsfjord just west of Nidaros. Magnus and his main force charged towards Sverre's standard on the right flank of the Birchlegs, only to find that Sverre was not there. Instead he was over on the left flank where he ordered his best troops to advance and surround the enemy. Magnus and his forces were trapped with their backs to the fjord, and the king fled in a small boat while losing most of his army and navy. Magnus headed for Denmark, and his supporter Archbishop Øystein Erlendsson left for exile in England, whereupon Sverre and the Birkebeinere occupied the city of Bergen. However, Magnus promptly raised a new army and navy with the assistance of the king of Denmark, and the bloody civil war in Norway continued.

Sverre almost always seemed to have good fortune on his side. He was so lucky that his enemies accused him of making a pact with the devil. For example, in a sea battle off the Norwegian coast, Sverre and his ships were far outnumbered and headed for certain defeat when a dense fog rolled in and allowed them to escape.

Despite his tenuous control over much of the country throughout his reign, Sverre began to appoint loyal *sysselmenn* to administer local areas on his behalf in place of Magnus' lendmenn. Whereas the lendmenn had been wealthy nobles from the local areas they controlled, Sverre's new sysselmenn typically came from other parts of Norway and were more closely tied to the king and his central administration. In addition, Sverre named new *lagmenn* as local judicial officers. So he created a new aristocracy under his own control, while removing or killing most of the old nobility and confiscating their lands.

The definitive battle of the war between Sverre and Magnus was the Battle of Fimreite on the Sognefjord in 1184. Sverre was in command of a small fleet of fourteen ships including his huge flagship called *Mariasuden*, a leaking hulk that was barely seaworthy. On June 15 they were surprised by a larger fleet of twenty-six ships commanded by Magnus. While Magnus tied his ships together in the traditional fighting platforms, Sverre let his ships sail independently, probing for weaknesses in the larger fleet and then attacking those weak spots. In this manner, Sverre's men managed to take Magnus' ships one by one. Magnus' men continued to retreat until several of his remaining ships were overloaded and suddenly sank into the waters of the fjord. In the process, Magnus jumped overboard and was killed along with hundreds of his men, including many members of his nobility. The Birchlegs had won the war, but new contenders to the throne and their armies continued to appear and challenge Sverre and the Birkebeinere from time to time.

Considering that he was a priest, King Sverre had a terrible relationship with the pope, the bishops, and the church in general, all of whom supported his enemies. The basic issue was that Sverre felt that the church should be subordinate to the king, whereas the church felt the exact opposite. Three years after he fled Norway, Archbishop Øystein returned from England, made peace with Sverre, and thereafter concentrated on his administrative church duties and the construction of Nidaros Cathedral.

However, after Øystein died in 1188, his successor Archbishop Eirik Ivarsson insisted upon retaining all of the rights and powers that the church had received in its prior agreement with Skakke and Magnus. He also believed that Sverre was an illegitimate fraud and a bigamist (Sverre having married the sister of the king of Sweden) who had unfaithfully abandoned the priesthood and was not worthy to be king. Therefore, Eirik steadfastly declined to hold a coronation ceremony for Sverre. Eirik and Sverre constantly argued over the church's right to name bishops and priests, the church's receipt of expensive fines, and even the allowable size of Eirik's hird. All of these issues created an irreconcilable conflict, and in 1190 Archbishop Eirik left Norway for exile in Lund, Denmark, where he lost his sight and stayed as the guest of the Danish archbishop for over ten years. In response, Sverre confiscated Eirik's property in Norway and declared that the archbishop's blindness was God's punishment for his unchristian attitude and behavior.

The archbishop then sent a complaint letter to the pope, who issued a papal bull authorizing Eirik to excommunicate Sverre. The archbishop promptly did so, and he was so angry with Sverre that he publicly recited the excommunication order once each week for several years at the altar of the Lund Cathedral. Back in Norway, Sverre had himself crowned by the remaining bishops, which led the pope to excommunicate them as well. Gradually the bishops all left Norway to seek the archbishop's forgiveness in Denmark. Sverre made matters worse by coming up with a fraudulent letter which stated that the pope had pardoned him. The pope angrily announced that the letter was a forgery. Sverre would not change his position, and one of his own priests wrote *A Speech against the Bishops* asserting that the king is God's chosen overlord over the church, that the king answers only to God, and that the church has a duty of loyalty and obedience to the king.

In the meantime, in 1196 the bishops raised their own army called the Baglers in support of Magnus' alleged son Inge. The fighting between the Birkebeinere and the Baglers was intense for many years. During the siege of a Bagler fortress at Tønsberg, Sverre became ill and he died in 1202. On his deathbed, he advised his son Håkon to make peace with the church. Håkon did so, but after his premature death less than two years later the war with the Baglers resumed and did not end until 1208.

3.2 *Birkebeinerne* by Knud Bergslien (1869) depicts Birchlegs taking Prince Håkon Håkonsson over the mountains to safety in 1206.

For the next several years, the Birchlegs and the Baglers observed an uneasy truce, and they each controlled different parts of Norway under their separate kings. When those kings both died in 1217, the Baglers agreed to recognize Sverre's grandson Håkon Håkonsson as the king of Norway, and the conflict between the Birchlegs and the Baglers was over. However, other rebel armies rose up periodically until 1240, when the last of them was defeated and the civil wars finally came to a close. Even though Håkon Håkonsson had already been king for thirty years, in 1247 he was crowned by a cardinal at a ceremony in Bergen after a large sum of money was paid to the pope.

Despite the fact that he was crowned by the representative of the pope, King Håkon made it clear that he was in no way subordinate to the church.

The Age of Greatness

The descendants of Sverre continued to rule Norway for another 140 years after 1247, and most of this period is called the Age of Greatness or the Golden Age, as Norway enjoyed mostly peace and stability and was considered one of the leading kingdoms of Europe. During the thirteenth century the Norwegian government grew and was strengthened under the firm, centralized rule of the king. The Kingdom of Norway, which already included Orkney, Shetland, and the Faeroes, was expanded to Greenland and Iceland in the 1260s, but shortly thereafter the Hebrides and the Isle of Man were transferred to the Scottish king. A new law of royal succession in 1260, which was actually similar to Skakke's law in the previous century, provided for more certainty and a hereditary monarchy. In the 1270s King Magnus the Lawmender codified all the laws of Norway and created a new penal system. The king assumed more power and authority to personally issue laws, decrees, and rulings instead of relying upon the tings to do so. The king's lagmenn gradually became local judges who could adjudicate cases on their own in place of the tings. In addition to the hird, each king began to appoint a Council made up of legal advisers, aristocrats, and later also bishops to advise and assist the king in governing the country. They worked on legislation, administration, finance, and foreign relations. The king also named a chancellor, an important adviser and official who kept the king's seal, issued royal documents, maintained administrative and financial records, and occasionally acted as the king's envoy in other lands.

At the local government level, the king's sysselmenn were given assistants called *lensmenn*, who were usually wealthy local farmers. The lensmenn collected taxes and fines, maintained roads and bridges, enforced the laws, and confiscated the property of outlaws. The old office of lendmann was changed to baron and then gradually phased out. In general, the aristocrats only made up about one percent of the population, and they were less wealthy and influential than the nobility in other European lands.

The northern border regions and the Sami

As the power of the chieftains declined in the eleventh century, it was the kings of Norway rather than the chieftains who began to assert control over the border regions of the Far North and to collect taxes from the Sami. The adjoining states such as Novgorod and later Sweden also took an interest in the same border regions, and in some cases the Sami were forced to pay taxes to two or three different countries at the same time. These taxes were normally paid in the form of furs, skins, tusks, and fish.

By the Middle Ages the Sami had formed *siidas*, which were groups of 20 to 150 family members and friends who lived and traveled together. Each siida was led by a council of older men. Some of the Sami lived in villages, while others continued to move from place to place as nomads following the herds of wild reindeer.

There were some violent conflicts in the northern border regions, especially in the thirteenth and fourteenth centuries, as Chudes and Karelians from Finland and Russia invaded the area to take control of the fur trade and to demand payment of taxes from the Sami. In the process, they committed some brutal atrocities against the peaceful Sami, which gave rise to the following Sami legend called The Pathfinder.

A band of Chudes attacked a Sami village and killed everyone except a boy who they wanted to use as a guide. They demanded that the boy take them to the next Sami village so they could attack that place as well. The Sami boy admitted that he knew where the next village was located, but he wasted time to delay the Chudes until the end of the day. He finally started to lead them as the day turned to night. The night was so pitch black that they could not see each other. The boy lit a torch and told the Chudes to follow the light of the torch, but they still had problems staying together. So then the boy told them to tie themselves together so that no one would get lost in the dark, and the Chudes followed his instructions. The boy continued to lead them through the mountains. He told them that he would start going very fast and that they should keep up by following the torch. He started running, and then he threw the torch over a cliff. The Chudes ran toward the torch and fell over the cliff. All of them died, and the boy and the Sami in the other village survived. The blood of the Chudes stained the rocks red, which they remain to this day.

In 1987 this story was made into a Sami-language movie with the same title. The movie was nominated for an Academy Award as Best Foreign Language Film. The disputes between the countries in the Far North continued for centuries despite treaties signed by Norway and the Russians from Novgorod in 1251 and 1326.

Changes in the countryside, along the coast, and in the cities and towns

By 1300 Norway's population had increased to about five hundred thousand. As a result, more land was cleared for farming, some farms were divided, and there were many more tenant farmers who leased land from the king, the church, the aristocracy, or the landowning farmers. The population growth even led to a scarcity of arable land, and some farmers had to try to eke out a living by cultivating less desirable land.

Farming became less profitable in the late thirteenth century when the weather turned colder and it became more difficult to raise crops in a northern climate. As government increased in size, the farmers had to pay higher taxes and fines, and the rents paid by tenant farmers also went up. Some of the new taxes were real estate taxes on the land to support the government and the military, and those taxes gradually replaced the leidang. In addition, the farmers had to pay tithes to the church. The rents and tithes were usually paid in the form of farm produce. So there was a heavy financial burden on the farmers. Some of them could not pay and lost their farms, and almost 70 percent of the farmland was now owned by the king, the church, and the nobility. Free farmers owned the other 30 percent, but some of their lands were less desirable or located in outlying areas. In fact, most farmers were tenants and not landowners.

Under the new rules of the church, women lost many of their rights, including the right to divorce their husbands. They still had limited rights to own and sell property, but their property, if any, was generally controlled by their husbands. On the farms, the women were responsible for preparing food, making and washing clothing, caring for the children, and feeding and milking livestock, including the dairy cows at the summer seter farms in the mountains. They also mowed hay and worked alongside their menfolk in harvesting the crops in the late summer and fall. Meanwhile, the men were engaged in working the fields, herding livestock, hunting, and fishing.

Slavery gradually went out of existence by the end of the twelfth century. The end of the Viking raids and the closing of the slave markets meant that fewer new slaves were available, except for the children of existing slaves. The church prohibited the ownership of Christian slaves and encouraged slaveholders to free their other slaves. Also, the population growth made non-slave male and female laborers and servants more available and cheaper to use, and most farmers preferred to employ and pay hired help rather than to own and care for slaves. More and more slaves were freed and became laborers, servants, or tenant farmers.

Fishing and exports of fish expanded substantially in the twelfth and thirteenth centuries, especially along the coast of northern Norway. To an increasing extent, the fish were preserved by drying and then transported as so-called stockfish to towns farther south for sale or export. Bergen became Norway's trading center for the export of stockfish and fish oil to Europe, and German merchants began to establish export offices in Bergen and other towns. Northern Norway was also a source of furs, ropes, and tusks. Of course, the king always took a piece of the action by taxing all such products and exports.

After being established by King Olav Kyrre in the eleventh century, Bergen grew into the largest and most prosperous city and the capital of Norway. In 1191 a traveler described Bergen as a wealthy city with impressive buildings, a large number of people, ships from many European countries, and a thriving trade in dried fish, honey, wheat, clothing, silver, and other products.

Other Norwegian towns included Oslo, Stavanger, Nidaros, Tønsberg, and Hamar, which grew as centers of government, trade, or the church. From 1100 to 1300, Norway experienced a building boom, and many large stone churches, monasteries, fortresses, castles, and other structures were constructed during this period. Some examples are Nidaros Cathedral, a section of Akershus Fortress in Oslo, and Håkonshallen (the king's hall) in Bergen. Growth of the cities and towns was also encouraged by new laws that gave them special privileges and trading monopolies. The residents of the cities and towns included landowners, merchants, craftsmen, storekeepers, aristocrats, government and military officials, and churchmen, as well as laborers and servants. Urban governments were created, and councilmen and bailiffs were appointed to govern the towns and cities and keep the peace.

So the population of the cities, towns, and countryside continued to grow through the end of the thirteenth century, and Norway was a unified and independent kingdom under an efficient administration.

CHAPTER FOUR:

Norway's Decline

During the period from 1300 to 1600, Norway lost most of its population and also lost control over its government and economy. The Norwegians were even deprived of their own religion and written language. This chapter examines the reasons for Norway's decline, as well as the beginning of a recovery in the seventeenth and eighteenth centuries.

The Black Death

In May 1349 a ship carrying wool left London on its way to Norway. One of the crewmen became seriously ill before departure, and at sea the sickness spread to the rest of the crew. Suddenly they began to die one by one, and within just a few days everyone on board was dead and the ghost ship was sailing aimlessly along the Norwegian coast. Finally it ran aground, and as local Norwegians began to unload the lifeless ship, the terrible disease infected them and quickly spread along the coast and throughout the valleys of Norway, causing widespread death of tens of thousands of Norwegians.

Another English ship with a cargo of grain made it to Bergen. But on arrival the crew was desperately ill, and the ship was only partially unloaded when everyone on board died. The cargo was delivered to the city, and many townspeople were stricken. So the residents of Bergen decided to sink the ship in the harbor in hopes of stopping the spread of the disease. Unfortunately, it was too late. Hundreds of people in Bergen were soon dead. A similar outbreak in Oslo the previous year ended only when the winter weather turned much colder.

The dreaded disease was the bubonic plague, also called the Black Death (*Svartedauen*). It originated along the Caspian Sea in Asia. The sickness was then carried by the Mongol army when it invaded southern Russia. In 1346 the Mongols besieged the city of Kaffa on the Crimean Peninsula. The invaders could not breach the strong defenses of the city, and their invasion force was gradually being weakened by the plague, so they started catapulting dead bodies over the city walls in an attempt to infect the defenders. The ploy worked, the city was ravaged by the plague, and the disease spread to the city's port on the Black Sea. From there it was taken by ships to Constantinople and then to ports along the Mediterranean Sea. Over the following five years, the plague spread throughout Europe. Eventually it reached Norway on ships sailing from Britain and Continental Europe.

The bacteria of the plague were carried by fleas that were attached to rats. Due to the lack of sanitation in the late Middle Ages, there were rats everywhere, which accounted for the rapid spread of the disease. After all the rats were infected and died, the fleas moved on to humans who suffered the same fate. The severe sickness was characterized by high fever, vomiting, dark sores on the body, and almost certain death within a period of hours to a few days. The survival rate was only 20 percent of those who were infected.

Norway suffered the highest death rate from the plague in all of Europe. In the spring, summer, fall, and early winter of 1349, the plague quickly spread throughout most of the country, and only two counties in the Far North were spared. In fact, in that one year, it is estimated that over one-half of the entire population of Norway died of the plague!

The cities and towns were particularly hard hit due to the unsanitary conditions and the proximity of the people. Medical treatment was virtually nonexistent, and there was no vaccine or cure. Bergen had only two small hospitals, and both were devoted to the care of lepers. So it was the church that took care of the victims of the plague. As a result, the archbishop, all but one of the bishops, and the vast majority of priests, monks, and nuns in Norway died. About 80 percent of the nobles and public officials also succumbed to the disease. Even the queen died, but King Magnus managed to survive by moving around Scandinavia to avoid the various outbreaks of the disease.

The plague also ravaged the Norwegian countryside, and entire valleys became depopulated and empty. In many places, no one was left to bury all the corpses. Agricultural production decreased substantially because crops were not planted or harvested and most of the livestock died. Consequently, the revenues of the king, the surviving nobility, and the church, in the form of rents, taxes, and tithes, were dramatically reduced. Some remaining members of the nobility became just ordinary farmers as their sources of income dried up. Many deserted farms (called *ødegårder*) were not resettled for centuries. However, the people who were fortunate enough to live through the ordeal had the opportunity to claim the best vacant farmland.

The plague did not end until the onset of cold weather in January 1350, when the bishop of Stavanger was the last recorded victim. While the plague in 1349 was the worst in Norwegian history, there were additional outbreaks of plague from time to time over the next 300 years.

There arose various stories and legends of desperate Norwegians who took extreme measures to try to avoid the plague. For example, a number of wealthy people moved their families and hid in a remote valley called Jostedal near Sognefjord. They agreed that no one would be permitted to leave the valley or receive any visitors. All messages with the outside world were left under a rock at the entrance to the valley. Even those precautions did not work, and everyone in the valley died except for one young girl who was found in a half-crazed state the following spring after she had spent several months among the dead bodies of family and friends.

The pope called the plague God's punishment of a sinful humanity in what he said were the last days of the world. He came up with a new mass to be sung by believers five times each week as they held a candle and knelt on one knee. Much to his dismay, that remedy afforded no protection from the disease. It is estimated that more than twenty million Europeans died of the plague.

No one realized that the plague was spread by fleas. Many erroneously thought it was a contagious disease that was spread from person to person. Others came up with more fanciful ideas of how the disease was transmitted. One prominent theory was that an ugly old woman named Pesta carried the plague from place to place. Trudging slowly but surely through the Norwegian countryside, the bent-over old hag carried a broom, a rake, and a large book that listed the names of everyone who was going to die. When she arrived at a village or farmstead, if she started sweeping with her broom, then everyone in that place would die. But if she used her rake instead, at least a few people would be spared.

In 1900 a Norwegian artist named Theodor Kittelsen published an amazing book of macabre stories and ghostly drawings called *Svartedauen*, which portrayed Pesta and the Black Death. Perhaps his best known story and drawing were called *Mor, der kommer en kjærring* [Mom, there's an old lady coming]. The story described the arrival of Pesta at a small farm up on a hill:

> Strangers don't come very often to the old, dark and modest wooden cottage up on the hillside. If it ever happens that an acquaintance strolls by, they already see him from a distance, long before he reaches the brook. And they wonder and they try to guess, "Maybe it's Per down there – no, I'm sure it must be Bjørn?" On a beautiful fall day it's warm and clear, and the leaves are falling one by one – yellow, red leaves – quietly. The kids on the farm are just hanging around, staring down the hill. Never have they seen anything like it! Who is that coming over there? Looks like the ugly, disgusting pile of garbage behind the house, creeping along like a bunch of rags, slowly but surely, like a wretch. Now the ugly one is at the brook, walking carefully on the rotting, split planks of the bridge. A broom under one arm, and she also has a rake. Ugly birds flutter around her and clip her on the back of the neck. Oh, no! Now they're scared, and they all run inside to their mother. "Mom, mom, hurry, come out here. Down at the brook there's an old woman coming. She is so ugly and awful that we've never seen anything like it. Oh, we're so scared — that awful old hag! Let's lock the door and hide under the bed!" See, now she's looking up at the house with her evil green eyes. Maybe she'll go by. See, now she's starting to sweep; she sweeps so that dirt and leaves are brushed to both sides.[1]

---

[1] Th. Kittelsen, *Svartedauen* (Kristiania: Stenersen, 1900), translated by John Yilek.

The plague had an extremely significant and long-lasting effect on Norway, as most of its people died and the economy deteriorated. As a result, the Kingdom of Norway, once considered to be one of the leading kingdoms of Europe, fell into rapid decline.

4.1 *Mor, der kommer en kjærring* by Theodor Kittelsen (1900)

The Hanseatic merchants

Apart from the loss of most of its population, Norway also lost control over its own economy as a result of the rise and dominance of the Hanseatic merchants from the cities of northern Germany along the Baltic Sea. Norway did not produce enough grain to feed its population. In fact, Norwegian grain production actually decreased in the late thirteenth century due to colder weather. Most of the grain produced in Norway was barley, rye, and oats, and a large quantity of wheat had to be imported.

At this time, Norwegians typically ate two meals each day. Both the morning and evening meals frequently included porridge and bread made of grain. Therefore, grain was a staple of the Norwegian diet, and it was usually in short supply in many parts of the country.

Most of the grain was imported from the fertile plains of Germany, where the grain trade was dominated by the Hanseatic merchants. Beginning in the 1230s and continuing thereafter in several agreements and treaties, the king of Norway had to give the Germans special privileges in Norway in order to obtain access to German grain. Over time, more and more privileges were granted to the Germans, who gradually came to monopolize the Norwegian imports of grain, as well as the exports of Norwegian products such as timber and dried fish.

For example, Hanseatic merchants from the city of Lübeck in Germany dominated the import-export trade in Bergen. There was no bank in Norway, so the Germans provided the only source of credit to the Norwegian fishermen along the west coast of Norway to finance their purchases of boats, equipment, food, and clothing. In return, the Germans required the Norwegians to sell all of their dried fish to them for export to other countries. Consequently, the Norwegian fishermen became totally dependent on the Germans, who were able to fix the prices of both exports and imports. Other Germans from Rostock had a similar arrangement and dominated the timber trade in the towns of Oslo and Tønsberg. In addition, the Germans had the advantage of owning large, well-built, enclosed ships called cogs that could safely transport substantial cargo to and from other lands. The Norwegian economy was stimulated by the Germans' trading activities. But the Germans kept most of the profits, whereas the Norwegian farmers and fishermen remained relatively poor.

The Hanseatic merchants settled along the wharf in Bergen in an area called Bryggen, where they built distinctive, triangular-shaped wooden buildings. Each building contained living quarters, an office, a meeting and dining room, and a warehouse, and the Germans used cranes to load and unload goods to and from their ships along the adjacent piers.

The Lübeck Germans in Bergen formed an association called the *Kontor*. The Kontor independently ruled the Germans' own community of over a thousand traders and craftsmen under German law. They lived and worked separately from the Norwegians in Bergen, and they were not subject to Norwegian laws, courts, or taxes. As a result, there were many cases of lawlessness and brutality, even murder and rape, by the Germans against the Norwegians that went unpunished. Furthermore, if the Germans failed to pay their debts to Norwegians, they could not be sued.

For example, a Norwegian named Olav Nilsson was a wealthy landowner and shipowner who was the leading government official in Bergen and a member of the Norwegian Council. He wanted to reduce the Hanseatic privileges in Bergen and prosecute the Germans for various crimes. In fact, he went so far as to raid some of the German ships. In response, in 1455 the Germans attacked and plundered Nilsson's ships. Nilsson and his son escaped and hid in a monastery. The Germans stormed into the monastery and cut off the hand of the bishop who tried to protect Nilsson's son. Then the Germans killed the son and set the monastery on fire. Nilsson, who was hiding in the tower of the monastery, asked the Germans for three hours to confess his sins. The Germans patiently waited for three hours and then rushed into the tower and murdered Nilsson and about sixty priests and nuns. No German was ever punished for this heinous act, although the Germans eventually contributed some money to rebuild the monastery.

The Hanseatic merchants dominated the Norwegian economy for over two hundred years. From time to time the kings of Norway tried to limit or abolish the Germans' privileges and monopolies. In each case the Germans would stop trading, the Norwegian economy would grind to a halt, and the king always had to back down and grant them even more privileges. The German Baltic cities were also city-states that controlled their own armies and navies. In 1367 the

Hanseatic cities went to war against Norway. The German merchants left the Norwegian cities, and the Norwegian grain imports were halted. The following year the Hanseatic fleet and their Dutch allies attacked, burned, and looted the city of Bergen. Norway had to sue for peace, and when the war ended the Hanseatic merchants returned to Norway with more rights than ever before.

The Hanseatic domination of the Norwegian economy finally began to diminish in the sixteenth century. Dutch, Danish, Scottish and English trading firms set up offices in Norwegian ports and provided new competition for the Germans whose special privileges were eliminated. Many Germans stayed in Norway, accepted Norwegian citizenship, and became a part of Norwegian society. The integration of the Germans and the influx of other foreigners created a new middle class of merchants in Norway.

Pietro Querini

In 1431 a Venetian nobleman and ship captain named Pietro Querini and his crew were shipwrecked in the North Sea. Abandoning their sinking ship, they manned the lifeboats, and the ocean current carried them north all the way to the Lofoten Islands, where Querini and ten other survivors finally came ashore. They were discovered by Norwegian fishermen from the island of Røst, and they lived with the Norwegians for the next three months. The subsequent writings of the Venetians provide an insightful glimpse at the daily lives of Lofoten fishing families in fifteenth century Norway.

At this time there were about 120 people living on the island. They caught a lot of fish, mostly cod and halibut. The cod was dried in the sun and wind without salt in order to preserve the catch as stockfish. The Norwegians ate some of the cod with butter and spices, and the halibut with salt. They also ate rye bread, meat, and porridge made of barley and oats, and they drank beer and milk. There were even pancakes made of the huge supply of bird eggs on the island. Apart from fishing, the fishermen raised rye, barley, and oats, and each family had five or six cows that provided dairy products.

The families lived in round wooden houses, each with an opening in the ceiling above the hearth. Due to the cold weather, the Norwegians were usually dressed in clothing made of wool from England. They were also described as devout Catholics, and the Venetians were impressed by their generous hospitality.

In May the fishermen loaded a large boat with dried fish and sailed all the way to Bergen, where they traded the fish for wool, grain, and other products that they used in their daily lives. All of the goods were traded by barter, and money was not used. Then the fishermen sailed back to Lofoten, where the annual cycle of life started all over again.

During this period there were high prices for the fish. Even though the Hanseatic merchants in Bergen profited handsomely, the Lofoten families were able to thrive with a reasonable standard of living and probably lived better than most of the farmers in inland Norway.

Queen Margrete

On October 18, 1370, the teenage queen of Norway, a former Danish princess named Margrete, was living in dire straits at Akershus Fortress in Oslo. She was pregnant, and her husband King Håkon was off fighting a war in Sweden. Margrete was literally trapped in the fortress, as the plague raged once again in the town, and her friend the archbishop had just died. She and her servants had little or nothing to eat, and Margrete had no money to pay them or to buy any food. So on that date the young queen wrote a letter to the king in which she described her plight and begged him for money and assistance. Even though she sounded like a meek, desperate girl who was totally dependent on her husband, she would later turn out to be the ambitious, strong-willed and shrewd ruler of all of Scandinavia and the most powerful woman in Scandinavian history.

At the time she wrote the letter, her husband the king was also in a desperate financial state because the royal treasury was bankrupt as a result of his many costly wars. To raise some money, King Håkon had to pawn his golden jeweled crown and other valued possessions to the local German merchants. However, before long the fortunes of the royal family would begin to improve.

Later in 1370 Håkon and Margrete celebrated the birth of their son Olav. Five years thereafter, Margrete's father King Valdemar of Denmark died. Margrete's nephew was the leading candidate to be the next king of Denmark, but he was a member of the Mecklenburg family that was largely despised throughout Scandinavia. Even though her son Olav was the underdog, Margrete was determined to expand her family's rule to Denmark.

She immediately got to work by contacting the most influential people in Denmark who would be instrumental in electing the next king, including the Danish nobility, the Danish Church, and the Hanseatic merchants. First Margrete provided some of her family's Danish castles and lands on favorable terms to leading members of the nobility and the church, and she promised to exempt the church from taxation and to provide the church and the nobility with other rights and privileges. Then she agreed to give the Hanseatic merchants more privileges in Denmark and Norway. Through her efforts, the election of her son Olav as the next king of Denmark became a reality in 1376. For good measure, she and her husband were named the regents of Denmark; that is, the temporary rulers of the country until their son reached the age of maturity. When Håkon died in 1380, Olav became the king of Norway, and one of Margrete's followers assumed the position of regent in Norway. So Margrete had essentially become the ruler of both Denmark and Norway.

However, tragedy struck in 1387 when young Olav suddenly died. All of Margrete's efforts seemed to be for naught, but she was not discouraged. On the contrary, within one week after Olav's death she managed to have herself named as the ruler of Denmark. The following year Norway followed suit, as the Norwegian Council named her ruler of Norway for life. In fact, the Norwegian law of royal succession, which provided for a hereditary monarchy, was ignored so that Margrete could be elected ruler of the country. The leaders of Denmark and Norway clearly preferred Margrete and rejected the hereditary claims of the Mecklenburgs.

Margrete's next objective was to take over the crown of Sweden, which was held by the hated Mecklenburgs. At the time, the nobility and the people of Sweden were rebelling against the rule of the Swedish king Albrekt of Mecklenburg, who had raised taxes, expropriated land, and appointed Germans to high positions of nobility. In March 1388 they decided to depose Albrekt and elect Margrete as the ruler of Sweden. She and the Swedish nobility then joined forces and went to war against Albrekt. In 1389 they were successful in capturing Albrekt and laying siege to Stockholm, which still supported the former king. The siege was broken by pirates called the Victual Brothers, who delivered food to Stockholm and also repeatedly attacked the Norwegian and Danish coasts, including the city of Bergen.

In the meantime, Margrete realized that she needed to find a male heir to become the next king of all of the Scandinavian countries. She selected her closest male relative who was not a member of the Mecklenburg family. He happened to be a seven-year old boy named Bugislav, who was the grandson of Margrete's sister and the son of a Polish duke. In 1389 the young Slav moved to Denmark, took the more Scandinavian-sounding name of Erik of Pomerania, was adopted by Margrete, and was named king of Norway.

The war in Sweden raged on until 1395, when a peace treaty was signed. In 1396 Erik was elected king of Denmark and Sweden. However, that was not sufficient for Margrete, who wanted to consolidate her rule and the rule of her adopted son over all of Scandinavia. In 1397 she convened a meeting in the town of Kalmar in Sweden. Those in attendance at the meeting were Margrete, Erik, and leaders of the Councils in Denmark, Sweden, and Norway. At the meeting Erik was elected king of a joint kingdom of the three countries, and then he was crowned king at a grand ceremony.

This was the beginning of the Kalmar Union of Denmark, Sweden, and Norway. The union lasted until 1814, although Sweden temporarily left the union in the fifteenth century and eventually left for good in 1523. During the period of the Kalmar Union, Norway was ruled by the kings of Denmark.

Margrete had achieved her goal of consolidating the rule of her family throughout Scandinavia. Even though Erik was the king, Margrete continued to be the actual ruler, and she built up a central administration to govern all three countries from Denmark. Norway, already in steep decline due to the death of most of its population, was left in a subordinate position in the union. As most of the remaining Norwegian nobility gradually died out, she appointed Danes to high positions in Norway, and she began the policy of exploiting the Norwegians by imposing high taxes and other fees. Although Norway still had its own Council, the kings in Copenhagen often made decisions without consulting the Norwegian Council. In effect, Norway had lost its own government and was ruled for the most part by Denmark.

After Margrete died of the plague in 1412, Erik continued to rule as king of the three countries. But he was an extremely unpopular ruler who fought many wars and faced several rebellions in Norway and Sweden. He was finally deposed in Sweden and Denmark in 1439 and in Norway in 1441. He retired to the island of Gotland and became a Baltic pirate until he was finally exiled back to Pomerania. After being ruled by Erik's nephew Christopher of Bavaria for a few years, in the mid-1400s the three kingdoms elected a German count named Christian of Oldenburg as their new king. A branch of the House of Oldenburg continues to rule Norway to the present day, and the current King Harald 5 of Norway is a descendant of the Oldenburg family.

Shortly after Christian's coronation as king of Norway at Nidaros Cathedral in 1450, he met with the Danish and Norwegian Councils in Bergen. They entered into a union treaty that provided for a permanent union of the two independent kingdoms, with the future kings to be elected by the two Councils. So Norway formally became an elective monarchy instead of a hereditary monarchy.

The Reformation

By 1523 the only remaining independent Norwegian institution was the Norwegian Catholic Church, which selected its own archbishop and bishops and was strongly represented on the Norwegian Council. In that year there was a new archbishop at Nidaros, a Norwegian named Olav Engelbrektsson who also became the leader of the Council. From day one he was determined to defend Norway and the Council from the Danish king and nobility and to protect the Norwegian Catholic Church from the growing Protestant threat.

The Protestant Reformation was already underway in Europe. In 1517 a monk and theology professor named Martin Luther posted his ninety-five theses on the door of the church in Wittenberg, Germany. Luther protested various teachings and practices of the Catholic Church, including the widespread sale of indulgences. He did not intend to create a new religion, but that is exactly what happened, and the new Lutheran religion quickly spread throughout northern Germany and on to Denmark and Sweden. By the 1520s even the Hanseatic merchants in Norway were practicing the Lutheran religion after it reached their Baltic cities in Germany.

The Norwegian archbishop recognized that the rising tide of Protestantism in northern Europe could lead to the destruction of the Norwegian Catholic Church. So he took various steps to protect himself and other church leaders. He raised an army of mercenaries, acquired a navy of warships, and built a fortress called Steinvikholm on a peninsula in the Trondheimsfjord.

In 1523 Frederik 1 was elected king of Denmark. Before electing him as king of Norway in 1524, Engelbrektsson and the rest of the Norwegian Council required Frederik to make certain promises. At their insistence, Frederik agreed to protect the Norwegian Church from heresy (that is, Protestant teachings), he agreed to confirm and enlarge the powers of the Norwegian Council, and he agreed to appoint only Norwegians to high positions in Norway. Over the course of the next few years, Frederik would break all of his promises.

In fact, by the mid-1520s the Norwegian Church was already under attack by the king and his appointees in Norway. For example, the archbishop's rival on the Council was Vincens Lunge, a Dane who married into a Norwegian family and was appointed as the leading official in Bergen and later in other parts of Norway. With the king's approval, Lunge took possession of several churches and monasteries to enrich himself and his family. Later he declared himself to be a Lutheran, and that was enough to make him the archbishop's mortal enemy.

In 1529 King Frederik formally authorized Lutheran teaching in Norway, contrary to his earlier promise. He also sent Crown Prince Christian to Norway with a fleet of ships and an army that confiscated church property in Oslo. The Lutheran religion began to spread in parts of Norway, although the vast majority of Norwegians continued to be devout Catholics.

A desperate archbishop responded in 1531 by taking the extreme step of inviting Christian 2 to Norway. Christian was the former king of Denmark, Norway, and Sweden, who had been overthrown after he and his supporters murdered over eighty Swedish nobles, clerics, and commoners. Despite Christian's terrible reputation and past crimes, he claimed to be a Catholic (even though he had previously flirted with the Protestants), so at the archbishop's request the Norwegian Council decided to depose Frederik and elect Christian as the new king of Norway. Unfortunately, on his way to Norway, Christian lost a large portion of his fleet and army in a storm, and he was unable to take possession of the fortresses in Oslo and Bergen that were under the control of Frederik's army.

Christian's brief reign ended abruptly in 1532 when the Danes and the Hanseatic cities sent a combined fleet and six thousand mercenaries to Oslo. Christian was powerless to oppose this large force, and he agreed to step down from the throne of Norway when the Danes promised him safe passage out of the country. However, when Christian returned to Denmark he was imprisoned in a Danish fortress, and he remained a prisoner for the next twenty-seven years until he died. The Danes now controlled most of Norway, while the archbishop tried to plan his next move.

The situation became even more complicated in 1533 when Frederik died and civil war broke out in Denmark between the supporters of rival claimants to the throne. In the absence of a new king, the Norwegian Council ruled Norway for the next three years. But different members of the Norwegian Council supported different contenders to the throne. Lunge, by now a Lutheran, favored Frederik's son Duke Christian who was also a Lutheran. This was unacceptable to the archbishop, who started negotiating with other contenders and finally lent his support to an obscure Catholic count from Germany who was not even one of the leading candidates in Denmark.

With the Danish civil war still raging, the archbishop decided it was time for decisive action. He invited the other members of the Council to a meeting in Trondheim in December 1535, supposedly to discuss the election of the next king. However, a few days later in January 1536, the archbishop's men murdered Lunge and imprisoned all but one of the other members of the Council in a monastery. After this outrageous act, the archbishop appealed to the Norwegian people to rise up in rebellion against the Danish authorities and military. Only some Norwegian farmers heeded his call. The German count never showed up in Norway as planned, and the Danes remained in control of the Norwegian fortresses.

The Danish civil war ended in July 1536 when Duke Christian's forces entered the city of Copenhagen after a long siege. It was now apparent that Duke Christian, the Lutheran, would become the next king, and one of his first acts was to invite the Danish Catholic bishops to a meeting. At this meeting, Christian demanded that the bishops pay all amounts that he owed to his mercenaries who had won the civil war. When they did not do so, he promptly had the Danish archbishop and two other bishops arrested and thrown into prison in August 1536. He also confiscated their property and all other property of the church in Denmark.

Duke Christian was elected king of Denmark (as Christian 3) in October 1536. He issued a coronation charter which stated that Norway was now and forever a province of Denmark and not a separate kingdom, that Norway was to be governed by the king of Denmark and the Danish Council, and that the king of Denmark was automatically the king of Norway. At the same time, he issued a decree that imposed the Lutheran religion on Denmark and Norway.

Back in Norway, the archbishop's short-lived rebellion ended already in 1536. At that point the archbishop tried to seek a reconciliation with Christian, and the Norwegian Council (now freed from imprisonment in the monastery) pledged its loyalty to Christian as the new king. This was not enough for Christian, who sent his army and navy to attack western Norway, after which they sailed to Trondheim to try to arrest the archbishop. However, he knew they were coming and decided it was time to make a quick exit. In April 1537 Olav Engelbrektsson sailed out of the Trondheimsfjord and went into exile in the Netherlands, where he died the following year.

King Christian then acted promptly to abolish the Catholic Church and carry out the Reformation in Norway by force. In 1537 he issued a church ordinance that established the Lutheran state church with the king as its leader, and he expropriated all property of the Catholic Church in Norway. Since the church owned over 40 percent of the land in Norway, this was a huge windfall for the king, whose income increased substantially from the rents and other revenues on the land. Apart from land, all of the church's treasures were taken by the king's men. Even St. Olav's casket was shipped to Copenhagen and melted down for new coins, and the saint's body was later buried at a secret location somewhere on the grounds of Nidaros Cathedral. The king clearly intended to prevent any more pilgrims from coming to worship at St. Olav's shrine.

The bishops of Hamar and Stavanger were arrested, and the king later appointed Lutheran superintendents to replace all of the Catholic bishops. The Catholic churches in Norway became Lutheran churches, and the Catholic priests served as Lutheran pastors until they were gradually replaced by pastors educated at Lutheran seminaries. All saints and relics disappeared from the churches, along with the Latin language and the Catholic rituals. New Lutheran Bibles and hymnals were published in Danish and used throughout Norway. In order to prevent any possible Catholic revival, the king imposed strict censorship on all printed material in

Norway, and all books, pamphlets, and even songs had to be approved in advance by Lutheran authorities at the university in Copenhagen. Monks and nuns were not imprisoned, but they were effectively prevented from practicing their Catholic religion until they all died. Over time the religious laws became even stricter, and in 1624 the death penalty was proclaimed for any remaining Catholic priests and monks in Norway.

Along with the abolition of the Catholic Church, the Reformation removed the last vestiges of Norwegian self-government. The Norwegian Council was terminated, and from then on Norway was ruled exclusively by the Danes in Copenhagen. Danish nobles were awarded the highest positions in Norway. Beginning in 1572, the Danish kings began to appoint a Danish governor (called a *stattholder*) as their personal representative in Norway. However, even though Christian's charter called Norway a mere province of Denmark, it was still sometimes called the Kingdom of Norway, and the Danish kings occasionally referred to themselves as the kings of Denmark and Norway. Norway also kept its own laws, military, and currency.

Norway even lost one of its principal cities when Oslo burned to the ground in 1624. The Danish king Christian 4 rebuilt the city farther to the west around Akershus Fortress and named the new city Christiania after himself. The city would retain this name until 1925, when its name was changed back to Oslo.

The Reformation also meant the end of the written Norwegian language, at least for the next few centuries. Danish became the oral and written language of all official business and the church in Norway, as well as the language used in all literature written in Norway. In fact, very few writings in Norwegian had been produced ever since the Black Death decimated the population in 1349. By 1500 (even before the Reformation), Danish had already become the written and oral language of the government. Upper class Norwegians usually spoke Danish, but typically with some Norwegian words and pronunciation. However, other Norwegians continued to speak the Norwegian language in their various dialects, which were somewhat similar to today's dialects in Norway. In addition, Norwegian ballads, folk songs, and stories continued to be sung and spoken orally in Norwegian dialects as they were passed on from person to person.

Swedish wars

From time to time during the period from 1563 to 1720, the Kingdom of Denmark and Norway was embroiled in several wars, as the Danish kings foolishly and unsuccessfully tried to expand their territories in Scandinavia and the Baltic region. Several wars were fought against Sweden, which invaded Norway from time to time. It was the Norwegian farmers who usually had to bear the brunt of the fighting, while the Danish kings who started the wars sat safely ensconced in their opulent palaces back in Denmark.

The wars sometimes made for some unlikely heroes. For example, during the Kalmar War in 1612, a young Norwegian girl named Guri blew a birch bark horn to signal the approach of enemy Scottish mercenaries at the Battle of Kringen in Gudbrandsdalen. The Scots were trapped on a narrow path and surrounded by Norwegian farmers who attacked them with rocks, axes, scythes, and other crude weapons. Only 113 of the 550 mercenaries survived. They were all captured by the farmers, who decided to take their prisoners all the way to Akershus Fortress. However, they grew tired of their assignment as soon as they reached the next town. So they had a party, got drunk, and massacred almost all of the prisoners on the spot. Then they returned to their farms. Although Norwegians should not exactly be proud of this incident, the young girl is still hailed as a national hero, and her statue can be found at Otta. To commemorate the fate of the Scots, the women in that part of Gudbrandsdalen wear tartan as part of their traditional dress called the *bunad*.

Not all Norwegians acted like war heroes. In the Kalmar War the king relied on local militias of farmers to fight the battles. But occasionally the farmers refused to fight, and there were some mass desertions as Norwegian farmers preferred to go home and take care of their families and farms instead of fighting and dying in meaningless wars. As a result, King Christian 4 subsequently formed a regular Norwegian army, which became active for the first time in 1641. But the farmers still had to do most of the fighting because they were drafted into the army while the merchants in the towns and cities were exempt from military service.

If the Danish kings were good at starting wars, they were even better at losing wars, and the Danish empire actually shrank during this period of time. As a result, Norway lost some significant territories to Sweden, such as Jemtland and Herjedalen in 1645 and Båhuslen in 1658. Even Trondheim county and other parts of central Norway were ruled by the Swedes for two years in the late 1650s until they were retaken by the Norwegian army and recovered by the Danish king in a subsequent peace treaty. With only minor variations, the modern borders of Norway have remained essentially the same since 1660.

It was very expensive for the Danish kings to conduct the wars because they had to pay for mercenaries, other soldiers and sailors, weapons, supplies, ships, and fortresses. To finance the various wars, the kings of Denmark exploited the people of Denmark and Norway by charging them high taxes, fines, duties, and rents. To raise additional funds, the kings also sold some of their extensive landholdings in Norway to merchants and to local farmers who thereby established themselves as landowners or expanded their existing farms.

However, by 1660 the Danish royal treasury was in a crisis situation, and King Frederik 3 summoned leaders of the Danish nobility, church, and merchant class to a meeting to discuss possible solutions. Until then Denmark was an elective monarchy, and the nobility always exercised great influence in selecting the kings. However, the Danish nobility had recently lost much of its power as the king appointed Germans to key roles in the military and the government.

At the meeting in 1660, the king, the church, and the merchant class decided to make the Kingdom of Denmark a hereditary monarchy, so the oldest male heir of a deceased king would automatically become the next king, and the nobility would no longer have the power to elect the king. The king's advisers drafted the new law and included a provision for an absolute monarchy, which the church and the merchants felt compelled to support. In an absolute monarchy, the king would issue all the laws, make all final decisions, and appoint all government officials. This also had the effect of reducing the power of the nobility, who would no longer have a predominant role in making laws and decisions and who would not be assured of appointment to high positions. In addition, the nobility's exemptions from taxation were eliminated.

The hereditary absolute monarchy officially took effect in Norway in 1661 and lasted until the break-up of the Kingdom of Denmark and Norway in 1814. Norway was no longer governed by the Danish Council dominated by Danish aristocrats. The power of the nobility was broken, and the king began to appoint Danes and Norwegians who were not aristocrats to official positions in Norway. As usual, the Danes were given the highest positions, but some of them were merchants and not members of the nobility. The king also changed the local governments in Norway by appointing *amtmenn* instead of lensmenn to administer the local districts, and he appointed lawyers called *sorenskrivere* as local judicial officers. Each Danish king also continued to appoint a Danish governor as his personal representative in Norway.

Mining and society in Røros

The kings of Denmark in the seventeenth and eighteenth centuries found another way to finance their wars and other activities – by exploiting the natural resources of Norway. In 1623 a large deposit of silver was discovered near the present town of Kongsberg in southern Norway. This was unbelievably great news for King Christian 4, who promptly claimed ownership of the silver mine and began to reel in revenues from the enterprise. Believing that he was definitely on to something, the king instructed pastors throughout Norway to periodically announce from their pulpits that their parishioners should be on the lookout for other valuable minerals in the ground.

In 1644 an old ne'er-do-well named Hans Olsen Aasen was out hunting for his next meal when he came across a herd of reindeer. He fired a shot, and one of the reindeer jumped up and scraped its hoof against the earth before falling dead. When Aasen approached his prey, he noticed some metal shining in the ground. He had just discovered the largest lode of copper in Europe near the present town of Røros. Aasen reported his discovery to a local German prospector named Lorentz Lossius, who then claimed the land as his own without giving any compensation to poor old Aasen. In fact, Aasen never received anything for his discovery until he later sold his claim to a Dane named Joachim Irgens in exchange for a small farm. Irgens was a court chamberlain and a friend of the king. He was also an arrogant crook who profited handsomely by using Aasen's claim and his own influence with the king to steal the mining company from Lossius, who of course had already stolen the original claim from Aasen.

In any event, a company called the Røros Copper Works was established in 1644, and the first copper mine was already in operation by the summer of 1645. The following year the company built a smelting plant at the future site of Røros because of the abundance of wood fuel in the vicinity and the power generated by the river rapids. The company obtained a royal charter from the king. The charter gave the company the exclusive right to all minerals, forest products, and waterways within a radius of about thirty miles from the original mine. The Copper Works was an independent company owned by private investors, but each year the company was required to pay 10 percent of all copper production to the king.

Most of the owners of the company were wealthy merchants who lived in Trondheim. Bank financing was unavailable, so at the beginning of each year the investors had to pay in to the company a substantial amount of money or goods as capital. In return they received all the profits at the end of each year after payment of the king's portion. The company was very profitable, and it continued in operation for over three hundred years.

Shortly after the company was established, the town of Røros was built with parallel and perpendicular streets. The town grew rapidly as the mining company attracted workers from all over Norway, as well as Sweden, Denmark, and Germany. As a result of the mixture of peoples, languages, and dialects, the townspeople created their own distinctive Røros dialect (called *Rørosmålet*) containing words and phrases from different parts of Norway and other countries.

Over time more copper mines and smelting works were opened near Røros. The operation provided the employees with a steady source of work and income in what were often tough economic times when other employment was not available. Many workers were former tenant farmers, servants, farm hands, and younger sons of landowners. They worked for the company as mineworkers, smelting plant laborers, lumberjacks, coal burners, craftsmen, drivers, and day laborers. An added advantage was that company workers were exempt from military service and some taxes, although employees occasionally volunteered for the military, especially when the nearby Swedish army periodically invaded the town.

The company was run by a local director and other officers who lived and worked in Røros. The director was not only the manager of the company. He was also the mayor, judge, police chief, fire chief, religious leader, and military leader in the town. That is, the company owned and operated just about everything in town, including the stores, the police and fire departments, the jail, the court, the church, the poorhouse, and the school.

There were occasional worker strikes and other labor strife, especially when the company failed or refused to pay the workers. For example, in the 1660s Irgens loaned so much of the company's money to the king that he stopped paying the workers. Instead he gave them scrip that could only be used to buy products at exorbitant prices at the company-owned stores. The workers sent two representatives, including a fiddler and mineworker nicknamed Spell-Ola, to Copenhagen to petition the king for relief.

But the king did not issue an order for a long time, so in 1670 the workers decided to send Spell-Ola back to Copenhagen. When Irgens heard about it, he had Spell-Ola arrested and held in chains in the town jail. The workers confronted and beat up Irgens and his company manager, and then they proceeded to the jail with the intention of freeing Spell-Ola. But when they got there, they were afraid to break the king's seal on the lock of the jail. So instead they used crowbars and a jack to lift the entire jail building off the ground, and Spell-Ola was set free. The situation was resolved shortly thereafter when the king ordered the company to pay the workers in cash, to pay them for holidays, and to compensate them for work injuries. Over time the workers also began to receive pensions after retirement.

The company school taught the workers' children various subjects such as reading, writing, arithmetic, and Christian religion. This was a real benefit to the workers' families at a time when such schooling of lower class children was not available in much of the country. The wealthier families in town hired private tutors to teach their younger children and sent their older children to schools in Trondheim.

The surrounding area also grew in population, and many new farms were established. Some of the farmers worked part-time for the company as loggers and drivers, and many farmers sold and delivered charcoal and farm produce to the company. The company gave many of its workers small plots of land to farm when they were not working for the company. Some workers even took summer leaves from the company to work on their seter farms in the mountains. Most of the farms around Røros raised primarily livestock including dairy cows.

In 1784 the company completed construction of a beautiful Baroque church on the hill in Røros. The church was called Bergstadens Ziir, which means the beautiful adornment of the mountain town. Inside the church, the seating arrangements were made according to wealth and status. The upper class had private boxes with curtains and foot benches covered with reindeer hides to keep their feet warm in the winter. They also reserved a box for the king even though he never sat there. Other leading citizens sat in the front pews, while the common people sat farther back. Instead of pictures of religious figures, the church contained portraits of company officials. The graves in the cemetery were also placed according to hierarchy. The richest people were laid to rest next to the church, while the poor people were buried way up on top of the hill in back of the church. The church bells were used to call church services, but also to warn the townspeople of fires, floods, and wars.

The well-preserved old town of Røros still stands and has been designated as a UNESCO World Heritage Site. Walking along the old streets, visitors feel like they are back in eighteenth century Norway as they view the cross-timbered smelters' cottages, storehouses, and workshops, as well as the mansions of the upper class residents of the mining town.

Norway in 1700

In 1700 the vast majority of Norwegians still lived on farms. Despite a series of famines and epidemics, Norway's population had grown substantially to about five hundred thousand, or approximately the number of people before the Black Death in the 1300s. The larger cities and towns, including Bergen, Christiania, Trondheim, Tønsberg, Skien, Stavanger, Fredrikstad, and Christianssand, were growing but only had a combined population of about twenty-five thousand. The cities and towns had become administrative centers for the expanding local governments, and their residents included a larger middle class of craftsmen, storekeepers, merchants, and traders, as well as lower class laborers and servants. A royal charter in 1662 had given certain cities and towns the exclusive right to export products from their surrounding areas, but some trade had to be sent through Denmark and not directly to other countries. The major Norwegian exports consisted of dried fish, timber products, furs, and minerals. On the other hand, much more grain had to be imported at high prices to feed the growing population.

The development of the water-powered gate saw in the sixteenth century allowed the owners of sawmills to increase their profits by exporting mass-produced finished boards instead of raw timber. More and more sawmills were built to meet the huge demand for finished lumber in the shipbuilding and construction industries of Europe.

The Norwegian nobility had almost vanished, and nearly all members of the nobility were Danes or their descendants. The public officials, leaders of the church, and wealthy merchants made up most of the upper class. The growing Norwegian army was led primarily by German officers appointed by the king. The king also appointed all other public officials, who were mostly Danes but also included some Norwegians.

In the countryside, virtually all of the farms that had been deserted in the Black Death were now reoccupied, and other land was being cleared for farming. The king still owned considerable land in the country, and much of that land was leased to farmers. However, available farmland was becoming limited, and many farms were divided, which made them less profitable. There were more and more tenant farmers called *husmenn*. A husmann leased a modest cottage and a small parcel of land for farming, and paid rent and provided labor to the landowner. All farmers had a huge financial burden because they had to pay a large amount of taxes and fees, while also providing soldiers and sailors for the army and navy.

Fishing had become more efficient with the introduction and expanded use of nets and long lines instead of just lines with single hooks. Apart from individual fishermen, there were also companies that owned fishing boats and engaged in fishing for cod, halibut, and herring in the waters off the Norwegian coast. Like the farmers, the fishermen had a heavy burden of high taxes and fees. But the standard of living for the hard-working farmers and fishermen improved, as more houses were built with fireplaces and chimneys (instead of open hearths and holes in the ceiling), wooden floors, glass windows, and better furniture, and the people wore better clothing.

4.2 *Munken gård i Esefjorden* by Adelsteen Normann shows a small farm
and a fishing boat on a fjord in the mountains of western Norway.

The Norwegian merchant marine and shipbuilding industry
grew substantially in the seventeenth and eighteenth centuries. Most
of the ships were owned by merchants in the towns and cities. Other
industries had also grown, such as mining, manufacturing,
ironworking, and salt works, so there were increased employment
opportunities for laborers and servants in the lower class. However,
Norway was a stratified society, and it was virtually impossible for a
member of the lower class to raise his or her status in life and join the
middle or upper class of society.

Changes in Sami life and customs

The Sami of northern Norway continued to live in groups called
siidas, and most of them were engaged in their traditional
occupations of fishing, hunting, trapping, and reindeer herding.

However, by about 1500 the Sami had domesticated their reindeer herds, so they were no longer following herds of wild reindeer.

In the seventeenth and eighteenth centuries the Lutheran state church sent missionaries to northern Norway to try to convert the Sami to Christianity. They were supported and encouraged by the kings of Denmark-Norway, who wanted to limit Swedish influence in the Far North. One of the most active missionaries was Thomas von Westen, a Lutheran pastor from Trondheim who was called the Apostle to the Sami. He built several churches in northern Norway, as well as schools for Sami children. He also gave outdoor sermons to Sami in their own language, and he established a seminary to train more missionaries.

Previously, the Sami had religious beliefs that were connected to nature. They considered the sun to be a heavenly god and the bear a sacred animal. Their religious ceremonies were led by shamans who also served as wise men and healers. A shaman communicated with the supernatural through trances and by the use of chants, drums, and other sacred objects.

So it was quite an adjustment for the Sami to come into contact with the missionaries who preached Christianity and the Bible. The church prohibited shamans, drums, and other religious customs and practices of the Sami, and many Sami men and women were executed for witchcraft. Nevertheless, some of the Sami converted to the Christian religion, and many Sami remain devout Christians to the present day.

CHAPTER FIVE:

Norway in 1814

Why do Norwegians celebrate syttende mai — the 17th of May — each year? This chapter tells the story of how people and events in Norway and the rest of Europe caused Norway to gain its independence from Denmark and adopt its own constitution in 1814. The story actually begins a few decades before that fateful year. It winds its way through palace intrigue, the battles and hardships of the Napoleonic Wars, changing loyalties and secret agreements, and the defiance and determination of a prince and the citizens of a small country that led to an unexpected turn of events and the founding of Norwegian democracy on May 17, 1814.

By the late 1700s Norway had been ruled by the kings of Denmark and mostly Danish nobles and bureaucrats for four hundred years. During that time, the kings had clearly exploited Norway and the Norwegians by levying high taxes, fines, and duties, by taking large shares of the profits of Norwegian silver and copper mines, and by starting dynastic wars that cost the lives of many Norwegians and the loss of various regions of Norway.

Norway continued to be a relatively poor country. While the vast majority of Norwegians were engaged in agriculture in the countryside and fishing along the coast, an upper class of merchants, government officials, and clergy began to prosper in the growing towns and cities. Most members of the upper class were educated in Denmark and spoke and wrote in the Danish language, which was the language used in official business and the church. There was still no written Norwegian language, although most people who were not of the upper class commonly spoke Norwegian in their various regional dialects.

Norwegian agriculture did not produce enough food to feed the population, so Norway relied on imports of grain and other commodities from Denmark, Germany, and other European countries. At the same time, there was heavy demand in Europe for Norwegian dried fish, lumber, iron, and minerals, and Norway had already built up an impressive fleet of merchant ships that transported cargo throughout Europe.

Challenges, protests, and rebellions

The high taxes, fines, and duties and the other government restrictions on economic and religious life occasionally led to challenges, protests, and even rebellions by various Norwegians against the established order. There were local protests and strikes in Christiania (now called Oslo) and other towns, and from time to time the miners in Kongsberg and Røros went on strike due to unpaid wages and other grievances.

In the 1760s there were tax protests by farmers in Bergen and Stavanger in response to a new poll tax that was used to pay for improving the military. The farmers' anger was stoked when government officials confiscated the property of farmers who could not or would not pay the tax. In Bergen this protest was known as the Stril War, as a mob of farmers physically attacked a tax official and made him pay their taxes. The military was called out to put down the rebellion, a few leaders of the revolt were imprisoned, and some overzealous bureaucrats were transferred or forced to resign.

In southern Norway a successful farmer and businessman named Christian Jensen Lofthuus led a widespread farmers' revolt against the heavy taxes and fines, as well as the government-imposed grain monopoly that gave special preferences to citizens of certain towns and cities. The revolt died out after Lofthuus was imprisoned, and he was chained to a stone pillar in Akershus Fortress for eleven years until he died in 1797. But his efforts led to the abolition of the grain monopoly and the dismissal of several public officials.

Without a doubt, the most significant challenge to the authorities came from a most unlikely source. Hans Nielsen Hauge was the lowly son of a farmer near Tune in southeastern Norway. In 1796, at the age of twenty-five, he was out plowing his father's fields. As he worked, he kept thinking about a hymn that he had sung many times in the local church, especially the following verse:

> Strengthen my soul, so I can understand what the Spirit can do. Guide my words and my thoughts, lead me and call me as weak as I am. I would gladly sacrifice myself and my possessions if You would dwell in my soul. And finally steal away everything that disturbs my innermost peace.[2]

Suddenly he had a religious reawakening. When he came home that night and over the next several weeks, his family and even the

---

[2] Verse 2 of the hymn "Jesus din søde forening at smage", original German lyrics by J.L.C. Allendorf (1712), translated into Danish by Peder Hygom (1740), translated into English by John Yilek.

neighbors noticed that he was a changed man. He was almost in a daze as he constantly prayed, read the Bible, and sat fixated in thought for hours at a time.

Hauge had never attended the university, and he was definitely not considered an educated man, but he started writing pages and pages of text that he sent to publishers in Christiania. Amazingly, they actually liked what he wrote, and they began publishing his books and pamphlets, which became bestsellers throughout Norway. In addition to his deeply devotional religious writings, Hauge harshly attacked the state church and its Lutheran pastors. He described the church as cold and impersonal and the pastors as greedy and arrogant, all contrary to the teachings of the Bible. Through his writings, Hauge gained a large following of supporters all over Norway.

He left the farm and traveled by foot all across the country, and he inspired thousands of people with his lay preaching. Most of his adherents were members of the lower class of society, including husmenn (tenant farmers) and common laborers and servants. In many communities, Hauge established societies of friends that held prayer meetings in homes and other places. In this manner, he created a huge national religious revival movement.

Apart from his strong religious beliefs and activities, Hauge felt that the lower class should no longer be dominated by the upper class of society. He thought that the poor people should raise their economic and social standing even in a stratified, class-based society like Norway, where people in the lower class were expected to accept their place in life and never amount to anything. So he became a successful businessman, leading his followers into many business ventures. He founded or purchased sawmills, farms, mining and shipping companies, construction firms, paper mills, hotels, trading houses, newspapers, and publishing companies.

Hauge's religious and business activities posed a serious challenge to the government, the merchant class, and the state church. They responded by having him arrested from time to time for vagrancy and for violation of the Conventicle Act. This law prohibited anyone other than ordained pastors of the state church from preaching or leading religious services. As a lay preacher who frequently led prayer meetings, it was quite clear that Hauge breached the Conventicle Act, but he defiantly refused to cease his religious activities.

Finally in 1804, at the urging of the bishop of Christianssand, the authorities sent Hauge to prison at Akershus without trial for seven years. His imprisonment was particularly harsh, as he was not permitted to read or write, to have any visitors, or even to exercise in fresh air. In prison he suffered from scurvy and other illnesses, and his physical condition deteriorated. He was finally released from prison in 1811, but by then he was a broken man and he died in 1824. However, Hauge's movement lived on in Norway and later in America, where various churches and colleges were founded by his followers. Even today, Hauge is considered an inspiration to members of the Norwegian Lutheran Church.

5.1 *Haugianerne* by Adolph Tidemand (1848) depicts a prayer meeting of a friends society established by Hans Nielsen Hauge.

The Danish king and his court

Since 1661 the king in Copenhagen had been an absolute monarch who issued all laws and decrees and made all other final decisions in Denmark and Norway. He was advised by his appointed ministers, and public officials in both kingdoms carried out the laws, decrees, and decisions.

In 1766 the king died prematurely, and his sixteen-year old son was elevated to the throne as King Christian 7. The royal advisers in Copenhagen had not paid much attention to Christian as he was growing up, but when he became king they discovered to their horror that he was mentally ill. Mental illness was a condition that afflicted various royal families in Europe at the time. The most famous example was George III, the king of England during the American Revolution, who descended into insanity over time. Christian of Denmark suffered from severe schizophrenia characterized by strange episodes of childlike behavior, drinking binges, and embarrassing sexual acts, often in the presence of Danish and foreign dignitaries. This was a real problem for the Kingdom of Denmark-Norway because the king was the sole governing authority. An absolute monarchy quite simply could not function with a king who was mentally ill.

The king's advisers hoped that his marriage to an English princess would help solve the problem, but his carousing and bizarre behavior got worse. So the advisers decided that they had to find some medical assistance for the king. They summoned an able German physician named Dr. Johann Struensee to Copenhagen. Struensee engaged in long conversations with the king, and Christian's condition seemed to improve slightly.

The king came to rely on Struensee, and he decided to appoint the good doctor as the leading minister in his government. Struensee proved to be a capable politician and administrator. He had the king sign progressive decrees that reduced trade restrictions and provided for freedom of the press in Denmark and Norway.

Unfortunately, Struensee also had an eye for the ladies, and it did not take long for him to develop a relationship with the lonely queen. Their affair became public knowledge and most likely resulted in the birth of the new Danish princess. This scandal was too much for the royal family, and in 1772 the king's stepmother had Struensee arrested and publicly beheaded on the charge of usurping the king's authority. The young queen was imprisoned, divorced, and then exiled to her family's estate in Germany, where she died shortly thereafter. The stepmother and her advisers took over the government of Denmark-Norway and reversed many of Struensee's progressive reforms.

That regime lasted until 1784, when a palace coup overthrew the government and gave the ruling authority to the king's son, sixteen-year old Crown Prince Frederik. He ruled on behalf of his father until 1808, when Christian died and the crown prince was named king.

Frederik of Denmark was an unusual-looking character who was secretly mocked by his own advisers and military leaders. Like most of his predecessors, his primary motivation seemed to be to preserve the dynasty of his family and its control over Denmark and Norway and other possessions. Although he ruled both kingdoms, he only traveled to Norway on one occasion. He did gain popularity by making some progressive reforms, such as lifting press censorship and reducing state monopolies and tolls in both kingdoms, but most of the reforms were later reversed.

Moreover, Frederik did not respond positively to the Norwegians' repeated requests for a bank and a university in Norway. For years, the Norwegian economy suffered from the absence of bank credit, and Norwegian officials, merchants, and farmers had to send their sons all the way to Copenhagen to study at a university. Frederik did not want Norway to have its own bank or university because he thought it might impair the unity of the two kingdoms and the future of his royal family in Norway.

Despite the Danish exploitation of Norway for hundreds of years, and the affairs and stubbornness of the Danish royal family, the vast majority of Norwegians in the late eighteenth century remained incredibly loyal subjects of the king. To them, an absolute monarchy was actually considered an advantage because any Norwegian, as a citizen of the dual kingdom, could directly petition the king in Copenhagen to solve problems and reverse unfair and arbitrary actions by unreasonable bureaucrats in Norway. On more than one occasion, the king or crown prince ruled in favor of the petitioners and corrected abuses of power by the local officials. Norwegians frequently complained about the authorities, but their complaints were generally directed at the bureaucrats in Norway and not the royal family in Denmark. No one could have predicted that the Norwegians would be seeking their independence within a couple of decades.

The Napoleonic Wars

After the French Revolution that overthrew the monarchy in France, the British declared war on republican France, and a series of wars would ravage the Continent of Europe for the next twenty-three years from 1792 to 1815. These periodic bloody conflicts were collectively called the Napoleonic Wars despite the fact that Napoleon Bonaparte did not actually rise to power in France until 1799. Nevertheless, these conflicts would ultimately play a vital role in determining the future of Norway and the Norwegians for many years to come.

In the Napoleonic Wars, Britain fought against France. The other Great Powers of Europe, including Russia, Prussia, Austria, and to a lesser extent Sweden, fought from time to time on one side or the other. Therefore, it was a period of shifting alliances between countries, and treaties of alliance were constantly signed only to be broken at the first opportunity. So sometimes one or more of the other countries fought on the side of France until one or more of them would change sides and join the British alliance.

High society

During the initial period of war from 1792 to 1807, Denmark-Norway remained neutral and did not fight on either side of the war. This proved to be of great economic benefit to the dual kingdom, which could trade with countries on both sides of the conflict. The almost constant state of tension and war substantially raised prices for commodities, and that also benefited the neutral countries. In this fifteen-year period, Norwegian merchants made huge profits by exporting dried fish to Continental Europe and lumber to Britain, not to mention the lucrative exports of Norwegian copper and iron. Meanwhile, Norwegian shipowners profited handsomely from inflated wartime freight charges of Norwegian merchant ships that delivered cargoes throughout Europe.

The lumber trade created massive wealth among the merchants of Christiania and the rest of southern Norway. These rich lumbermen purchased huge estates and built stately mansions with formal gardens and statues, and they hosted lavish parties and various public events. There arose in Christiania a high society of merchants, government officials, and clergy.

One of the wealthiest men in the world was a Norwegian named Bernt Anker. He owned twenty-seven ships and huge tracts of forest land in southern Norway, and he employed over twenty thousand people in many different industries such as lumbering, shipping, manufacturing, mining, and armaments. He was so rich that he sent his shirts and underwear to London to be laundered. His home in Christiania, called the Palace, was later the residence of the king whenever he visited Norway. It contained glittering chandeliers, granite staircases, Chippendale furniture, a theater, a library open to the public, and a collection of art by Italian masters. Anker hosted plays, concerts, scientific lectures, and of course parties, and his household included thirty servants and ten carriages.

Bernt's brother Peder Anker, who was also a rich lumber merchant, owned a large estate called Bogstad, which can still be seen just northwest of Oslo. An English traveler who visited Peder Anker at Bogstad in 1799 later described the scene:

> He received us with as much magnificence as any foreign Prince, but with all the hearty welcome and hospitality of his country, added to the splendor of a King. The suite of apartments was quite princely, and

they were fitted up in the most elegant style. His
gardens were laid out in the English taste; and the
situation of his mansion, upon the borders of a lake at
the foot of a rocky mountain, gave to the whole an
appearance of great grandeur. ... The dinner was
preparing in large airy apartments, where every thing
was in the utmost order. ... In the greenhouses were
[pineapples], apples, melons, and peaches. ... [T]he
grand [salon] ... filled several chambers ... as one sees
in the Italian palaces. ... One room was entirely filled
with original drawings of the old Masters.[3]

The same Englishman, after attending a dinner party at a
Christiania mansion, noted that his own king of England could not
provide a more elegant feast with such delicacies, wines, and
expensive liqueurs and confections. [4] Unfortunately, such
extravagance among the Norwegian elite was about to come to an end.

The Continental System, war, and blockade

The beginning of the end of Norwegian prosperity came in the
fall of 1806 when Napoleon announced the Continental System.
This was a policy of economic warfare against Britain in which all of
the ports in Continental Europe were to be closed to British ships
and goods, and all trade with Britain was prohibited. Napoleon
wanted to force Britain out of the war by destroying or severely
damaging the British economy. Britain retaliated by using its large
navy to try to blockade the ports of France and its allies. Each side
pressured Denmark-Norway to cease trading with the other side.
Consequently, it became more difficult and hazardous for Norway to
import, export, and ship products in Europe.

---

[3] E.D. Clarke, *Travels in Various Countries, Vol. X* (London: Cadell, 1824), 388-391.

[4] Clarke, *Travels in Various Countries, Vol. X,* 382.

Danish-Norwegian neutrality ended abruptly in 1807. The British had received information that Napoleon was building a northern army so he could threaten to invade Denmark if Denmark-Norway did not join his alliance and the Continental System. This was alarming news to the British, who feared that if Denmark joined the French alliance or if France occupied Denmark, then France would have control of Denmark's navy and merchant fleet. This would threaten British dominance on the high seas, close the sound between Denmark and Sweden to British ships, and prevent the British navy from operating in the Baltic Sea.

Britain promptly demanded that Denmark-Norway join the British alliance against Napoleon, or, as an alternative, deliver its entire navy and merchant fleet to the British for safekeeping to guarantee that Denmark-Norway would remain neutral in the war. Frederik of Denmark rejected those demands, as he had no intention of taking sides in the war or handing over the fleet and leaving his country defenseless.

In response, Britain sent a large naval fleet and army to Denmark and invaded that neutral country in a massive, unprovoked surprise attack in August 1807. The British military occupied parts of Denmark and unmercifully bombarded Copenhagen. The city was set on fire, and there was extensive damage and loss of life. The British finally left Denmark after six weeks, destroyed several Danish ships, and took the rest of the Danish fleet with them back to Britain.

This outrageous action by the British angered Frederik, and he declared war on Britain and joined the French alliance and the Continental System in October 1807. As a result, Denmark-Norway was no longer a neutral country in the Napoleonic Wars. Britain then sent its large navy to blockade all Danish and Norwegian ports. The British blockade and attacks on shipping off the Norwegian coast effectively prevented Norway from importing grain to feed its population, and also blocked the export of Norwegian dried fish, lumber, and other products. This was a disaster for Norway, as the economy collapsed and many merchants went into insolvency. At the same time, there was an untimely famine in Norway when the crops failed in 1807 and 1808 and the Norwegian people faced starvation. Food was so scarce that Norwegians began to grind up tree bark and mix it with their meager supplies of rye flour to make bark bread to feed themselves and their families. There were also epidemics in Norway, and many people died.

Furthermore, the British blockade effectively cut the lines of communication and transportation between Denmark and Norway, and Frederik and his advisers could no longer govern Norway from Copenhagen. Fortunately, when Britain invaded Denmark, Frederik appointed a temporary government commission in Christiania to run the affairs of state on his behalf in Norway. He named Danish Prince Christian August as chair of the government commission and military commander in Norway. This was the first time that Norway was allowed to have its own government since the Reformation. The government commission worked diligently to try to relieve the food shortage by sending representatives to purchase grain and other products to be slipped through the blockade or transported through Sweden.

Norway's problems were compounded in 1808 when Frederik foolishly declared war on Sweden. The Swedes had been attacked by the Russians, and Frederik had visions of raising an army to invade southern Sweden and reclaim territory that Denmark had previously lost to the Swedes. Frederik's plans never materialized, and the Norwegians had to bear the brunt of the war when Sweden attacked Norway. The Norwegian army fought valiantly and drove the Swedish army back to the border. But for several months, Frederik would not permit the Norwegian government commission to negotiate an armistice with Sweden and Britain. As a result of Frederik's actions, the Norwegians faced economic ruin, starvation, and a lengthy war that prevented Norway from importing or exporting goods through Sweden or across the sea.

At this point, some of the loyal Norwegians started to wonder why they were still in a union with Denmark that seemed to cause them nothing but trouble and hardship and provided them with little or no assistance. That sentiment was especially held by some leading members of the Norwegian merchant class, who began to have discussions about whether Norway might be better served in a union with Sweden or some other alternative such as independence.

One of those leaders of the merchant class was Count Herman Wedel Jarlsberg. He was one of the last remaining members of the Norwegian nobility. As the son of a diplomat, he grew up in England and did not permanently live in Norway until his mid-twenties. He owned a large estate and served as the leading official of Buskerud in southern Norway, and he married the daughter of Peder Anker. He also became a member of the government commission, where he worked feverishly to purchase and ship food supplies to Norway. At this difficult time, he became an advocate for terminating the union with Denmark and entering into a union with Sweden because he felt that the latter arrangement would be better suited to avoid economic, political and military problems for Norway in the future. He was never a popular figure in Norway because of his leanings toward Sweden and the fact that he spoke Norwegian with a foreign accent. But he was a true Norwegian patriot who would play an important role for the country in the years ahead.

By 1809 it occurred to Frederik and his advisers in Copenhagen that times were tough in Norway and that the loyalty of some of his Norwegian subjects and the unity of his dual kingdom might be at risk. So he finally decided to provide the Norwegians with some relief and assistance. Although they were on opposite sides of the war, Denmark-Norway and Britain entered into a licensed trade agreement. This agreement allowed Norwegian ships to obtain licenses to ship lumber from Norway to Britain and to ship grain and other products from Denmark to Norway. In this manner, the British blockade of Norway was partially lifted, continued starvation was averted in Norway, and the Norwegian economy showed some improvement.

Frederik addressed another longstanding concern of the Norwegians. In 1811 he summoned Wedel Jarlsberg to Copenhagen, where Wedel Jarlsberg thought he might be reprimanded or even imprisoned by the king for his political beliefs and his dealings with Sweden. Instead, Frederik informed him that Norway would at last be permitted to have its own university. As a longtime advocate of a Norwegian university, Wedel Jarlsberg was thrilled with the news. He returned to Norway, where he and other wealthy Norwegians raised the necessary funds for the university. The Royal Frederik's University opened in Christiania in 1813. It remained Norway's only university for over a century, and its name was changed to the University of Oslo in 1939.

The licensed trade agreement was not renewed in 1812. So the British blockade resumed, and Norway could no longer import or export goods. It was also a year of poor fishing, the crops failed again, and hungry Norwegians rioted and raided government and private grain storage warehouses in different parts of Norway. The new Danish governor of Norway, who had replaced the government commission, called out the military, and there were armed confrontations between farmers and soldiers. The return of good fishing and better harvests in 1813 relieved the food situation somewhat, but more Norwegians had become dissatisfied with Denmark, and sick and tired of war, blockade, starvation, and the poor economy.

Changes in Sweden affecting Norway

In 1807 the king of Sweden was Gustav Adolf, a stubborn man who seemed to frequently make bad decisions and consequently was not respected by most of the military leaders, nobles, and government officials in Sweden. Gustav hated Napoleon and revolutionary France, and he rejected any suggestion that he should abandon his alliance with Britain, even though Napoleon and his allies clearly seemed to have the upper hand in the war.

Napoleon and the Russian tsar Alexander settled their differences and entered into the Peace of Tilsit in July 1807. They were now allies, and in a secret agreement Napoleon consented to a Russian attack on Finland. Finland had been part of the Swedish kingdom for centuries, and many Swedes had settled in Finland. Alexander was supposedly going to attack Finland in order to force Sweden into the Continental System, but in reality he intended to take Finland away from Sweden and make it part of the Russian Empire.

So in February 1808 Russia invaded Finland with a large force. The Swedes were unprepared for the war, and by the end of the year the Russians had overrun most of Finland and were invading northern Sweden. It was clear that Russia was now in possession of Finland and was not about to give it back to Sweden. Sweden had thereby lost one-third of its territory, transforming it into just another minor European state.

The Swedish military and civilian leaders blamed King Gustav for this debacle because he had refused to join Napoleon's alliance and he had diverted a large part of the Swedish army to attack Norway instead of concentrating his forces to defend Sweden and Finland. The Swedish generals took action in March 1809 by staging a coup that overthrew the king. They arrested Gustav, imprisoned him for a few months, and then shipped him off to Germany in exile. Gustav's elderly uncle Karl was elected king of Sweden. Unfortunately, King Karl was not only old. He was also ill and half senile, and more importantly he did not have any children who could inherit the throne. So the Swedes decided to find a new crown prince who would be the future king of Sweden.

Most of the Swedish generals and nobles wanted to find a strong crown prince who was an experienced military leader, and who would build up the army, attack the Russians, and take back Finland. They decided this even though Sweden had just signed a peace treaty awarding Finland to Russia in September 1809.

Their choice turned out to be Christian August, the Danish prince who was commander of the military in Norway. Christian August accepted the appointment, moved to Stockholm, changed his name to Karl August, was adopted by old King Karl, and became the new crown prince of Sweden. He was a popular choice, a friendly person with impressive military credentials. But unfortunately the new crown prince was overweight, and he loved to indulge in too much food, drink, and tobacco. In 1810, just a few months after he took office, the crown prince suddenly had a stroke or heart attack, fell off his horse, and died instantly at a military parade. Now the Swedes were back to square one, and they were not very enthused about the remaining candidates to fill the position of crown prince.

At that point, a young Swedish nobleman and military officer named Baron Lieutenant Carl Otto Mörner took it upon himself to find an acceptable candidate. On his own initiative, and without any authority whatsoever from the king or anyone else, Mörner started meeting with some of Napoleon's generals in Paris. One day he showed up at the office of Jean Baptiste Bernadotte, a great marshal of France who had successfully led several French military campaigns. Bernadotte had been one of France's best generals, but he was currently out of favor with Napoleon as he awaited his next assignment. After just a few minutes of conversation, Mörner was impressed and he asked Bernadotte if he would consider becoming crown prince and the next king of Sweden. Bernadotte did not say no to this surprising offer, but he said that he could not take such a step without Napoleon's consent.

Mörner returned to Stockholm and proudly announced to the Swedish leaders that he had found the ideal candidate in Bernadotte. Instead of thanking Mörner for his efforts, they arrested the young upstart for acting without authority. But the more the Swedish leaders thought about it, the more they liked Mörner's idea. Bernadotte seemed to be the strong military leader who could reconquer Finland from the Russians and restore Sweden to its former glory. The Swedish leaders made contact with both Napoleon and Bernadotte. Napoleon gave his consent. Bernadotte would not have been his first choice, but he felt that it could be advantageous to have a Frenchman on the Swedish throne.

Bernadotte also said yes, and in fact he had already been lobbying for the position. In October 1810 he traveled to Stockholm, took the Scandinavian name Karl Johan, converted to the Lutheran religion, was adopted by King Karl, and became the new crown prince of Sweden. As such, he was now the undisputed leader of Sweden, with primary responsibility for the military and foreign affairs.

The Swedish generals tried to impress upon Karl Johan the necessity of retaking Finland. But after reviewing the situation, Karl Johan came to the conclusion that going to war again with Russia was unwise and unrealistic. Russia was an ally of France and had a formidable army. And even if it were possible for the Swedes to somehow retake Finland, Sweden would thereafter live under the constant threat of another Russian invasion for years or even decades to come.

At the same time, Karl Johan did not accept his new position as crown prince just to sit still, especially considering the opportunities that might arise in a war of shifting alliances. He realized that the Swedes expected him to do great things and that some Swedish nobles were not all that excited about having a commoner as their crown prince. If he did not do something to compensate Sweden for the loss of Finland, they could send him back to France just as quickly as he had come.

Karl Johan ultimately decided that the best way to bring glory to both Sweden and what he hoped would be his Bernadotte dynasty was to take Norway away from the king of Denmark. This would have the added benefit of weakening Denmark, reducing the chances of another Danish war against Sweden, and establishing Sweden as the dominant power in Scandinavia.

A possible Swedish takeover of Norway was not a novel idea in Sweden. The deposed King Gustav had fancied this notion enough to invade Norway during the war with Russia, and a minority of Swedish nobles and generals had also favored the Norwegian option instead of slogging through another war with Russia to reclaim Finland. But to the extent possible, Karl Johan wanted to achieve his goal of taking over Norway through alliances and diplomacy, although he realized that some sort of military action might also be required to accomplish his goal. The crown prince explained his ideas to the Swedish leaders and they agreed. Over the next three years, virtually all of Karl Johan's efforts were directed toward Sweden's new top priority of taking Norway away from King Frederik of Denmark.

Swedish diplomacy

Karl Johan's diplomatic efforts got underway in 1811 when he asked Napoleon for his consent to a Swedish takeover of Norway. Napoleon declined to give his consent, for once deciding not to double-cross one of his allies, namely the king of Denmark. So Karl Johan secretly made contact with the other Great Powers of Europe, and eventually he switched sides in the Napoleonic Wars. First he entered into a secret agreement with Russia, which agreed to Sweden's takeover of Norway in exchange for Karl Johan's assurance that Sweden would not make any future claim to Finland. By 1813 he also secretly obtained the consent of Britain and Prussia by agreeing to send Swedish troops to Continental Europe to fight as part of the British alliance against France.

During the period from 1810 to 1813, Karl Johan sent his spies into Norway to obtain information on the Norwegian military forces and installations and to find out the Norwegians' attitudes toward Denmark and Sweden, respectively. The spies found that most Norwegians were still generally loyal to King Frederik and the union with Denmark. But Karl Johan's representatives also had secret meetings and even negotiations with leading Norwegian merchants who favored some arrangement with Sweden instead of the union with Denmark. Those merchants included Peder Anker and Wedel Jarlsberg, and the Swedes promised them that Norway could have its own constitution, laws, and legislature and even equal status with Sweden in a future union of the two countries.

Napoleon's invasion of Russia

The turning point of the Napoleonic Wars was the French invasion of Russia in 1812. Napoleon left France with over four hundred thousand troops and made good progress as the Russian forces retreated. The French made it all the way to Moscow, but the Russians burned the city, and Napoleon decided to retreat in the middle of the frigid Russian winter. The French withdrawal from Russia was a complete disaster, as not more than ten thousand soldiers in Napoleon's original invasion force made it back to central Europe.

In the course of this invasion and retreat, Napoleon managed to alienate almost all of his former allies, including Russia, Prussia, Austria, and Sweden. They all joined an alliance with the British and made preparations to defeat France and finish off Napoleon once and for all. Meanwhile, Napoleon was back in France raising yet another army to go on the attack through Germany once again.

By 1813 the only significant remaining ally of France was Denmark-Norway. In Copenhagen, King Frederik started to come to the realization that France and its allies were likely headed for an ignominious defeat that could result in the loss of all or part of his kingdom. He also got wind of Karl Johan's plans to take Norway away from him.

For months Frederik's advisers had been telling him to get out of the French alliance, and finally the king began to heed their advice. He tried to switch sides and join the British alliance in order to avoid defeat and the loss of Norway, but he was too late. Both the Russians and the Swedes demanded that Frederik give up Norway, or at least Trondheim county and northern Norway, as a prerequisite to joining their alliance. Frederik refused this demand and thereby cast his lot with Napoleon, win or lose.

Christian Frederik to Norway

At this point, King Frederik came up with a new strategy. In May 1813 he sent his cousin and heir to the Danish throne, Prince Christian Frederik, to Norway as governor and military commander. He hoped that somehow Christian Frederik could hold onto Norway for their family dynasty. The prince made it through the British blockade to Norway, dressed as a common sailor on a fishing boat.

5.2 Portrait of Christian Frederik by J.L. Lund (1813)

Christian Frederik was an unusual choice for the positions of governor and military commander in that he had little or no experience in government or the military. But at the age of only twenty-six, he was young, articulate, smart and ambitious. The Norwegian public liked him because he was handsome and personable. He was also hard-working, and within a short period of time he managed to create several functioning Norwegian government departments and he became a popular figure in Christiania. Later in the same year, Frederik once again declared war on Sweden, and he ordered Christian Frederik to invade that country. But the prince was intelligent enough to ignore the order, knowing that the Norwegian military was not up to the task and that such an invasion would fail and would interfere with his immediate priority of building up the Norwegian government and the trust and support of the Norwegian people.

From Leipzig to Kiel

By May 1813 Napoleon had raised another large army and was advancing through Germany, while Karl Johan took his Swedish army across the Baltic Sea to join the forces of the British alliance. The decisive battle of this campaign took place near Leipzig. Karl Johan and his army played an important role in the allied victory over Napoleon's forces at the Battle of Leipzig in October 1813. Once again, Napoleon was forced to retreat towards France.

This time the allies saw their opportunity to pursue Napoleon all the way to Paris and end the war right then and there. As part of their plan, Karl Johan was given command of the Northern Allied Army, made up largely of Swedish and Russian troops. He agreed to lead the army through northern Germany and Holland to the French border, where they would halt. Karl Johan did not want to invade France because he was a Frenchman with hopes of becoming the next ruler of France after Napoleon was captured or killed.

The Swedish crown prince moved the Northern Army through northern Germany, but before they reached Holland he diverted from the allied plan and ordered the army to turn north towards Denmark. He decided the time had come to defeat Denmark and force King Frederik to relinquish Norway. On December 1, 1813, his forces attacked the Danish army in Holstein, a duchy just south of Denmark that was ruled by Frederik. Badly outnumbered by fifty thousand allied troops, the Danish army quickly withdrew, and almost all of Holstein was occupied by Karl Johan's army within just a few days. Both sides agreed to an armistice that was signed on December 15, 1813.

Russia had secretly consented to Karl Johan's attack northward through Holstein, but Britain and the other allies knew nothing about it beforehand, and now they were extremely angry that Karl Johan had not followed the original plan and agreement to pursue the French army directly to France. By going off on his own without their consent, Karl Johan had alienated the British and those other allies and thereby sacrificed his remote chance of becoming the next ruler of France. So the next step for the Swedish crown prince was to negotiate a peace treaty with Denmark that would allow him to take over Norway.

When the treaty negotiations got started after the Swedish-Danish armistice went into effect, a representative of the Austrian Empire showed up and offered to mediate a settlement between Sweden and Denmark. The Austrian pressured Frederik to give up Trondheim county and northern Norway in exchange for a peace treaty. But Karl Johan was in no mood for mediation or compromise. He insisted upon receiving nothing less than all of Norway as the price of peace, and he threatened to resume his attack and invade and occupy Denmark if he did not get his way. Frederik had no alternative except to agree to the terms demanded by Karl Johan, even if it meant giving up the Kingdom of Norway that had been ruled from Denmark since 1380.

The Treaty of Kiel between Sweden and Denmark was finalized and signed in the night between January 14 and 15, 1814. There were no Norwegians present at the negotiations or the treaty signing, and clearly no one had asked Norway to consent to the treaty. Under the treaty, King Frederik of Denmark granted Norway to King Karl of Sweden (and not to Sweden itself) as a kingdom in union with Sweden. Denmark kept the ancient Norwegian possessions of Iceland, Greenland, and the Faeroe Islands, and also received some small Swedish lands along the Baltic Sea. It was agreed that the Norwegians would keep all of their laws, rights, privileges, and freedoms. King Karl, as the new king of Norway, promised to pay Denmark a portion of the Danish national debt. Finally, Denmark joined the alliance against Napoleon. Even though Britain and the other allies (except Russia) were still upset with Karl Johan, they felt obligated to go along with the transfer of Norway to the Swedish king in accordance with their secret agreements with Sweden.

The treaty was a great triumph for Karl Johan and the culmination of his efforts to take over Norway as compensation for the loss of Finland. His next priority was to finalize the union of Sweden and Norway.

Norwegian reaction to Kiel

Sweden and the Great Powers of Europe assumed that the Norwegians would willingly submit to the Treaty of Kiel and join the union with Sweden, and that Christian Frederik would promptly close up shop in Christiania and return to Denmark. That was not going to happen.

When the Norwegians learned the details of the Kiel Treaty, the vast majority were indignant and furious. They had been loyal subjects of the kings of Denmark for centuries, and they had faithfully stuck with Frederik through all the wars, blockades, famines, and other problems of the past few years. So how could he treat them so shabbily and just hand over Norway to the king of Sweden without even consulting with them or obtaining their consent? And how could Sweden and the Great Powers expect them to join a union with Sweden, a country that had repeatedly attacked them and occupied and even taken away parts of their country over the past two hundred years? They were not cattle that could be bought and sold! Their only consolation was that the treaty did not break up their beloved country as they had once feared. But they were also angry that Frederik had the audacity to keep the ancient Norwegian lands in the North Atlantic, including Iceland, Greenland, and the Faeroes.

As far as almost all Norwegians were concerned, the Treaty of Kiel was not binding on Norway because they were not a party to the treaty, and they would never join a union with Sweden. On the streets of Christiania and other cities and towns, there was a spontaneous new feeling of national enthusiasm and pride for Norway. Now that the king of Denmark was no longer king of Norway, the overwhelming sentiment was that Norway should declare its independence. Of course, there were a few upper class Norwegian merchants like Wedel Jarlsberg who favored a union with Sweden, but they were a small minority compared to the large numbers of Norwegians who now demanded independence.

The mood of the Norwegians darkened even further, and their determination grew, when Karl Johan sent them a public announcement. It stated that Norway was now an independent kingdom in a union with Sweden, that the Swedish military would occupy the Norwegian military fortifications, and that he was appointing a Swedish governor of Norway to take control of the government in Christiania. If Karl Johan thought the Norwegians would gladly receive this announcement, he was sorely mistaken.

Christian Frederik did not leave for Denmark. Rather, he continued to run the government in Norway, and he started making arrangements with the Norwegian military to defend the country from any attack by Sweden. Karl Johan and the bulk of the Swedish army were still occupied in Continental Europe while the British alliance tried to finish off Napoleon and win the war. Therefore, Christian Frederik saw this as an ideal opportunity to create an independent Norway under his leadership as king.

King Frederik of Denmark, after just agreeing to the Treaty of Kiel, supported Christian Frederik's plan to become the king of an independent Norway and thereby save the country for the family dynasty. If Frederik could no longer be the king of Norway, he hoped that Christian Frederik, as heir to the Danish throne, could eventually become king of both countries and create a new union of Denmark and Norway sometime in the future.

So Frederik was playing a dangerous double game of pretending to cooperate with Sweden and the Great Powers while actually supporting Christian Frederik behind the scenes. In January, at Sweden's request, Frederik sent an official message to Christian Frederik ordering him, as soon as possible, to appoint commissioners to hand over the Norwegian fortresses to Sweden, to resign as governor of Norway, and to return to Denmark. But in secret correspondence between Frederik and Christian Frederik, the king of Denmark apparently expressed his support for Christian Frederik's plan to become the ruler of Norway. And since the British blockade of Norway had been suspended, Frederik also supported Christian Frederik by shipping large quantities of much-needed grain to Norway over the next several months despite British objections to the shipments while Christian Frederik was still in charge.

The first Eidsvoll meetings and the proclamation

Christian Frederik acted immediately and decisively on his new plans for Norway. Already in late January, he met with a few of his best friends and supporters in Norway. They met at the estate of Carsten Anker, Christian Frederik's longtime friend and mentor, about forty miles north of Christiania at Eidsvoll. At this meeting, the prince expressed his view that he should proclaim himself to be the new king and absolute monarch of Norway since he was the legitimate heir to the throne and Frederik had relinquished his title as king of Norway. Those in attendance did not object, and they generally supported Christian Frederik's plans.

Christian Frederik then traveled through southern and central Norway to Trondheim, Røros, and other towns. He wanted to get a feeling for Norwegian public opinion. Throughout the country, he was met with a warm reception and a few cheering crowds. He concluded that the Norwegians wanted independence with him as their new king.

Upon his return to the Christiania region, Christian Frederik held another meeting at Eidsvoll on February 16, 1814, which was later called the meeting of notables. This was a larger meeting with twenty-one prominent Norwegians. They were all high officials, military leaders, or merchants from places in and around Christiania. Almost all had been supporters of Frederik and the union with Denmark, and many of them had been born in Denmark, were descended from Danish families, or otherwise had close ties to Denmark.

At this gathering Christian Frederik described his plans to become the new king and absolute monarch of an independent Norway. But while everyone in the room except Peder Anker was in favor of Norwegian independence, to the surprise of Christian Frederik the vast majority opposed his plan to become an absolute monarch in Norway. After what the previous absolute monarch had just pulled at Kiel, they did not want to be ruled by yet another absolute ruler who had unchecked and unlimited power and authority.

As eloquently stated at the meeting by Professor Georg Sverdrup from the new university in Christiania, in the Kiel Treaty the king of Denmark had given up his family's right to rule Norway, so the absolute monarchy in Norway had ended, and the sovereignty of the country was now held by the Norwegian people. Therefore, it was up to the Norwegian people to decide how they would be governed and who would be their new king. The general consensus of the meeting was that Norway should have its own constitution and elect its own king as a constitutional monarch and not an absolute monarch. Sverdrup cushioned the blow to Christian Frederik's pride by expressing the belief that the Norwegian people would undoubtedly select him as their new king.

Christian Frederik could see the handwriting on the wall, and he was persuaded not to proclaim himself as the new king and absolute monarch of Norway. Instead, he and the others at the meeting decided to call for an election of delegates to a constitutional assembly that would draft a Norwegian constitution and elect a new king of Norway. They also named Christian Frederik as regent to temporarily run the Norwegian government along with several ministers.

A few days after the second Eidsvoll meeting, Christian Frederik issued a proclamation to the Norwegian people that called for the election of a constitutional assembly to decide on a new form of government for Norway, with Christian Frederik to govern as regent in the meantime. He also appointed ministers to head the various departments of government, except for foreign affairs which he decided to handle on his own.

The proclamation was received with great enthusiasm and celebration throughout Norway. It was clear that the overwhelming majority of Norwegians, like the dignitaries at the second Eidsvoll meeting, felt that Norway should have its own constitution like the United States, France, the Netherlands, Poland, Spain, and various other countries. Even conservative Sweden had a new constitution since 1809. Many common people throughout Norway, in addition to various members of the upper class, started writing their own drafts of a Norwegian constitution, and there were countless discussions among Norwegians as to what kinds of provisions the new constitution should contain. One prominent Norwegian newspaper even ran a contest and offered a money prize for the best constitution. The newspaper received nine entries, but no winner was announced because none of the constitutions was deemed to be worthy of the prize.

Meanwhile in Stockholm, the king of Sweden had appointed Swedish Field Marshal Count Hans von Essen as the governor of Norway under the union with Sweden, with the responsibility first to take over the Norwegian government and fortresses and later to draft a Norwegian constitution. At the end of February 1814, the newly-appointed governor sent a Swedish delegation to Christiania to start making the arrangements. They scheduled a meeting with Christian Frederik. But when they arrived for the meeting, they were surprised to see not just Christian Frederik but also a number of prominent Norwegians. At Christian Frederik's request, Carsten Anker read to them the proclamation for a constitutional assembly. The regent and the Norwegians made it clear that the Norwegian people would draft their own constitution for an independent Norway and select their own king instead of serving under a Swedish governor. The Swedes were speechless, shocked and angry at these unexpected revelations, and they stormed out of the meeting without further discussion and returned to Sweden.

Anticipating that he had not heard the last from the Swedes, Christian Frederik then ordered the Norwegian military to defend the border with Sweden and take over the Danish-Norwegian naval ships in Norway. Over the next several weeks, Sweden did nothing other than send a few notes to Christian Frederik demanding compliance with the Treaty of Kiel. Of course, the new regent and the Norwegians refused to comply with those demands.

In February and March, in accordance with the proclamation, Norwegians met at special services in their local churches or military units throughout the country. At each meeting, the Norwegians first took an oath to defend Norway's independence and to risk their lives and blood for their beloved country. Then they elected local electors who subsequently met and elected the delegates to the constitutional assembly.

The Eidsvoll assembly

Norway's constitutional assembly met and conducted its business from April 10 to May 19, 1814, at Carsten Anker's mansion at Eidsvoll. There were 112 delegates from all parts of southern and central Norway. They were all men, and most of them were government officials including pastors and members of the military, but there were also many merchants, landowners, and farmers. There were no representatives from north of Trondheim county because, in an age of slow communications and transportation, they simply could not arrive in time to participate. Norway experienced an early spring thaw that year, and the roads that were normally covered with ice and snow in early April now contained a lot of slush and mud that made travel by horse-drawn sleigh or wagon very slow and challenging.

Eidsvoll was chosen as the site of the assembly because it was in a central location, at least for most of the delegates. It was also away from the major towns and cities so that the delegates could speak their peace and work freely and not under the constant scrutiny of the public and the press. Moreover, Eidsvoll was safely removed from the Swedish border in case of an invasion from the east.

On the other hand, the rural location posed its own problems. It was difficult to find enough accommodations for all the attendees. Many shared rooms in farmhouses. Some slept on beds of hay on the floor, at least for a few nights. Quite a few delegates had to walk long distances to and from the meetings each day.

Carsten Anker's mansion house was being renovated, and the meetings took place in the second floor ballroom and art gallery, where the representatives sat close together on uncomfortable wooden benches without writing tables. The walls of the hall were decorated with pine boughs and a risqué painting of Venus that had to be replaced when it became a distraction for some of the delegates.

Despite the travel difficulties and the rough accommodations, the mood of the assembly was upbeat, as the representatives were eager to draft a constitution, and they knew they were participating in an important, historic event for the future of their country. Christian Frederik gave the opening and closing addresses and reviewed various drafts of the Constitution, but he did not otherwise participate in the deliberations of the assembly.

The representatives were divided into two different factions or parties with different views. The majority party led by a country judge named Christian Magnus Falsen was the so-called independence party. Its members made up over two-thirds of the representatives in the assembly and were mostly government officials, military men, and farmers. They believed that Norway should be an independent country led by Christian Frederik as king. The minority union party for the most part consisted of merchants and wealthy landowners, and they were led by Wedel Jarlsberg. Their view was that Norway should enter into a union with Sweden, and that it was unrealistic for Norway to reject the position of Sweden and the Great Powers and declare its independence. However, the members of both parties agreed that Norway should have its own constitution, government, and laws. All were in agreement that Norway should be a constitutional monarchy.

On April 12 the assembly elected a committee to draft a proposed constitution for consideration by the full assembly. There were fifteen members on the drafting committee, including Falsen and Wedel Jarlsberg, and they came from the various regions of the country that were represented in the assembly. Oddly enough, there were no farmers on the committee. Most of the members of the committee were from the independence party, and the committee selected Falsen as its chairman.

Falsen and a teacher named Johan Adler had already prepared a proposed draft of the Constitution, and their draft was used as a model by the committee. The Falsen-Adler draft and Falsen's influence on the drafting process later caused him to be called the Father of the Constitution. While several provisions of the Falsen-

Adler proposal were incorporated in some form in the Constitution, many of its provisions were changed or removed and other provisions were added.

Even though his union party was outnumbered on the drafting committee, Wedel Jarlsberg played an important role in the drafting process. He concentrated on the constitutional powers of the king, and he tried to persuade the committee to adopt provisions that he thought might be acceptable to the Swedes if Norway subsequently joined a union with Sweden.

5.3 *Riksforsamlingen på Eidsvoll 1814* by Oscar Wergeland (1885) shows the Norwegian constitutional assembly in 1814. Christian Magnus Falsen is standing and reading, and W.F.K. Christie is seated to his right. Standing on the far right is Peder Anker.

The committee completed a first draft of the Constitution on April 26. This draft was reviewed by Christian Frederik who gave the committee his comments and suggestions. A few changes were made, and the committee's proposed Constitution was finalized on April 30 and submitted to the full assembly on May 4. There followed a lively debate in the assembly, and then a redaction committee including Professor Sverdrup made the final changes.

On May 16 the Norwegian Constitution was unanimously approved by the Eidsvoll assembly. The document was dated May 17, 1814, and was signed by the officers of the assembly on that date. Therefore, *syttende mai* (the 17th of May) would later become Norway's National Day or Constitution Day. The rest of the delegates signed the Constitution on May 18.

In addition, on May 17 the assembly unanimously elected Christian Frederik as king of Norway. He accepted, and on May 19 he took the oath of office and gave his final address to the Eidsvoll assembly. The assembly members also took an oath and then shouted "*hurra!*" as cannons were shot off outside. The king adjourned the assembly, and the delegates departed Eidsvoll the next day. They had completed their assignment to draft the Norwegian Constitution in less than six weeks.

Provisions of the Eidsvoll Constitution

The Eidsvoll Constitution provided for a free and independent Norway, so it was also Norway's declaration of independence. At the time, it was considered a very progressive constitution, and many of its provisions were based on the Constitutions of France and the United States. For example, like the US Constitution, the Norwegian Constitution applied Montesquieu's doctrine of separation of powers. Thus, the Norwegian government was separated into three independent branches, including an executive branch, a legislative branch, and a judicial branch.

The executive branch of government was to be run by the king of Norway and his appointed ministers. Norway became a constitutional monarchy, not an absolute monarchy. The monarchy was to be hereditary, and upon the king's death his male heir would become the next king of Norway. The king was in charge of the military and foreign policy, and he and his ministers were otherwise responsible for carrying out the laws of Norway. But the king did not have the right to grant any new titles of nobility.

The *Storting* was to be the legislative branch of government elected by the Norwegian people. The name Storting was coined by a delegate and pastor named Nicolai Wergeland, who had used the term in his own draft of the Constitution. The right to vote was given to any Norwegian man (but not any women) over the age of twenty-five who had resided in Norway for over five years and either: (a) was an existing or former public official, or (b) owned or leased (for a term of at least five years) any land that was on the tax rolls, or (c) was a citizen of a town, or owned a house or land with a specific minimum value in a town or port. Consequently, only about 10 to 15 percent of the Norwegian people initially had the right to vote. Women, servants, laborers, husmenn, and many others were excluded. The right to vote was gradually expanded over time, but Norway did not adopt universal suffrage for all men and women until 1913.

The Storting was to meet every three years to pass laws and appropriate money. If the Storting passed a bill, the king did not have the absolute right to veto the bill. But the king could issue a veto and thereby delay the enactment of the bill. However, if the Storting passed the same bill in three consecutive sessions, the king could no longer make a delaying veto, and the bill became law.

The Constitution provided for a court system as the judicial branch of government. It also provided individuals with certain basic rights, including freedom of expression. Even though the Eidsvoll assembly had voted to include freedom of religion for Christians in the Constitution, for some unknown reason the redaction committee took it out of the final version. Consequently, until the 1840s there was no freedom of religion in Norway, except for members of the Lutheran state church.

The Constitution was not totally enlightened because it excluded all Jews, Jesuits, and monastic orders from the Kingdom of Norway. The Jewish question was debated in the assembly. Wedel Jarlsberg and several others thought it was wrong to ban an entire group of people from the country. But the majority ruled in favor of the exclusion. The prohibition against Jews was finally removed from the

Constitution in 1851, but the exclusion of Jesuits lasted all the way until the 1950s!

The reaction of the Great Powers and Sweden

As the Eidsvoll assembly was working on Norway's Constitution, Norwegian envoys were asking the Great Powers to recognize a fully independent Norway. For example, in March Christian Frederik sent Carsten Anker to London, and he stayed there for several weeks. Anker met with various members of the British Parliament to lobby them on Norway's behalf. However, he ran into some problems, as the Swedes tried to have him deported from Britain, and he even had to spend some time in an English debtors' prison for the unpaid obligations of one of his former companies.

Anker successfully persuaded several members of Britain's opposition party to support an independent Norway, and they gave impassioned speeches in favor of Norway in the Parliament. But ultimately his mission was unsuccessful because the British government felt that it had to keep its promise to Sweden to support the union. The same was true of the other Great Powers. Britain did agree to send special commissioners to Norway in order to state the position of the British government in favor of the union of Norway and Sweden, to find out the sentiment of the Norwegian people, to protect Norway's rights in any arrangement with Sweden, and to try to mediate an agreement between Sweden and Norway.

By late May of 1814, Karl Johan and his Swedish army were back in Sweden. The crown prince was indignant that the Norwegians had defied him and the Treaty of Kiel by declaring independence, approving their own constitution, and electing Christian Frederik as their king. He was also upset with his appointed governor and others in the Swedish government for basically doing nothing in his absence to force Christian Frederik and Norway to comply with his wishes. He prepared his military for an invasion of Norway, and he vowed to teach the Norwegians a lesson and force them to accept the union.

In May the Great Powers compelled King Frederik of Denmark to stop his grain shipments to Norway, and Britain reimposed its naval blockade of the Norwegian ports. Frederik's double game was over, and now he would have to comply with his treaty obligations instead of secretly supporting Christian Frederik and an independent Norway.

Britain, Russia, Prussia, and Austria sent commissioners to Norway in May, June, and July. Before they went to Norway, they were convinced that all the talk of Norwegian independence was just the work of Christian Frederik and a few rebels. But when they arrived in Christiania, they discovered to their surprise that nearly all the Norwegians strongly favored independence and the new king, and that they were dead set against joining a union with Sweden. The commissioners also found that Norway already had a fully functioning government with several departments and active public officials, all operating under the new Constitution, plus a Norwegian military and fortifications defending the border with Sweden. They were quite taken aback and even impressed by what they saw and heard.

Nevertheless, the Great Powers were still intent on finalizing a union of Sweden and Norway, but as part of a peaceful agreement that they offered to mediate. The British were clearly in favor of allowing the Norwegians to have their own government in such a union. Over several weeks in June and July of 1814, the Great Powers tried to mediate the dispute between Sweden and Norway, and they spoke with Christian Frederik and representatives of Sweden.

In early June Christian Frederik was still hoping for a miracle to save his throne, as he felt there was a remote chance that the British might come around to the Norwegians' position. He tried to delay the process, and he refused to abdicate or change the Constitution without approval of the Storting. He also asked for two or three months to hold a Storting election and to call the Storting into session. Of course, all of this was unacceptable to Karl Johan. He insisted that Christian Frederik leave Norway immediately, that the Eidsvoll Constitution be replaced by a new Norwegian constitution to be drafted by the Swedes, and that the Swedish military be permitted to occupy the Norwegian border fortresses to guarantee a union of the two countries.

The parties continued to negotiate. By July it had become clear to Christian Frederik, if not to the Norwegians, that he would have to leave the throne. But to his credit, he still tried to work out the best deal possible for Norway. That is, Christian Frederik expressed the willingness to abdicate and leave Norway, and to allow the union with Sweden to take place with Storting approval. But he argued that Norway must keep its existing Constitution and continue to occupy at least some of the border fortifications. Karl Johan was not willing to accept this proposal, and the mediation and negotiations ended without success.

The Swedish invasion and the Moss Convention

On July 30, 1814, an impatient Karl Johan sent his Swedish army across the Norwegian border and invaded Norway in order to enforce compliance with the Treaty of Kiel. The ensuing conflict was known as the August War or the War of the Cats because the two sides just pawed at one another. The soldiers of the Norwegian army were eager to defend their country. Although outnumbered by the Swedes, the Norwegian army was well-trained, and its generals had formulated a plan to mount an effective defense. The major problem was that the Norwegian army was not well supplied with ammunition, clothing, or food, and the supplies would likely begin to run out in a couple of weeks.

In southeastern Norway, as the Swedish army advanced farther into Norwegian territory, a wary and inexperienced Christian Frederik kept ordering his army to retreat even before any battle was engaged, except in one place where the Norwegians fought bravely but had to withdraw. This was not the plan that he and the generals had worked out, and the generals objected to the withdrawals, but to no avail. The Norwegians gave up Fredrikstad after firing only a few shots, and their army finally withdrew to the west bank of the Glomma River.

The strategy of Christian Frederik (or the lack thereof) enraged the common Norwegian soldiers, who were spoiling for a fight with the invaders. They started calling Christian Frederik a coward and a ballroom king or theater king who was better suited to a ballroom or a theater than a battlefield. Farther north around Kongsvinger, where Christian Frederik was not present, the Norwegians held their ground and won three skirmishes, and the Swedish invaders had to withdraw back across the border.

On the Swedish side, after just a few days, the war against Norway was becoming expensive, and Sweden had just spent a lot of money in the war against Napoleon. So Karl Johan started to have second thoughts about the invasion of Norway. He was also concerned about the possibility of having to fight a protracted war (especially a cold winter war in the mountains) against a country that he was trying to incorporate into the union. He did not want to be despised by his future Norwegian subjects. Finally, he knew that in the fall the Great Powers were going to meet at the Congress of Vienna to decide the outcome of the Napoleonic Wars and to redraw the boundaries on the Continent of Europe. If his war with Norway was not won before the Congress got started, Karl Johan was worried that the Great Powers might change their minds about the Swedish-Norwegian union and, heaven forbid, recognize an independent Norway.

Based on these considerations, on August 7, just a few days after the start of the invasion, Karl Johan and the Swedes agreed to negotiate an armistice with the Norwegians. Karl Johan then proposed a compromise. He demanded that Christian Frederik call an election of the Storting to approve the union with Sweden, transfer his powers to the Storting once it was in session, and then leave Norway. In return, Karl Johan promised to accept the Eidsvoll Constitution with only such amendments that might be required to accomplish the union with Sweden. In the meantime, the Swedish army would continue to occupy some but not all of the Norwegian border fortifications. Christian Frederik agreed to those terms, and the Moss Convention was signed on August 14, 1814, to end the war.

The Norwegian military and the general public were furious over the terms of the Moss Convention, and there were demonstrations against the agreement and the union throughout the country. They blamed Christian Frederik for giving up without a fight, and mobs even attacked the homes of one of the Norwegian generals. Despite the widespread dissatisfaction, Christian Frederik probably did the Norwegians a great service by sacrificing his crown to save the Eidsvoll Constitution and a large measure of independence for Norway, albeit in a union with Sweden.

In a secret addendum to the Moss Convention, Christian Frederik agreed to transfer his powers immediately. So when he returned to Christiania from the war zone, he feigned illness and assigned his powers to the Norwegian government ministers. He abdicated in early October, and he left Norway for good on October 26, 1814. In 1839 he succeeded Frederik as king of Denmark.

It might seem strange that Karl Johan was willing to sign the Moss Convention on essentially the same terms that he had rejected two weeks earlier. However, apart from the considerations mentioned above, he wanted to get a deal done and finalize the union as soon as possible, even if he had to approve the Eidsvoll Constitution in amended form. He hoped that any provisions of the Constitution that were not agreeable to him could be changed to his satisfaction in the future.

The first Storting and the union with Sweden

The union of Sweden and Norway was not yet in place because the terms of the union had to be negotiated and approved by the Storting and the Swedish government. The election of representatives to the first Storting was held in September 1814. Since the vast majority of Norwegians still opposed the union, the newly-elected Storting representatives were even more radical and independence-minded than the delegates in the Eidsvoll assembly. In fact, the residents of Bergen made their representatives promise to vote against the union. Wedel Jarlsberg was the only union party member at

Eidsvoll who was elected to the Storting, although the Storting did include some other advocates of the union with Sweden.

For his part, Karl Johan tried to hold his temper so that the Storting would go along with the Moss Convention and approve the union, but he was clearly disgusted with the attitude of the Norwegians. In a letter to the Russian tsar, he complained that the Norwegians did not seem to understand that the Great Powers had already forced them to give in. In the same letter he also insulted the intelligence of some Norwegians who thought they were supposed to elect Karl Johan or even his son instead of Sweden's King Karl as the new king of Norway.

The Storting met for the first time in October 1814 in Christiania, and before long the members realized that there was no realistic alternative other than to vote for the union. That was accomplished on October 20, just before the deadline set by the Moss Convention. There were, however, some representatives who voted against the union, including the delegation from Bergen.

The next step for the Storting was to negotiate with the Swedish commissioners on the necessary amendments to the Eidsvoll Constitution. During the negotiations, the Swedes kept two army divisions in Norway, just close enough to Christiania to appear intimidating, but the rest of the invasion force was withdrawn to Sweden.

After a false start, the final Norwegian negotiating team was led by Storting President W.F.K. Christie, who proved to be a patient, shrewd negotiator. The Swedish commissioners presented broad proposals made by Karl Johan in an attempt to increase the king's powers at the expense of the Storting and to limit the independence of Norway in the union. But those proposals were all rejected by Christie and the Norwegians.

At one point in the negotiations, a Swedish commissioner had a letter delivered to Christie's apartment late at night. The letter contained an ultimatum that if the Norwegians did not agree to a certain position of the Swedes the following day, then the Swedes would immediately terminate the negotiations and the Swedish army would overrun Norway. The issue was who should have the power to naturalize foreigners who could then become government officials in Norway. Christie read the letter over and over again and paced back and forth in his apartment for most of the night. Finally, having made his decision, he crumpled up the letter, threw it into the fire, and went to bed. The next morning at the negotiating table, he acted as if nothing had happened, and he continued to reject the Swedish position. The Swedish commissioners backed down, and that point was resolved in favor of the Norwegians.

When the negotiations were completed, it was agreed that the Constitution would be amended to accommodate the union with Sweden, but Christie had actually managed to reduce the powers of the king. There was to be a divided Norwegian council of ministers who would serve in Christiania and Stockholm, respectively. The king retained control of Norwegian foreign relations, and he could also appoint a governor as the king's representative in Norway. But the king's military powers were limited in that he could not declare an offensive war without the approval of the Storting, and the use of the Norwegian military outside of Norway was severely restricted. In addition, the king could only appoint Norwegians to be public officials in Norway. Almost all the provisions of the Eidsvoll Constitution remained unchanged, including the reference to Norway as a free and independent state. The Norwegian Constitution of 1814 has since been amended many times, and some of its provisions are obsolete, but it still remains in effect today.

On November 4, 1814, the Storting approved the amended Constitution and unanimously elected Sweden's King Karl as the king of Norway. The king appointed Peder Anker as his first minister of the Norwegian government in Stockholm and Wedel Jarlsberg as Norway's finance minister. He also appointed a Swedish governor in Christiania.

A few days later, Karl Johan traveled to Christiania along with his son Oscar and the appointed governor Count von Essen. Karl Johan was there to take the oath of office as Norway's new crown prince. He wanted his entrance into the Norwegian capital to be a great ceremony, so his carriage was beautifully decorated and his procession included smartly uniformed soldiers on horseback. He was hoping to be greeted by cheering crowds of Norwegians. But when he arrived in Christiania, it was a bleak and rainy day. Hardly anyone turned out for the procession, and the Norwegians who saw the crown prince were unenthusiastically silent. On November 9 he took the oath, including a promise to uphold the Norwegian Constitution.

On his way to Christiania, Karl Johan had stopped for the night in Moss. At a gathering in the town, he greeted each person that he met with the same two Norwegian phrases, asking them if they were married and had any children. Those were the only Norwegian words that he knew. He never learned Swedish either, and all business at his court was conducted in his native French language.

An Act of Union (*Riksakt*) was approved by the Storting and the Swedish Parliament (the *Riksdag*) in early 1815. It provided for a dual monarchy, two countries with a common king, united in war, but otherwise equal and independent.

So after all was said and done, Norway was an independent kingdom that shared a common king with Sweden. Norway had its own constitution, legislature, court system, laws, currency, military, and bureaucracy, as well as control over its own domestic affairs. But Norway was still in a secondary position in a union with another country because it had a Swedish king who controlled Norway's foreign relations.

The economy after the war

Shortly after the Napoleonic Wars ended, Norway suffered an economic depression. Among other problems, Norway's lumber exports to Britain never recovered from the British blockade because Britain started importing most of its lumber from Canada, while imposing high duties on its imports from Norway. Denmark raised its duties on other Norwegian products, and Norwegian fishermen experienced new competition from North America that resulted in less demand and lower prices. There was hardship and deprivation from the lower class to the upper class in Norway, and many Norwegian merchants whose businesses had survived the wars now went into bankruptcy.

In tough economic times, it was a challenge for the new Norwegian government to make ends meet. The government had to raise taxes on the struggling Norwegian general public. In 1816 the government founded the Bank of Norway and established a new national currency, but those efforts did little to end the economic downturn. In fact, the Norwegian economy did not fully recover for the next twenty-five years.

The Treaty of Kiel required the king, in his capacity as king of Norway, to pay Denmark a substantial portion of the Danish national debt, and Frederik of Denmark was now demanding payment. Karl Johan expected the Norwegian government to pay the debt. But the Norwegians could not afford to pay, and in fact they refused to pay because they did not recognize the validity of the treaty and they were not a party to the treaty. They felt that the debt, if any, had been assumed by the king of Sweden and not the Kingdom of Norway, so therefore Sweden should pay. They also claimed that Frederik had no right to demand payment because he was the one who had incurred the national debt. Finally, they said that it was Frederik who owed a substantial sum to Norway, not the other way around, because he had taken Norway's ancient possessions in the North Atlantic.

Karl Johan also made claims and demands against Denmark by alleging that Frederik had breached the treaty and therefore could not claim money under the treaty. In the end the Great Powers stepped in to mediate the dispute. Denmark was forced to compromise by accepting only 30 percent of its original demand at a low interest rate over ten years. After some threats by Karl Johan to stage a coup in Norway, terminate the Norwegian Constitution, and fully unify Norway and Sweden and their finances, the Storting finally relented in 1821 and Norway paid the reduced amount over time.

Constitutional issues

King Karl died in 1818, and Karl Johan ascended to the throne in Sweden and Norway. He was crowned at separate ceremonies in Stockholm and Trondheim. He had originally accepted the Eidsvoll Constitution with just minor amendments in order to finalize the union, but he had always hoped to change the Constitution more to his liking. Now that he was the king, at every session of the Storting until he died in 1844, Karl Johan proposed amendments to the Norwegian Constitution to increase his own power at the expense of the Storting.

For example, he wanted the Storting to meet every five years instead of every three years, and he wanted the power to appoint the Storting's president and to dissolve the Storting. He also wanted to have an absolute veto instead of just a delaying veto of all bills passed by the Storting. Finally, he demanded expanded rights to issue emergency decrees and control the press, the right to appoint nobility, and the right to dismiss government officials other than judges. All of these demands and proposals were rejected by the Storting even though Karl Johan threatened a coup backed by the Swedish military. The Norwegian Constitution remained unchanged. In fact, by 1821 the Storting had abolished all titles of nobility in Norway over the objections and delaying vetoes of the two Swedish kings.

Foreign relations and the Bodø Affair

On another constitutional issue, it was the Norwegians who were dissatisfied. Under the Constitution, the king controlled Norway's foreign relations. Moreover, the king delegated that responsibility to the Swedish Foreign Ministry even though the Norwegian Constitution said nothing about the Swedish Foreign Ministry. Karl Johan was determined to allow the Swedes to control the foreign and consular affairs of both kingdoms, and in any event Christian Frederik had never created a Norwegian Foreign Ministry. While some Norwegians were employed by the Swedish Foreign Ministry over time, all of the leading positions in the ministry were held by Swedes as long as Karl Johan was the crown prince or the king. The

Norwegians did not like this arrangement at all, and they suspected that the Swedish Foreign Ministry would primarily look after the interests of Sweden and not Norway. Those suspicions were confirmed by the Bodø Affair just a few years after 1814.

In 1818 the Norwegians arrested an Englishman who tried to smuggle goods into Norway without paying the required tolls. The smuggled goods were seized by Norwegian customs and stored in a warehouse at Bodø in northern Norway. After the smuggler was set free on bail, he and his accomplices kidnapped the local Norwegian sheriff and his men, broke into the warehouse and stole some of the confiscated goods, and set sail for England. They left the Norwegian captives adrift in a small boat off the Norwegian coast, but fortunately the Norwegians got back to Norway unharmed.

When the smuggler reached England, he asked the British government to demand compensation from Norway for harassment and for loss of goods. The British Foreign Ministry sent a message to the Swedish Foreign Ministry, which in turn asked the Norwegian government for an explanation. In their response, the Norwegians rejected the demand for compensation, which they found to be outrageous since Norway did nothing wrong and the smuggler had clearly violated a whole host of criminal laws and had been caught red-handed. Norway treated the case as a criminal matter and demanded that Britain prosecute the smuggler.

At this point, the smuggler and his agent bribed Norwegian officials to obtain access to government documents and then presented falsified documents to the British government to substantiate their claim. They also substantially raised the amount of compensation that they demanded from Norway. Based on the falsified documents and a pack full of lies, the British government took the side of the smuggler and pressed Sweden to pay the inflated amount of the claim. The British also threatened economic sanctions if the claim was not paid in full.

The Norwegians continued to reject what they considered to be a totally bogus claim. But the Swedish foreign minister expressed to Karl Johan his fears that the affair could damage Sweden's relations with Britain, at which point Karl Johan ordered a Norwegian official to sign an agreement that caved in to all of the smuggler's demands. In 1821 the Norwegian government was forced to drop all charges against the smuggler, return the rest of the smuggled goods to him, and pay him a huge amount in damages.

The Norwegians felt betrayed and humiliated at the outrageous outcome dictated by the Swedes. For the next eighty years, Norwegians brought up the Bodø Affair whenever they complained about Sweden's control of Norway's foreign relations. In the end, it was the Bodø Affair and other incidents and issues relating to foreign and consular affairs that led to the breakup of the union in 1905.

Syttende mai

In the years after 1814, Norwegians throughout the country began to privately celebrate the 17th of May (syttende mai) as the date of Norwegian independence and the Constitution. Syttende mai started to become an informal national day of celebration in Norway. Karl Johan strongly objected to the celebrations, which he felt were traitorous to the union with Sweden. Instead, he wanted Norwegians to celebrate November 4 as the date on which Norway first elected the Swedish king as its own and approved the amended Constitution that recognized the union.

On May 17, 1824, the students' union held a celebration in Christiania, and in 1827 the first large public celebrations of syttende mai took place in Trondheim and Christiania. Karl Johan was angry, and he vowed never to permit those celebrations again. However, on the evening of May 17, 1829, a large crowd of Norwegians gathered to celebrate in a square in Christiania, where they were cheering and singing songs. The Swedish governor of Norway ordered the cavalry to charge and disperse the crowd. The ensuing melee was referred to as the Battle of the Marketplace (*Torvslaget*) even though no one was killed and only a few Norwegians suffered minor injuries.

This event caused public outrage that the governor had sent the military to attack Norwegians who were peacefully celebrating. Even Karl Johan thought the governor had gone too far. Shortly thereafter the governor died, and the king did not appoint a new governor until 1836. That new governor was Wedel Jarlsberg, and from then on the Swedish kings only appointed Norwegians to that position.

After 1829 Norwegians held public celebrations of syttende mai every year. The day became a national holiday in 1836, and it is properly referred to as Norway's National Day or Constitution Day, not Independence Day because full Norwegian independence was not achieved until a different date in 1905. In 1870 the popular children's parades on syttende mai got started, and since then parades of children or adults waving Norwegian flags have been a regular part of the celebration on the 17th of May throughout Norway and among Norwegians and their descendants in the rest of the world.

Despite Karl Johan's attempts to amend the Constitution and his aversion to syttende mai, over time he became a popular king in Norway. He had a formal demeanor and a tendency to fly off the handle at times, but the Norwegians found that deep down he had a warm heart. Toward the end of his reign, he was more popular in Norway than in Sweden. In fact, a Scottish visitor to Sweden wrote that Karl Johan should give up the Swedish throne and just be the king of Norway, where he was liked by the people.[5] Today Oslo's main street is called Karl Johans gate, and a statue of the popular king mounted on his horse appears in front of the Norwegian Royal Palace.

---

[5] Samuel Laing, *A Tour in Sweden in 1838* (London: Longman, 1839), 423-424.

CHAPTER SIX:

From Nationalism to Independence

The events of 1814, which led to the establishment of Norway's own government and limited democracy, created a feeling of pride among Norwegians that culminated in the full independence of the country in 1905. On the other hand, many Norwegians left their native land for a better life in America, and there was discrimination in Norway against the Sami. This chapter examines various developments in Norwegian government and society during the nineteenth and early twentieth centuries.

Now that Norway had its own constitution and government, throughout the 1800s and into the 1900s there was a new sense of Norwegian identity and an enthusiasm for all things Norwegian. The nationalistic feeling among the Norwegian public was especially apparent in the flowering of the arts, language, and literature in a manner that was typically and uniquely Norwegian.

Some examples were the artist Johan Christian Dahl who painted majestic landscapes of Norwegian mountains and valleys, and another artist named Adolph Tidemand who drew scenes of life in the Norwegian countryside. Much later they were followed by the renowned Edvard Munch who painted *The Scream*, and Gustav Vigeland who created the wonderful sculptures at Vigelandsparken in Oslo's Frogner Park.

The author, poet, and playwright Bjørnstjerne Bjørnson wrote vivid stories of rural Norway and won the Nobel Prize for Literature. Norwegians were even proud of Henrik Ibsen, the great playwright, despite the fact that he spent many years out of the country in Italy and Germany and he wrote plays that were very critical of Norwegians. In the early twentieth century, Norwegian author Sigrid Undset won the Nobel Prize for her marvelous stories of a medieval heroine named Kristin Lavransdatter.

Edvard Grieg

Edvard Grieg was Norway's greatest composer, who brought Norwegian folk music to the concert hall. He grew up in Bergen in a well-to-do family. His father was a descendant of Scottish merchants who had settled in Norway and became part of the middle class. But Edvard's greatest influence was his mother, who was a pianist and an accompanist and who was widely considered to be the best piano teacher in Bergen.

Needless to say, Edvard learned to play the piano at a young age. According to legend, when he was a boy his parents would frequently invite musicians to their home for evenings of chamber music. Edvard was supposed to be asleep in bed upstairs, but he could not resist the temptation to sneak downstairs and listen to the beautiful music.

As a teenager he was already an accomplished musician whose composing and keyboard skills impressed a family friend and distant relative named Ole Bull, the leading violinist of his day. It was Bull who recommended that his parents send Edvard to a music conservatory. Edvard and his brother both studied at the Leipzig Conservatory in Germany, where Edvard further developed his interest in composition and studied under some of the finest German instructors. After obtaining his music degree, he moved on to Copenhagen and joined a thriving arts community of young men from Norway, Denmark, and Germany. For part of that period, Edvard studied the works of Danish composer Niels Gade, who wrote classical music in the traditional German style.

On a visit to Bergen, Grieg was asked to play one of his compositions for Ole Bull, who listened intently and was somewhat less than fully impressed. In a stern voice, Bull told young Grieg that he must develop his own distinctive Norwegian style of music and that if he continued to write music like Gade he would only be stuck in the mud.

The great violinist took his young protégé under his wing, and he instilled in Grieg a true appreciation for the unique style and sound of traditional Norwegian folk music. He led Grieg to a cave where he played Norwegian melodies about trolls and goblins, and he introduced Grieg to several Hardanger fiddlers.

At that point, according to Grieg, the scales fell off his eyes, and he started to develop his own style of music in the Norwegian tradition. Grieg studied the collections of Norwegian folk tunes compiled and arranged by the Norwegian organist and composer Ludvig Mathias Lindeman, and he incorporated many of those pieces in his classical compositions. Over time Grieg became internationally famous and successful by combining elements of classical music and Norwegian folk music in his works for piano, choir, ensemble, and orchestra.

Throughout his life, Grieg loved to hike with his friends in the Norwegian mountains. From time to time they would encounter singers and other musicians, and Grieg would write down the songs that he heard and later arrange the same melodies for piano or other instruments. In 1891 Grieg and his friends were hiking in the Jotunheimen mountains when they stopped at an inn and heard the beautiful soprano voice of a young milkmaid named Gjendine Slaalien. She was singing a lullaby to her sister's baby. Grieg was entranced by the beautiful song, and he made it one of his favorite piano arrangements called "Gjendine's Lullaby". In fact, Gjendine taught him many other songs that he used in various compositions.

Grieg's most well-known work was the *Peer Gynt Suites*, which he wrote for the play by Henrik Ibsen about a devil-may-care Norwegian who never takes anything seriously and wastes his entire life. Grieg's home called Troldhaugen near Bergen is a favorite attraction for tourists to the present day.

The new Norwegian language

Since the 1500s, Norwegians had no written language of their own, although most of them spoke Norwegian in various dialects that were not uniform or consistent. Even in the years after 1814, Danish continued to be the only written language in Norway, as well as the language of government, business, and the church.

That began to change in the 1830s and 1840s when Norwegians started writing books in their own language. For example, two Norwegians named Peter Christen Asbjørnsen and Jørgen Moe collected oral folk tales from various parts of the country. In 1845 they published those stories in written Norwegian, and their books became bestsellers in Norway. After Asbjørnsen and Moe and various others broke the ice, more authors began to publish books and other writings in Norwegian.

Many of the folk tales collected by Asbjørnsen and Moe were about life in the Norwegian countryside. The stories were imaginative and funny, but they also contained a spice of satire and irony as well as feelings of guilt and morality. There were several stories about a family that included a father and his three sons. Two of the brothers were conscientious and hard-working, while the other son named Askeladden (the Ash Lad) just sat around the fire and poked at the ashes with a stick. However, when a crisis arose and the two responsible brothers tried to take care of it, they always failed miserably. At that point, Askeladden would finally get involved. He would then outwit his brothers, kill the trolls, and win the hand of the princess and half the kingdom. Some of the stories were illustrated by Norwegian artists Erik Werenskiold and Theodor Kittelsen (also of Black Death fame), and the illustrated folk tales of Asbjørnsen and Moe are considered national treasures in Norway.

Despite the efforts of Norwegians such as Asbjørnsen and Moe, there was still no uniform written Norwegian language until a young private teacher from western Norway named Ivar Aasen decided to do something about it. He was a self-taught philologist who studied Old Norse and other languages, and he decided to undertake the monumental task of creating a new written Norwegian national language.

After receiving a stipend from an academic society, Aasen traveled throughout most of Norway in the 1840s. At each village and farmstead, he listened to how Norwegians spoke, and he compiled a long list of words, phrases, sayings, and definitions, as well as word endings, conjugation, inflection, and grammar. A lot of people thought it was pretty strange that he just wanted to hear them talk, but they were generally accommodating.

During his travels, Aasen spent almost all of his time in rural areas because he felt that the dialects of the farmers were the purest form of Norwegian and were the least influenced by Danish and other foreign languages. However, even the rural dialects were somewhat different from each other, and in narrowing down his final list of words and phrases Aasen had to choose from many different alternatives.

Once his research was done, Aasen created a brand new written Norwegian language that he called *landsmål* — the language of the country. He published a grammar book in 1864 and a dictionary in 1873 for the new language. His artificial language became very popular among Norwegians, especially in western Norway from which he borrowed most of his words and rules of grammar.

However, many people in the cities and eastern Norway did not like Aasen's new language, and they felt that the written Norwegian language should be based on Danish, modified by Norwegian spelling, pronunciation, and grammar and containing various Norwegian words and phrases. So they supported a written language that was called Dano-Norwegian or *riksmål*.

The controversy continued, and in 1892 both languages were given equal status in the Norwegian elementary schools. There are presently two written national languages in Norway. *Nynorsk* (new Norwegian) is based on Aasen's landsmål, and *bokmål* (book language) is derived from riksmål or Dano-Norwegian. So Norway is one of very few countries in the world to have an artificially-created language — nynorsk — as a national language. In school, students in Norway are given the opportunity to take their classes in either bokmål or nynorsk. About 87 percent select bokmål, although all students must show proficiency in both languages. Bokmål is also used in most newspapers and books, as well as Norwegian language classes for Americans, Brits, and other foreigners. But in Norway, bokmål and nynorsk are considered written languages, and most Norwegians like to speak in their own native dialects that are not identical to either of the two written languages.

The great upheaval

During the nineteenth century there was a huge increase in the population of Norway. In fact, the number of people in the country doubled from about 900,000 in 1800 to about 1,800,000 in 1865. As a primarily agricultural society, this was a significant problem for Norway because all of the available farmland in southern and central Norway was occupied, and there was no place to build new farms. Norway never had the best land and climate for farming, and now many existing farms were divided to the extent that farming became unprofitable for many landowners and their tenants. At the same time, there were fewer employment opportunities for farm hands as agriculture became more mechanized with the introduction of the threshing machine and other new equipment. Throughout the country, more and more farmers, tenants, laborers, and others were simply unable to support themselves, and Norway was reaching a point of widespread poverty among its rapidly growing population.

6.1 A husmann's cottage from Skarderud, Ringsaker

For example, tenant farmers called husmenn each leased a cottage and a small plot of farmland from a landowner. The husmann paid rent and provided labor to the landowner in addition to working his own modest plot of land, which was often in an undesirable location on the outskirts of the farm. The husmann frequently needed to work other jobs such as lumbering, mining, or fishing in order to support his family and make ends meet. So a husmann was a hard-working member of the lower class who often lived nothing more than a hand-to-mouth existence and had no real hope of improving his lot. Although a husmann normally had a lease of his small parcel of land for the lives of himself and his wife, his grown children could not inherit the lease, so they were even lower on the totem pole and typically had to work as common laborers or servants.

The problem of a growing population and scarcity of available farmland in Norway was solved in three ways – by clearing more land for farming, by moving to the cities or northern Norway, and by mass emigration from Norway to America.

Nybrottsmannen – the man who clears the land

In nineteenth century Norway, there were men with a specialized occupation that were called *nybrottsmenn*. They were the men who cleared the swamps and wetlands by digging trenches to drain the water and by removing stones and stubble, all for the purpose of creating new meadowland for cultivation and pasture. This was backbreaking work that was heavily in demand and resulted in the creation or expansion of hundreds of new or enlarged farms in southern and central Norway.

The most famous nybrottsmann in all of Norway was Lars Nilsson Nesheim, a wealthy bachelor farmer from Voss. Despite his family's well-to-do status, he enjoyed the hard work of digging trenches and draining swamps from early spring to late fall every year for several decades. When he worked, he wore waterproof oilskin clothing over his other clothes and several pairs of socks under his knee-length boots. So he kept himself dry and warm even if he had to toil in water and mud all day long. He dug long trenches that were about three feet wide and six feet deep.

Nesheim lived a simple life in his own one-room house on the farm of his sister and brother-in-law. His only furnishings were a bed, a stove, a small table, a couple of chairs, and floor-to-ceiling bookshelves on all the walls. He was an avid reader and singer who collected hundreds of books and songs, and he loved to sing a song about himself and his work that was written by a local schoolteacher. Despite his life of hard, tedious work, Nesheim was always in a good mood, and he had many friends. He also collected letters from Norwegians in America, and he was even a correspondent for a Norwegian newspaper in Chicago, but he never made it to the New World.

On to northern Norway and the cities

When farmland was scarce or times were tough in southern or central Norway, many nineteenth century Norwegian families moved to northern Norway where available farmland and hopefully a better life were waiting for them. Despite the shorter growing season in the northern climes, some families thrived in their new homes, as shown by the following story about Ole Olsen.

Ole Olsen was a poor husmann at a farm called Trallerud near Biri in southern Norway. In the 1820s he and his wife Ingeborg decided to move their family north. It was a very long journey over valleys and mountains. First they went over the Dovre Mountains and then past Trondheim to a place called Beitstad, where Ole was a tenant farmer for a few years. But then in the spring of 1831 Ole learned from a man who had just come from Sweden that there was a place farther north in a valley called Susendalen that was without snow, and that the place had green, leafy trees and a creek with good water that came down from the mountains.

So in the spring of 1833, Ole and Ingeborg once again moved their family, this time to Susendalen, south of present-day Hattfjelldal in Nordland. They brought their livestock with them, including a horse, three cows, and some sheep and goats. Along the way, there were not many places with good trails, and in the last part of the journey they had to go over a mountain. It was also difficult for them to cross the river in Susendalen because it was flooded, and they had to borrow a boat from a Sami. When they finally reached the place they had heard about, they settled there and called the place Trallerud after the farm they had come from near Biri. Things went well for Ole in Susendalen, and he was the owner of a large farm in the valley. When he died in 1876, he was considered a rich man.[6]

With the advent of the Industrial Revolution and the construction of new plants and factories, other Norwegians from the rural areas migrated to the cities and towns of Norway. There they

---

[6] Many thanks to my Norwegian cousin Reidar Sagmo for most of this story about our great-great-great grandfather.

found employment and steady income as industrial workers or as servants in the homes of the upper class. For example, there were new textile plants in Christiania and Bergen, paper and cellulose factories in southern and eastern Norway, and fish canneries in Stavanger. In the last half of the nineteenth century, roads and railroads were built throughout the country, steamships lines were established along the coast, fishing and whaling were expanded, and the Norwegian merchant marine grew substantially to meet the demands of increased trade throughout the world. In addition, communications improved with the introduction of the telegraph in the 1850s and the telephone in 1880. All of these activities provided more jobs, especially in the cities and on the high seas. In fact, the population of Christiania (spelled Kristiania after 1877) increased from 75,000 to 235,000 during the period from 1870 to 1900, and other cities experienced similar growth.

The expansion of the industrial and agricultural workforce led to labor unrest. In 1848 a young journalist named Marcus Thrane started a labor movement that promoted universal suffrage, better schools, pensions, land reform, and other pragmatic policies in support of the lower class. Within just a few years, about three hundred new workers' unions attracted thirty thousand members who were primarily laborers, craftsmen, and husmenn. Despite Thrane's moderate stance, some of the union members began to speak of revolution. As a result, Thrane and other labor leaders were thrown into prison for several years, and their movement fell apart. Thrane later left Norway for the United States where he participated in socialist groups in New York, Chicago, and Wisconsin.

Emigration from Norway to America

Although clearing new land and moving to other parts of the country relieved some of the pressure of a growing population, it was mass emigration from Norway to America that ultimately solved the problem of scarcity of jobs and farmland in Norway.

A few Norwegians had emigrated to Dutch settlements in America as early as the seventeenth century. But more widespread movement of Norwegians across the Atlantic Ocean really began in 1825.

In that year a small sloop called the *Restauration* left Stavanger with fifty-two people on board. The undersized ship was not designed for an ocean voyage and it was barely seaworthy on the high seas, but the passengers were determined to make it to the New World. Some of them were Quakers who were looking for religious freedom that was not available in Norway. That is, until 1845 it was unlawful for anyone to establish a church outside of Norway's Lutheran state church. Other passengers on the *Restauration* were just seeking a better life in a new place with more prospects and opportunities. The cargo of the ship included iron bars that the passengers hoped to sell to generate money to buy farms in America. However, the long voyage was not without its problems.

First they headed to England, where some passengers illegally sold brandy to the local population, and the ship left port just before the English sheriff was about to arrest them. Then instead of sailing west toward America, for some unknown reason they sailed south toward Africa. Just off the Madeira Islands they found a barrel of wine floating in the sea. They hauled the barrel aboard, and then the passengers and crew got so intoxicated that no one was steering the ship, which somehow made its way into the nearest harbor. After enjoying the generous hospitality of the local islanders for one week, they left for America and finally arrived in New York City more than three months after they had left Stavanger.

Unfortunately the ship and the cargo were immediately confiscated and the ship captain was arrested by United States customs officials for violation of several laws. Thanks to the efforts of some wealthy American Quakers, the ship, the cargo, and the captain were eventually released by an order signed by US President John Quincy Adams.

But by then the Norwegians had already made their way up the Hudson River to their first settlement in upstate New York. However, as a result of the delays, they did not have time to plant or harvest any crops the first year, and they experienced hunger and sickness over the harsh winter. They actually faced serious hardships over the following ten years until they finally moved to the Fox River Valley in Illinois, where they established the first permanent Norwegian settlement in America.

After this inauspicious beginning, Norwegians continued to emigrate to the United States and Canada during the period from the 1820s to the 1860s. In fact, Norwegians fought on both sides of the American Civil War from 1861 to 1865.

However, it was after the end of the Civil War that the great wave of migration from Norway to America took place. In almost every year until the 1920s, thousands of Norwegians came to the New World. In fact, as many as a million Norwegians emigrated to America between 1825 and 1929, and the vast majority of them came after 1865. Except for Ireland, Norway had the highest percentage of its population that emigrated to America. The numbers varied from year to year, depending upon economic conditions in America and Norway. More Norwegians would emigrate in years when times were tough in Norway and the American economy was booming. The largest number occurred in 1882, when 28,804 Norwegians left for America.

The Norwegians settled primarily in Minnesota, Wisconsin, Iowa, Illinois, the Dakotas, Montana, and Washington, but many found their way to Canada, Texas, California, and other states as well. Most of the immigrants were young individuals and families from rural areas of Norway. They were predominately farmers, but there were also fishermen, doctors, engineers, and pastors. Later there were people from the cities and towns of Norway, and many of them found jobs in industry in cities such as New York, Chicago, Minneapolis, and Seattle. The mass exodus relieved the pressure of a growing Norwegian population and helped to solve the problems relating to the lack of jobs and farmland in Norway, but Norway also lost a lot of talent and energy as the result of the departure of so many young Norwegians.

It was not surprising that these Norwegians left their country because America had so much to offer them. First, there were millions of acres of cheap agricultural land that were there for the taking. The US Homestead Act of 1862 gave 160 acres of government land west of the Mississippi River to any settler who intended to become a US citizen and who agreed to live on and cultivate the land for five years, and the settler only had to pay a small fee to claim the land. This was almost too good to be true. Any poor Norwegian husmann or laborer could own a free farm in America that was larger than just about any farm back in Norway. Not only that, but in contrast to much of the rocky, mountainous land in Norway, the available land on the American prairie was mostly fertile, flat land on which plentiful crops and livestock could be raised.

Second, industrial workers and other laborers in US cities earned much higher wages than in Norway. Furthermore, America gave the Norwegians freedoms and rights that they did not enjoy in Norway. Any adult male US citizen could vote in elections. There was freedom of religion. Perhaps most importantly, there were no permanent classes of people in America. It was the land of opportunity where even a poor person could work hard and become wealthy or at least a member of the middle class.

In view of these advantages, many Norwegians who settled in America wrote letters back home and encouraged their families and friends to join them, and the great wave of immigrants continued until the 1920s. At that point, the enactment of more restrictive American immigration laws finally halted the massive flow of people from Norway.

A typical farmer in Norway who wanted to move to a new farm in the American Upper Midwest in the late nineteenth century would first have to sell his Norwegian farm or terminate his lease, pack up some food and a few of his personal belongings (oftentimes in just one trunk or suitcase), and sell or give away everything else. After some tearful, permanent farewells to parents and others to be left behind, he traveled to the coast, bought a ticket, and boarded a ship for a voyage of two to eight weeks.

While at sea, he prepared his own food, slept on a bed of straw, and sometimes experienced seasickness or disease. Some passengers never made it and were buried at sea. But there were also good times on the ship, with dances, fiddlers, and singing, especially on the 17th of May.

The Norwegian did not need a passport or a work permit to enter the US. However, once he reached New York or another American or Canadian port, he still had over a thousand miles to travel to the Upper Midwest. Fortunately, states like Minnesota and Wisconsin sent representatives to New York to assist immigrants with their travel arrangements. But there were also plenty of conmen and land speculators who tried to take their money.

The immigrant often met family or friends at his final destination. Then he had to find a new place to farm, register his land claim, build a temporary sod house on the prairie, and start farming. He also met new neighbors, including not just Norwegians but also Americans, Swedes, and Germans, and he had to learn some English to survive in the new land. Much of his social life revolved around the local Lutheran church.

There might be years of hardship, and not all Norwegians found the New World to their liking. Some even returned home to Norway after a short time. But most Norwegian immigrant farmers became successful American farmers. Others started businesses and newspapers, and some even became politicians. In addition to churches, Norwegians also established several colleges in America with names like St. Olaf, Concordia, Augsburg, Luther, Augustana, and Pacific Lutheran. In fact, Norwegian pastors generally did not like the American public schools because, of all things, many of the teachers were women and they did not even teach religion! In some places, the Norwegian children took two weeks off from the public school to be taught religion and Norwegian language by their pastors.

Nevertheless, Norwegians were quickly assimilated into the American population. While they continued to write letters back to Norway and they preserved some of their Norwegian ways, they were proud to be Americans in their new lives.

Parliamentary democracy

Oscar 2, the grandson of Karl Johan, became the king of Sweden and Norway in 1872. As a younger son of the family, he never expected to be king until his older brothers died. Oscar was raised as the "Norwegian prince". Both before and after he became king, he spent a lot of time in Norway, and he spoke and wrote fluent Norwegian. He also felt that he had a favorable relationship with the Norwegian people.

When he became king, Oscar decided to create more good will with the Norwegian people by giving them a "morning gift". He approved a Storting bill that abolished the office of governor (stattholder), who was the personal representative of the king in Norway. In recent years the position was somewhat meaningless because it was held only by Norwegians since 1836, and it had actually been vacant since 1856. But the Norwegians still complained about it and felt it was an unnecessary, humiliating sign of Norway's subordinate position in the union with Sweden. In place of the governor, there was a new position called minister of state, essentially the new prime minister of the Norwegian government who would serve in Norway. So for the first time the leading government minister of Norway would be in Christiania and not in Stockholm.

Oscar must have thought that the Norwegians were ungrateful subjects because they pretty much ignored his gesture, and they merely switched their attention to their other grievances against Sweden and the king. That was particularly true in the Storting, which had recently become more powerful.

In the first major change to the Norwegian Constitution, in 1869 the Storting began to meet every year instead of once every three years, so the Storting was given more control over the government's budget. This amendment had been passed largely through the efforts of Johan Sverdrup, a liberal politician in the Storting. Backed by an alliance of liberals and farmers, Sverdrup intended to place even more power in the hands of the Storting vis-à-vis the king and his appointed ministers.

Ever since Norway's Constitution was created in 1814, the king only appointed government officials and not members of the Storting to his cabinet of ministers, and those ministers never attended sessions of the Storting. This system was originally preferred by the members of the Storting because they did not want the king and his ministers to be dictating or interfering in the deliberations of the Storting.

But now many representatives in the Storting had changed their minds, and they wanted the government ministers to be permitted to attend the Storting so they could be asked to explain and justify their actions and decisions. In fact, the actual goal of Sverdrup and the liberals was to transform the Norwegian government into a parliamentary democracy in which the cabinet ministers would all be members of the Storting and would represent a majority of the Storting. Therefore, the executive branch of government would in reality become part of the legislative branch, and the powers of the king would be reduced. Sverdrup disliked the separation of powers, but it was clearly a part of the Norwegian Constitution. So the liberals essentially wanted to change the Constitution to give virtually all powers of government to the Storting.

In the 1870s and 1880 the Storting repeatedly passed a bill to authorize cabinet ministers to participate in sessions of the Storting. This bill was always vetoed by the king, who wanted to retain the right to appoint and control the government ministers. In 1880, when the bill was passed by the Storting for the third time, the Storting also passed a resolution declaring that the bill had become law.

King Oscar vetoed the bill again anyway, and he asserted that the bill was a constitutional amendment and that he had a right to an absolute veto of any such amendment. However, the Constitution expressly gave the king just a delaying veto of bills passed by the Storting, and there was no language in the Constitution that gave the king an absolute veto.

The liberals in the Storting took the position that the king only had a delaying veto of any Storting bill including a constitutional amendment, and that the delaying veto could not be used in the present case because the Storting had passed the bill three times. Therefore, they argued, the king's veto was ineffective and the bill was now a legally valid law. The farmers in the Storting went even farther than the liberals and asserted that the bill was law because the king had absolutely no right to veto a constitutional amendment.

So the king and the Storting were at odds. Of course, the king's appointed ministers sided with the king. They refused to comply with the new law, and they did not appear in the Storting. This impasse lasted until the next Storting election in 1882, which the liberals won convincingly over the conservatives who supported the position of the king. On the heels of their impressive victory in the election, the liberals decided to press their case.

They did so by voting to impeach all of the cabinet ministers and remove them from office because the ministers had advised the king to veto the bill, allegedly in violation of the Constitution. In May 1883 the cabinet ministers went on trial before a Constitutional Court that was comprised of the members of the Supreme Court and liberals from the Storting. The Supreme Court judges wanted to acquit the ministers, but the liberals constituted a majority on the Constitutional Court. Consequently, in March 1884 the Constitutional Court found all of the ministers guilty of abusing the royal veto, removed them from office, and ordered them to pay fines.

The king was clearly upset with this decision, but he felt that he had no alternative other than to dismiss the cabinet. He appointed a new cabinet of obscure bureaucrats, but the liberals threatened to impeach them, too. The king then considered the possibility of a military coup in which he would take over the Norwegian government by force and abolish the Storting. However, after two more months of indecision, Oscar gave in to the demands of the liberals. He asked Sverdrup, as the majority leader of the Storting, to form a new cabinet of government ministers.

In June 1884 a new cabinet of liberals who were members of the Storting took office as government ministers, led by the new prime minister Johan Sverdrup. The Storting once again passed the bill giving the ministers access to the Storting, and this time the king approved the bill. Since then, Norway has been a parliamentary democracy in which the government ministers are selected by the Storting, and all ministers are members of the Storting. So the separation of powers was terminated, and the king's powers were drastically reduced. The king's only significant remaining powers in Norway were the right to delay the enactment of Storting bills for a couple of years and the right to control Norway's foreign and consular affairs. Both of those remaining powers would later be at issue in the fateful year of 1905.

The year 1884 was also when the first official Norwegian political parties were formed, including the Liberals (*Venstre*) and the Conservatives (*Høyre*). Emboldened by their success in creating a parliamentary democracy, the Liberals, as the majority party in the Storting, passed a number of progressive laws, such as expanding the right to vote to about half of all Norwegian men and providing for jury trials in criminal cases. They also improved the elementary school system by specifying seven years of compulsory education and by providing for local school boards elected by the voters. The Liberals and the Conservatives alternately controlled the Norwegian government from time to time until 1905.

Norwegianization of the Sami

While the members of the Storting were expanding the rights of Norwegians, they were also intent upon severely limiting the rights of the Sami. After a minor Sami rebellion in Kautokeino in northern Norway in 1852, the Norwegian government embarked on a longstanding policy of forcing the Sami to abandon their language and culture and become Norwegians. So Norway effectively tried to destroy the Sami language and culture and to Norwegianize the Sami.

6.2 A Sami family in Vesterålen in the 1890s

The Norwegian government sent Sami children to boarding schools where they were indoctrinated on how to be Norwegians. They were only permitted to speak Norwegian, and all Sami language and culture were excluded. In addition, the government prohibited the use of the Sami language in the public schools, awarded the best land and all government positions in northern Norway to Norwegians, severely limited the right of the Sami to own or use any land, and even restricted the allowable size of Sami houses. This discriminatory anti-Sami policy continued in Norway until after the Second World War.

Polar explorers

On a more positive note, polar exploration by various Norwegians in the late nineteenth and early twentieth centuries became a source of national pride and scientific achievement. The two most famous and successful Norwegian polar explorers were Fridtjof Nansen and Roald Amundsen.

Nansen was a handsome, athletic doctor of zoology from a well-to-do family who was also fearless. As a young man, he had joined a sealing expedition in the Arctic that traveled near the east coast of Greenland, and he became fascinated with the polar regions.

In the 1880s Nansen, himself an expert skier, decided to form a team of skiers that would be the first to make it all the way across the frozen island of Greenland. Other explorers had tried unsuccessfully to walk or ski across Greenland by starting on the west coast of the island where the climate was much better. In contrast, the east coast was filled with ice, snow, and glaciers. But Nansen did not like the idea of starting an expedition on the west coast, skiing to the east coast, and then having to ski all the way back to the west coast to be picked up by a ship. He preferred to plan an expedition that would start on the east coast and travel west, so it would only be necessary to cross Greenland once. However, that meant that the expedition would have to make it to the west coast or they would face certain death, because even if they retreated to the east coast they could not be picked up by a ship there. So Nansen developed his lifelong theory of polar exploration – only go forward, no turning back.

The Storting did not agree to finance the expedition, which they thought was a suicide mission. Nansen's boss at the Bergen Museum felt sorry for him and gave him some extra time off because he was sure he would never come back alive. Finally a Danish coffee merchant came up with the necessary funding, and Nansen completed his plans.

Nansen selected five other expert skiers to join him on the expedition, including two Sami. A Swedish-Finnish explorer had recommended the Sami because he said they always found the right way. However, when the two Sami finally showed up late, Nansen wished he had never asked them because one was too young and the other was too old and married. This broke Nansen's cardinal rule of never taking married men on a polar expedition, conveniently disregarding the fact that he was married himself.

In 1888 a ship took the six explorers to a point off the east coast of Greenland, where they left the ship in two small rowboats that they paddled north for a few days before landing on the ice-filled coast. Then they got on their skis and began the arduous task of pulling sleds with their supplies up tall mountains to the interior. At the time some scientists theorized that the interior of Greenland contained beautiful, warm, green meadows, but Nansen and his men only encountered ice and snow. Their trek was extremely strenuous, and they had to deal with strong winds, extreme cold, and burning sun.

After six weeks of skiing, they descended the last mountain and made it to the west coast. There they built a small boat which Nansen and another man rowed for four days to the village of Godthåp – now called Nuuk, the present capital of Greenland. The last ship of the year had just left, but some Inuit caught it in their kayaks to report to the world that Nansen's team had made it safe and sound.

They spent the winter at Godthåp, where Nansen stayed with the Inuit and studied their language and way of life. Among other things, he learned how to paddle a kayak and drive a dogsled. In the spring of 1889, the expedition returned to Norway, where they were met by a cheering crowd of fifty thousand people in Kristiania. Nansen and his men had accomplished what seemed impossible, and he instantly became world famous and a national hero.

A couple of years later, Nansen decided that his next polar mission would be to reach the North Pole, something that no one had done, primarily because of the moving ice and open channels of water on the polar ice cap. The wreckage of a ship that was destroyed in a storm north of Siberia had recently been found on the other side of the North Pole near Greenland. Based on this strange occurrence, Nansen had a theory that a ship entering the polar pack ice north of Siberia would float with the ice to the North Pole and then out the other side of the ice cap. So that became his plan for the North Pole expedition.

To almost everyone else, this theory and plan seemed even crazier and more dangerous than the Greenland expedition. If a ship entered the pack ice, wouldn't it be crushed by the ice? And even if the ship was sturdy enough to withstand the ice, who knew where the ice would take the ship or if it would ever emerge from the ice cap? The whole enterprise seemed like a one-way disaster that promised only certain death. Nevertheless, this time the Storting voted to provide the necessary funds. They wanted this expedition to be solely Norwegian, including the financing. Nansen made arrangements to build a new ship called *Fram* – meaning forward, consistent with his plan to go forward and never turn back. It was a strong ship with round sides that would be lifted up and not crushed by the pack ice. Unfortunately, the rounded sides caused the ship to roll in the open sea, making for an uncomfortable voyage.

Nansen and twelve other explorers left Kristiania on the *Fram* on June 24, 1893, and entered the ice north of Siberia on September 22. Amazingly enough, Nansen's theory proved to be right – the ship floated with the pack ice toward the North Pole.

However, by 1895 it was apparent that the ship would miss the North Pole by hundreds of miles. At this point, Nansen and a colleague named Hjalmar Johansen did something even more bizarre and dangerous. On March 14, 1895, they left the ship to travel by skis and dogsled over four hundred miles to the North Pole. They said goodbye to the others because there was no way they would be able to find the moving ship again.

On April 8 Nansen and Johansen made it all the way to a latitude of 86 degrees 14 minutes, the farthest north of any human up to that time. They had to turn back because they could not get past huge walls of ice. So then they went south toward Franz Josef Land (north of Russia), and they finally reached terra firma on July 24, 1895. From there they made it to Jackson Island where they spent the winter in an improvised shack that they built. On May 19, 1896, they left for Spitzbergen in kayaks. Finally, on June 17, 1896, the two were discovered and saved by sheer miracle by an English exploration team led by Frederick Jackson. It was about fifteen months since they had left the *Fram*. Nansen and Johansen arrived back in Norway by ship on August 13, 1896. Coincidentally, the *Fram* had been freed from the pack ice and reached northern Norway just a week later on August 20. The following day all members of the expedition were reunited in Tromsø. They had almost made it to the North Pole, and all of them had survived the incredible ordeal. They sailed the *Fram* down the Norwegian coast to Kristiania, and on the way they stopped at many ports where they were met by cheering crowds. Needless to say, Nansen's fame was even greater than before, and the expedition had also managed to collect reams of scientific data.

In 1909 another Norwegian polar explorer named Roald Amundsen borrowed the *Fram* from Nansen and the Norwegian government. He intended to complete the task of reaching the North Pole. However, there was bad news for the Norwegians when it was announced that an American named Robert Peary had just accomplished that feat.

Now that Amundsen could no longer be the first to reach the North Pole, he secretly changed his plans. The ship left Norway on August 9, 1910, and in the Madeira Islands on September 6 Amundsen informed the crew that they were on their way — to the South Pole! No one had yet reached the South Pole, and the crew enthusiastically agreed to the new plan.

The *Fram* reached Antarctica at the Ross Ice Shelf on the Bay of Whales during the southern summer on January 14, 1911. Over the next few weeks, the men built a base camp and a few other camps on the route toward the Pole. At the same time there was also a British expedition led by Robert Falcon Scott in Antarctica. Both the Norwegians and the British intended to try for the Pole. So it was to be a race to the South Pole between the Brits on foot and the Norwegians on skis and dogsleds.

On September 8, 1911, Amundsen and a few of his men started their journey to the South Pole, but it was too early in the season and they had to turn back to the base camp due to the terrible weather. Finally, Amundsen and five others left the camp on October 20, and they skied and rode dogsleds all the way to the South Pole by December 15. Amundsen's best camera did not work, so they had to take pictures with a small Kodak camera. But they had won the race and were the first to reach the South Pole. After spending three days there, they traveled back to the base camp, left Antarctica on January 30, 1912, and returned to Norway. The British reached the South Pole about five weeks after Amundsen. But tragically Scott and all other members of his expedition died on the way back.

Independence in 1905

Ever since 1814, Norwegians were constantly disturbed that Norway's foreign relations were controlled by the Swedish king, who had delegated that responsibility to the Swedish foreign minister. As a result of the Bodø Affair and other incidents, Norwegians were convinced that the Swedish Foreign Ministry only looked out for the interests of Sweden and not Norway.

Although some Norwegians were employed by the Swedish Foreign Ministry, most of the diplomats, including those with the highest ranking positions, were upper class Swedes. All business in the Foreign Ministry was conducted in the Swedish language. When a Norwegian diplomat named Sigurd Ibsen (the son of Henrik Ibsen) started writing his reports in Norwegian instead of Swedish, he was bluntly informed that he would never be promoted, so he was forced to resign from the Swedish Foreign Ministry in 1890.

The Swedish consular service was part of the Foreign Ministry, and it handled business transactions for Swedes and Norwegians abroad. While the staff of the consular service was more evenly balanced between Swedes and Norwegians, the general consensus in Norway was that the consular service was designed solely to serve Sweden and not Norway. For example, Norway had a much larger merchant marine than Sweden, but the offices of the consular service were located in places that would best support Swedish businesses instead of the merchant marine.

Moreover, Norwegians resented the fact that their lack of control over their own foreign and consular affairs had placed them in a subordinate position in the union with Sweden. They wanted to have their own Foreign Ministry and consular service, but the Swedes insisted upon retaining full control over the foreign and consular affairs of both countries. In the latter part of the nineteenth century, this became the dominant issue in the relationship between Norway and Sweden. As with the conversion to parliamentary democracy in Norway, it was the Norwegian Liberals who took the lead in advancing Norwegian interests relating to foreign and consular affairs.

In the 1880s the Liberals began to call for an independent Norwegian foreign minister and a separate Norwegian foreign and consular service. The Swedish and Norwegian governments formed a joint committee to try to resolve this matter. By 1890 the committee reached a possible compromise solution that provided for a joint council of Swedish and Norwegian ministers to handle foreign affairs, but the tentative agreement broke down when the Swedish government declared that the Swedish foreign minister must still be in charge of the joint Foreign Ministry.

After the committee's negotiations ended in 1892, the Storting decided to take action on its own by passing a bill for an independent Norwegian consular service and by appropriating money to form the new consular service. King Oscar vetoed the bill, but then his cabinet of Liberal ministers refused to countersign the veto and they all resigned their positions. However, the Liberals had second thoughts when they learned that the king was prepared to appoint a cabinet of Conservative ministers and that ultra-conservative politicians in Sweden were discussing the possibility of going to war against Norway. So the Liberals backed down and withdrew their resignations, and no Norwegian consular service was formed.

But the issue did not go away. Once again in 1893 the Storting passed the same bill to authorize a Norwegian consular service, and the king vetoed the bill. This time the Liberal prime minister of Norway resigned, and the king appointed a minority Conservative government. This action seemed to fly in the face of Norway's recent adoption of parliamentary democracy in which a majority of the Storting was supposed to form the government. In any event, the Conservatives had to resign in 1894 when they lost the next election, and the Liberals were back in power.

In 1895 the Liberals tried one more time to bring the issue to a head. The Storting passed a new bill to terminate the combined consular service of Norway and Sweden. This time the ultra-conservatives who controlled the Swedish government had enough. In cooperation with the king, they passed a bill to terminate the free trade agreement with Norway and another bill to increase Sweden's military expenditures. Sweden also made plans to mobilize its military for a war against Norway.

The Norwegian Liberals realized that Norway was in a weak military position compared to Sweden, so on June 7, 1895, they backed down once again and agreed to negotiate with Sweden on the issue of control over foreign and consular affairs. A joint committee of negotiators from Sweden and Norway met for the next three years. But by 1898 they had made absolutely no progress in resolving the issue because the Swedes would not budge from their position that Sweden should retain full control over both countries' foreign and consular services. Furthermore, in 1897 the Swedish government allowed the free trade agreement with Norway to expire, and that action proved to be detrimental to the Norwegian economy.

During this period the Storting voted to strengthen the Norwegian army, to enlarge Norway's naval fleet, and to build or modernize Norway's fortresses on the border with Sweden. Even though Norway was in a union with Sweden, as a result of periodic Swedish threats of invasion it was apparent that Sweden had become Norway's main potential military adversary. Norway wanted to avoid a repeat of 1895 when the Swedes prepared for an invasion of Norway and the weakness of the Norwegian military caused the Norwegians to back down from their efforts to create their own consular service. In 1899 the Norwegian government also made plans for a future Norwegian Foreign Ministry by creating a new Department of Foreign Affairs under the leadership of Sigurd Ibsen.

Two years later Ibsen wrote a treatise that proposed a new compromise solution. His idea was that Norway and Sweden should have separate consular services, but a combined diplomatic service. This proposal seemed to have some appeal in both countries, and in 1902 the Swedish and Norwegian governments formed yet another committee called the Consulate Committee to discuss and negotiate the issue based on Ibsen's treatise. The Consulate Committee made progress and issued a communiqué on March 24, 1903, containing an agreement that Norway and Sweden would have separate and independent consular services, each under the control of its own government. The communiqué was then signed by the Swedish and Norwegian prime ministers, and the prospects for a final solution seemed promising.

In the fall of 1903, a new coalition government of Conservatives and moderate Liberals took office in Norway on a platform to negotiate a final peaceful solution with Sweden. In May 1904 the Storting drafted a bill to approve the communiqué. But by then Sweden had a new ultra-conservative government led by Prime Minister Erik Boström, and they were steadfastly opposed to the communiqué that the previous Swedish prime minister had signed.

The coup de grâce came in November 1904 when Swedish Prime Minister Boström showed up in Kristiania and announced his "principles of dependency" (*lydrikepunkter*). His proposal was that Norway could have its own consular service but that it should be under the control of the Swedish Foreign Ministry. The Norwegian government rejected that proposal because it was clearly inconsistent with the communiqué, which provided that Norway's separate consular service would be controlled by Norway's own government. In January 1905 the Norwegian government sent a letter to the Swedish government stating that negotiations would not continue unless Boström's proposal was changed to conform to the communiqué. When the Swedish government's answer was negative, the Norwegians announced that the negotiations with Sweden were over.

At this point, Norwegians of all political stripes agreed that there was no reason to negotiate with Sweden any longer. The negotiations had lasted for years and had gone nowhere, and the Norwegians felt that the Swedes had acted in bad faith by reneging on their agreement to an independent Norwegian consular service that was under the control of the Norwegian government. So the Norwegians felt betrayed, and their bitterness increased when King Oscar told the

Norwegian government that he would not agree to a separate Norwegian consular service. Now that there was no point in further negotiations, it appeared to the Norwegians that their only remaining alternatives were to create their own separate consular service or to dissolve the union with Sweden.

Sweden's Crown Prince Gustav, who was temporarily serving as regent while the king was ill, came to Kristiania in February 1905 and was treated coldly by the Storting and the Norwegian public and press. Gustav found that the general Norwegian sentiment was in favor of taking strong action on the consular issue that would probably lead to a break-up of the union. He returned to Stockholm, where he tried unsuccessfully to negotiate a compromise with Boström. Then he sent a letter to the Storting in which he argued for more negotiations and preservation of the union. The Norwegians thought that the letter had a somewhat threatening tone, and that had the effect of moving the Norwegian politicians and public even closer toward the idea of full Norwegian independence.

In March 1905 a new coalition government of Liberals and Conservatives took office in Norway. It was led by a wealthy Bergen shipowner named Christian Michelsen, who promptly designed a strategy to dissolve the union. He also mobilized the Norwegian military to defend the country from any Swedish invasion. In addition, he spoke with Gustav and told him that the only remaining hope for continuation of the union would be for Norway and Sweden to have totally separate foreign ministries. But the king, Gustav, and the Swedish government would never agree to such a plan.

To bring matters to a head, in May the Storting unanimously passed a bill to establish a separate Norwegian consular service. As expected, the king vetoed the bill on May 27. Jørgen Løvland, Norway's chief minister in Stockholm, warned the king that the veto would lead to a crisis and dissolution of the union, but the king was adamant and refused to withdraw the veto. Then, as already planned by Michelsen, all of the Norwegian ministers refused to countersign the veto and immediately resigned en masse. The king said he would not accept the resignations because he could not find any other ministers to form a new government. But the written resignations were submitted anyway, and on May 29 the Norwegian ministers in Stockholm left Sweden and returned to Norway.

The king's statement that he could not form a new government gave Michelsen an opportunity and a justification to finalize and implement his plan to dissolve the union. He acted promptly in early June by informing the Storting of his new strategy. Michelsen and the Storting did not want their new plans to leak out, so they shut down all mail service and telegraph lines to Sweden. Also, they did not want the king to show up in Norway, so on June 6 they blocked the railroad line from Sweden with an empty train.

The next day, at a short prearranged meeting of the Storting on June 7, 1905, the Storting unanimously approved a resolution that dissolved the union with Sweden because the king had ceased to function as the king of Norway by failing to form a government of ministers. That is, under the Norwegian Constitution, the king could only exercise his powers through a cabinet of ministers, and he failed to appoint any ministers, so he no longer functioned as the king of Norway and the union was null and void. The same resolution authorized the resigning Norwegian ministers to exercise the powers of the king so that the Norwegian government could continue to exist and function. In a second resolution, the Storting offered to elect a prince of the Swedish royal family as the new king of Norway. When those resolutions were announced to the Norwegian people, there were huge celebrations throughout the country. Norway had just declared its full independence. The Storting's action to dissolve the union was arguably of dubious constitutional validity, but now it had become a reality.

Oscar was shocked and distressed at the news even though the Norwegians had forewarned him what would happen if he vetoed the consular bill. The king sent a telegram of protest to the Storting. The Swedish ultra-conservatives demanded war against Norway, but the king rejected any military action. In the meantime, liberals and members of the labor movement in Sweden held mass rallies supporting the Norwegians and opposing any invasion. Outside of

Scandinavia, the Great Powers of Britain, Germany, and Russia strongly favored a continuation of the union, but they all had more pressing issues elsewhere, and more than anything they wanted to avoid war in Scandinavia.

After a lively debate in the Swedish Riksdag, Sweden and the king ultimately consented to the dissolution of the union, but only if it was approved by a plebiscite in Norway and if the details of the dissolution were worked out in negotiations between the Swedish and Norwegian governments. On August 13, 1905, a plebiscite was held in Norway, and approximately 85 percent of eligible voters voted 367,149 to 184 to dissolve the union. Even though women could not vote, the women's suffragettes in Norway collected 279,878 signatures of Norwegian women supporting dissolution of the union. So there was an overwhelming consensus in Norway for full Norwegian independence.

Beginning on August 31, 1905, representatives of Sweden and Norway met in Karlstad, Sweden, to negotiate an end to the union. There was heated bargaining, the Swedes threatened to invade Norway, and troops were mobilized on both sides of the border. The Great Powers urged moderation and compromise. Finally the two sides reached an agreement, and the Karlstad Convention between Norway and Sweden was signed on September 23, 1905. It provided for dissolution of the union, a demilitarized zone on both sides of the border, and arbitration of any future disputes between the two countries. In addition, Norway reluctantly agreed to dismantle some of its new border fortifications that had been built at great cost. On October 16 Sweden repealed the Act of Union. Finally, on October 26, 1905, Oscar renounced the throne of Norway, and, as expected, he declined Norway's offer to elect a Swedish prince as the next king of Norway. Norway was fully independent for the first time since 1380.

New royal family

Norway had made the offer to elect a Swedish prince as its new king to lighten the blow to Oscar and to appease the Great Powers.

But the Norwegians fully expected the king to decline the offer, so in the summer of 1905 they began the process of searching for another candidate to become the new king. There were, in fact, many members of the Storting who favored a republic without a king, but the majority felt that a monarchy would make an independent Norway more acceptable to the Great Powers.

At an early stage in the process, Norway focused on the Danish prince Carl as the leading candidate. He was the younger son of the soon-to-be king of Denmark. Perhaps more importantly, Carl's wife Maud was the daughter of King Edward VII of England, who therefore was strongly in favor of Carl's candidacy and became an advocate for Norwegian independence.

Carl was definitely interested, but he felt that he could not accept Norway's offer to become the new king until after Oscar renounced the throne. In addition, Carl knew that some Norwegians wanted to abolish the monarchy. So he asked the Norwegian government to hold another referendum, this time on the question of whether Norway should still have a monarchy. Norwegians once again went to the polls in November 1905, and a majority of about 80 percent voted in favor of the monarchy.

On November 18 the Storting voted unanimously to send an invitation to Carl to be the next king of Norway, and he accepted on the same day. He, his wife, and their son Alexander sailed to Kristiania on November 25, 1905. Despite a cold drizzle that day, there was a large cheering crowd of Norwegians on hand.

Carl changed his name to Haakon, and Alexander's new name was Olav. So the former Danish prince became King Haakon 7, and he and Maud were crowned king and queen in a ceremony at Nidaros Cathedral in 1906. The king adopted a personal motto – *Alt for Norge* [Everything for Norway], and he became an inspiration to the Norwegian people through two world wars over the next fifty years.

After 1905

As a newly independent country, Norway was recognized by the Great Powers of Europe and many other countries. Norway also created its own Ministry of Foreign Affairs and began to open embassies and consulates in other countries. Norway's foreign policy emphasized active international trade and neutrality in any war, although Norway developed close ties with Britain and implicitly relied on the British navy to protect the country from any invasion. In 1907 the Great Powers of Britain, Russia, France, and Germany signed an Integrity Treaty that guaranteed the territorial integrity of Norway. While the treaty was just a piece of paper that could easily be violated by any of the signing parties, it was important to establish Norway as a recognized independent neutral country.

Norway removed the Swedish colors from all of its flags both before and shortly after the declaration of independence in June 1905. The modern Norwegian flag, containing a blue and white Nordic cross on a red background, was first designed in 1821. The three colors represent freedom, inspired in part by the French and American flags. However, beginning in 1844, Norway's flag was required to contain a union symbol in the corner. The union symbol included Norwegian and Swedish colors and was commonly referred to as the herring salad because it looked like a popular Scandinavian breakfast dish. The Storting removed the union symbol from the Norwegian civilian and merchant flag in 1899 and from the military flag in 1905.

Despite some leftover hard feelings between Norway and Sweden, their relations gradually improved. In 1912 Norway, Sweden, and Denmark entered into a joint declaration to remain neutral in any war between the Great Powers.

During the period between 1905 and the beginning of the First World War in 1914, Norway experienced robust economic growth, and many of its industries were created or expanded. Several hydroelectric power plants were built along the country's rivers and waterfalls. One of Norway's largest corporations, Norsk Hydro, was founded in December 1905.

However, the Norwegians became concerned that investors and companies from foreign countries were purchasing and taking ownership of Norway's waterfalls and mines. As a result, in 1909 the

Storting passed the Concession Laws that limited private ownership of those resources to a period of sixty to eighty years, after which ownership would revert to the Norwegian government. In this manner, Norway managed to encourage private (including foreign) investment, while preserving Norway's ultimate control over its own natural resources.

The Great War

By 1914 two of Norway's leading trading partners were Britain and Germany. Norway imported coal, fuel, and machinery from Britain, and exported fish, ore, and nitrates to that country. Norwegian fish, ores, and other products were also sent to Germany. Unfortunately, the shadows of war were descending on Europe, and the two major rivals were Britain and Germany, who were building up their respective navies.

Although Norwegians were generally aware of the threat of war, as well as its possible negative effect on trade and the Norwegian economy, some of Norway's political leaders seemed rather oblivious to the danger. The Liberal government of Gunnar Knudsen relied on Norway's declaration of neutrality and the British navy to protect the country from war, and did not increase the military budget. In February 1914, when the Conservatives challenged this policy, Knudsen replied that the world was essentially free of political problems. Contrary to his assertion, within five months the First World War started in June 1914, and Norway's two main trading partners – Britain and Germany – were on opposite sides of the war. In early August, Norway declared its neutrality, and Norway and Sweden entered into another agreement to maintain their neutrality and not to go to war against each other. The government also imposed emergency price controls on various products, and appointed a commission to find and import grain because Norway still did not produce enough food to feed its population.

Almost immediately, Britain pressured Norway to stop sending exports to Germany, especially nitrates, pyrites, ores, and other products that could be used in the war industry. Both Britain and

Germany mined the North Sea, and the Germans initiated submarine warfare against British ships. Britain responded in November 1914 by declaring all ships in the North Sea to be at risk. Even though Norway was neutral and was not fighting on either side of the war, Norway's trade, economy, and shipping were at great risk. Nevertheless, Norway continued to trade with both Britain and Germany and actually benefited by charging high wartime prices for its exports and high freight rates for transporting goods on Norwegian ships.

A significant development took place in February 1915 when Germany started sinking ships near Britain, including Norwegian ships. The people of Norway were outraged that Germany was attacking their ships and killing their sailors. Although Norway would officially remain a neutral country in the war, from that point on the Norwegian government clearly favored its relationship with Britain over Germany. Beginning in 1916, Norway and Britain signed agreements that limited Norway's exports to Germany and required Britain to purchase Norwegian fish that otherwise would have been sold to Germany.

Things got worse on February 1, 1917, when Germany declared unrestricted submarine warfare against all ships in a large area around Britain and France. Germany began to sink many more Norwegian ships, and there was widespread public hatred of Germany all over Norway. Norway and Britain started a convoy system that largely moved the Norwegian ships out of harm's way and assigned British ships to carry most of the cargo between the two countries.

The United States entered the war against Germany in April 1917. For decades the United States had been the champion of the rights of neutral countries. But now that the Americans were no longer neutral they demanded that Norway – a neutral country – cease all trade with Germany. Norway sent trade representatives to the United States, and in April 1918 the two countries signed a trade agreement that significantly reduced Norwegian exports to Germany and increased American exports of much needed products to Norway.

As a result of its agreements with the United States and Britain and its anger at Germany, Norway became a "neutral ally" of the Western Powers for the rest of the war. By the time the war ended in 1918, Norway had suffered substantial losses, including half the tonnage of its merchant fleet and two thousand lives. Norway's economy also suffered, and many of its people found themselves close to poverty.

At the Paris Peace Conference following the Great War, Norway tried to obtain compensation for its losses during the war. But the victorious nations had other priorities, and all that Norway received in the peace treaty was sovereignty over the Arctic islands called Spitzbergen. In 1925 Norway took possession of the islands, now called Svalbard, but under the conditions that the islands would remain demilitarized and that other countries could continue their commercial activities including coal and uranium mining on the islands. In fact, the Russians are still mining on Svalbard to the present day.

The Labor Party

For over seventy-five years beginning in 1935, the Labor Party (*Arbeiderpartiet*) was Norway's largest political party that consistently dominated the government of Norway. The party was formed in 1887 as a socialist organization that supported workers and others in the lower class. At the beginning, the party promoted pragmatic policies and solutions by demanding such things as shorter working hours and universal suffrage.

Initially the party was not represented in the Storting. However, this changed over the next twenty-five years as more and more workers and other lower class people were given the right to vote. By 1899 there was universal suffrage for all men in Norway, and the right to vote was extended to all women in 1913. The Labor Party won four seats in the Storting in 1903, all elected by mineworkers, farmers, and fishermen in northern Norway. Over the following fifteen years the party's representation in the Storting continued to grow, and the party retained its moderate socialist agenda.

However, at the end of World War I in 1918, the policies of the Labor Party took an abrupt turn to the left. The Communists were now in control in Russia, and there were bad economic conditions and high unemployment in several European countries including Norway. The Norwegian Labor Party adopted a new radical agenda in support of revolutionary class warfare. In 1919 the party joined the Communist International (Comintern) promoting revolution throughout the world. But despite its support for revolution on paper, the Labor Party did little or nothing to foment a workers' revolution in Norway.

In 1920 the Russian Communists announced the Moscow Theses which authorized them to dictate policy to all members of Comintern. Many members of Norway's Labor Party resented this power grab by the Russians, and there were several splits in the party. The more moderate members left the Labor Party to form their own Social Democratic Party in 1921, and a leftist minority departed in 1923 to form the Norwegian Communist Party. But in 1927 the Social Democrats rejoined the Labor Party with a goal to gain broad electoral support for a more moderate socialist program.

This strategy proved to be beneficial, and the Labor Party had great success in the 1927 election and won fifty-nine seats in the Storting. The non-socialist parties were haggling with each other and could not form a majority government. So King Haakon surprisingly turned to the Labor Party to establish a minority government on January 27, 1928. But Norway was not ready for the socialist government, which lasted only three weeks. During that short period of time the Norwegian currency lost much of its value, several Norwegian banks went under, and capital fled the country. The non-socialist parties then got their act together and formed a new government, and the Labor Party subsequently lost many seats in the 1930 election.

By that time the Great Depression had hit Norway. As many as 42 percent of union workers were unemployed. The Labor Party then developed a more pragmatic program called Work for All to increase employment by expanded state investment in the economy. This program appealed not only to industrial workers but also to farmers and fishermen who were suffering from the economic downturn. The Labor Party had become a more moderate socialist party that supported reform instead of revolution and believed in working within the system. As a result, in the 1933 election the Labor Party scored a great victory, winning 69 of the 150 seats in the Storting, compared to no seats for the Communists. The representatives from the Labor Party began to more actively participate in the Storting and formed alliances with others including the Farmers Party to promote their ideas.

This effort resulted in the formation of a minority Labor Party government supported by the Farmers Party in 1935, beginning a period of Labor Party dominance of Norway's government that lasted almost to the present day. The new prime minister was Johan Nygaardsvold, and a distinguished history professor named Halvdan Koht became the foreign minister.

The new government raised the budget for agriculture, fishing, forestry, local government, and highway construction, all paid for by higher taxes and fees including a new sales tax. More significantly, the government created the social welfare state by enacting laws for old age pensions, unemployment insurance, paid vacations, health and safety in the workplace, health insurance, and educational reform. The welfare state would be expanded by successive Labor Party governments over the next several decades.

Over time, the high unemployment rate came down. Labor union membership increased, as did the broad popular support for the government and the Labor Party.

CHAPTER SEVEN:

World War II in Norway

The Second World War was the most traumatic event in Norwegian history, as Nazi Germany unexpectedly invaded and brutally occupied Norway. This chapter details the circumstances that led to the invasion, the efforts of the German occupiers and their Norwegian collaborators to Nazify the country, exploits of the Norwegian resistance movement, and the liberation and postwar trials.

Neutrality and disarmament in the interwar years

At the conclusion of World War I, the victorious powers wanted to make sure that such terrible death and destruction would never happen again. In addition to imposing punishing reparations on Germany and placing severe restrictions on the German military in the Treaty of Versailles, they founded an organization of states called the League of Nations, the predecessor to the United Nations, for the purpose of avoiding or peacefully settling disputes between nations. The League was the pet project of US President Woodrow Wilson, but he could not persuade his own country to become a member of the organization.

In 1928 many countries of the world went one step farther by signing the Kellogg-Briand Pact, a treaty that prohibited nations from going to war to resolve international conflicts. So at least on paper, the world had outlawed war, but it remained to be seen whether the League and the treaty would be effective in actually preventing another world war.

Norway had managed to stay out of the fighting in the First World War by declaring its neutrality, although the Norwegians suffered heavy losses of ships and sailors at sea. Based on its experience in the first war, Norway desired to maintain its neutral status in any future conflict, as well. In addition, the Norwegian government actively supported and placed great reliance on the League of Nations to keep the peace. The Norwegian government thought that the League and the treaty, when combined with Norway's neutrality, would keep the country out of any future war.

Consequently, in the 1920s the size and firepower of Norway's military were drastically reduced by successive governments of Liberals and Conservatives, and this governmental policy of virtual disarmament was also strongly supported by the Farmers Party. The other major political party, the Labor Party, adopted an even more extreme position that the entire Norwegian military should be abolished. As a result, in the twenty years after the conclusion of the First World War, Norway spent very little money on manpower, weapons, and ships for the military, and the country was left almost defenseless.

In the 1930s it became abundantly clear that the League and the treaty could not prevent war. In particular, three League members and treaty signatories – Germany, Italy, and Japan, called the Axis Powers – showed their total disdain for the League, the treaty, and their international obligations by invading other lands. Although Norway made some limited expenditures for torpedo boats and light land weapons in 1933, the Norwegian government essentially did nothing else to protect the country from the growing threat of war.

Outside the Norwegian government, there were Norwegians who perceived the danger posed by the aggressive Axis Powers and the possibility that Norway could be their next target. In 1936 a poem called "You must not sleep" by Arnulf Øverland appeared in Norwegian publications. In the poem, he warned his countrymen that the Germans and their leader Adolf Hitler were a threat to world peace and security. Similarly, Otto Ruge, the chief of the Norwegian general staff, warned the Norwegian government that southern Norway was dangerously vulnerable to attack and that the most likely attacker was Germany.

But those warnings were ignored by the government, which by then was under the control of the antimilitaristic Labor Party. Although the party removed unilateral disarmament from its platform in 1936, the Labor government still refused to support any appreciable military expenditures. The leadership and most of the members of the Labor Party were of the opinion that:

1. Military expenditures were a waste of money because Norway could not protect itself from attack by a major power anyway;
2. Building up the Norwegian military could alarm other nations and increase the chances that Norway could be attacked;
3. The Norwegian military was reactionary and could not be trusted because it had previously been used to put down labor strikes and arrest labor leaders;
4. Instead of spending money on the military, the government should use its available funds for social welfare programs and agriculture in tough economic times;

5. A larger military was not necessary because no one was threatening to attack Norway; and

6. The British navy would protect Norway from any attack by Nazi Germany, so a German invasion of Norway would be impossible.

Even though most of these opinions seem incredibly naïve and irresponsible in retrospect, they embodied the firm policy of the Norwegian Labor government in the late 1930s, and that policy was also supported by most of the political opposition. In summary, just a few years before Norway was invaded and occupied, Norway's leaders left the country undefended because they could not conceive of any possibility that Norway would be attacked.

Even after the League of Nations and the Kellogg-Briand Pact had proven to be ineffectual, Norway continued to rely on its status as a neutral country to protect itself from war. In May 1938 Norway, Sweden, and Denmark entered into another joint declaration of neutrality in the event of any war in Europe, but they did not make any plans for a military force to defend their neutrality. Under international law, a neutral country is obligated to have a military that can defend its neutrality. But Norway completely ignored this duty and was only prepared for a neutrality watch and not a neutrality defense. That is, Norway could only hope to watch and not defend itself if a foreign power invaded the country.

It was not until the Second World War was about to break out that the Storting finally approved some modest military expenditures, but much less than the amount recommended by the Norwegian military. For example, in 1939 the Storting appropriated 20 million Norwegian kroner per year for defense. However, Norway was still in the process of purchasing new weapons when Germany invaded Poland and the second great war in twenty-five years began on September 1, 1939. Within a few days, Britain and France declared war on Germany, and Norway once again declared its neutrality.

Prelude to war in Norway

Well in advance of the outbreak of hostilities in September 1939, both Britain and Germany recognized the strategic significance of Norway in a European war. First of all, Norway had a long shoreline that faced the North Atlantic shipping lanes. A Great Power with naval bases along the Norwegian coast would have a strategic advantage in any naval war and could also wreak havoc on the enemy's merchant ships at sea.

Second, both Germany and Britain imported iron ore from mines in northern Sweden, and much of the ore was shipped by train to Narvik in northern Norway, where it was loaded onto ships for transport to the two countries. In fact, Germany received over 80 percent of its iron ore from the Swedish mines, and the only other transportation route went through the Swedish port of Luleå on the Gulf of Bothnia between Sweden and Finland, which was blocked by ice in the winter. So for many months of the year it was vitally important for the Germans to ship iron ore through Narvik to supply their armaments industry in Germany. Without access to the port of Narvik in Norway, the German armaments industry and ultimately the German war machine would grind to a halt.

After Germany occupied Austria, Bohemia, and Moravia, US President Franklin Delano Roosevelt, on April 14, 1939, asked Hitler and Italian dictator Benito Mussolini for assurance that they would not invade a long list of other countries including Norway. In response, Hitler publicly mocked Roosevelt's request, while the German envoy in Oslo asked Norwegian Foreign Minister Halvdan Koht if Norway felt threatened by Germany and if Norway had asked Roosevelt to request such assurance. The Norwegian government was aghast that Roosevelt had even mentioned Norway by name, since Norway wanted to stay out of any discussion of war. So Koht answered the Germans by saying no, Norway did not feel threatened and definitely did not make any such request to the Americans. Nevertheless, a few days later Germany offered to sign a non-aggression treaty with Norway. The Norwegians politely declined the offer because they did not want to sign anything that might jeopardize their status of neutrality.

When the war began in September 1939 and Norway declared its neutrality, the Norwegian leaders only called up a few military units and put a few forts on alert. But they did not order a general mobilization of the military because they still did not feel that an attack on Norway was possible. Despite its declaration of neutrality, the Norwegian government also secretly continued to rely on the British navy for protection, and at Norway's request the British government gave Koht a written confirmation that Britain intended to defend Norway from any attack by Germany.

In the meantime, Britain was secretly making plans for Norway. Now that the British were at war with Germany, on September 19, 1939, Britain's First Lord of the Admiralty Winston Churchill submitted a proposal to the British government that called for a British naval action to block the transport of Swedish iron ore to Germany. Specifically, Churchill wanted Britain's government to authorize the British navy to mine the Norwegian territorial waters near Narvik so that German ore boats would be forced into the open sea where they could be destroyed by British naval ships. But the British cabinet was still led by Prime Minister Neville Chamberlain, who had already handed the Sudetenland in Czechoslovakia to Hitler at the Munich conference and who, even now after Britain's declaration of war against Germany, was doing little or nothing to wage war against the Nazis. So Churchill's proposal was not approved by the British government, and the Germans continued to ship large quantities of Swedish ore along the Norwegian coast from Narvik to Germany.

The complexion of the war changed considerably on November 30, 1939, when the Soviet Union attacked Finland. This brought the war much closer to home for the Norwegians, who were generally sympathetic to their Scandinavian neighbor. Many young Norwegian volunteers went to Finland to join the Finnish army in the Winter War against the Russians. Churchill viewed the Winter War as a new opportunity to convince the British government to do something about the ore shipments from Narvik to Germany. By December 1939 Britain and France were each separately making plans to send military units to occupy Narvik and the Swedish iron mines and to use the same area to ship military supplies through Norway and Sweden to the Finns. In February 1940 the Brits and the French got together and formulated plans for a joint military operation in northern Norway and Sweden. So they were planning to occupy an area of northern Norway, a neutral country, as part of their war effort against Germany.

At the same time, the Germans had their own plans for Norway. In October 1939 the staff of Admiral Erich Raeder, the commander of the German navy, urged Hitler to plan an attack on Norway. In World War I the surface ships of the German navy had been confined to the Baltic Sea. In the new war they wanted to establish naval bases on the Norwegian coast to protect their supply of iron ore from Sweden and to attack the British navy and merchant shipping in the North Atlantic. For example, Admiral Karl Dönitz, the commander of the German submarine fleet, wanted to base submarines in Narvik and Trondheim.

Hitler agreed to consider these proposals, but at this time he had other priorities in mind such as completing the occupation of Poland and planning to attack other countries. So as the Winter War between the Soviet Union and Finland progressed, Raeder and his staff became increasingly concerned about the possibility that Britain and France could beat Germany to the punch and occupy all or part of Norway.

In December 1939 a new player appeared on the scene when a Norwegian named Vidkun Quisling traveled to Berlin. He was a former military officer who was previously the Norwegian minister of defense for a couple of years. Now he was the leader of the Norwegian fascist party called the National Unity Party (*Nasjonal Samling* or NS). Founded in 1933, the NS had never caught on with the Norwegian public and had very little electoral support. By 1939 the party was actually losing members and was nearing the brink of dissolution. Quisling hoped that his visit to the leading fascist country would somehow reverse the waning fortunes of himself and his tiny political party.

First Quisling met with the Nazi ideologue Alfred Rosenberg, to whom he claimed that pro-British and Jewish elements in Norway's government were conspiring with the Western Allies against Germany. All of this was, of course, pure fantasy, but it sounded persuasive to a sympathetic and ill-informed Rosenberg. To avoid an Allied occupation of Norway, Quisling proposed to take over the Norwegian government in a coup and then invite the Germans to occupy the country. Later Quisling met with Raeder and gave him the same song and dance plus the fabricated revelation that the British and the Norwegians had secretly agreed to a British naval base at Kristiansand. He also emphasized the role he could play in establishing German naval bases along the Norwegian coast, and he assured Raeder that he had substantial support in Norway. This was just what Rosenberg and Raeder wanted to hear, and they enthusiastically suggested that Hitler meet with Quisling.

On December 14, 1939, Raeder introduced Quisling to Hitler. At two meetings Hitler and Quisling discussed Quisling's plan to take over the Norwegian government and invite the Germans to occupy Norway. But after politely listening to Quisling, Hitler's views on Norway did not change. For the time being, he was perfectly satisfied with Norway as a neutral country, and his first priority was to commit his military forces to an invasion of France. Moreover, Hitler was skeptical of Quisling's plan to take over the Norwegian government, and he knew that Quisling had little public support in Norway. But at the same time he was concerned about a possible British occupation of Narvik and the resulting interruption of Swedish iron ore supplies to Germany. So Hitler somewhat unenthusiastically asked his military staff to look into how an occupation of Norway could be accomplished. But he still had no immediate plans to attack Norway.

The British government finally took action in December 1939 to block the flow of iron ore to Germany by ordering the British navy to blockade the North Sea. German ships avoided the blockade by sailing in Norwegian waters all the way down the coast of Norway. British merchant ships also sailed in Norwegian waters, and three of them were attacked and torpedoed by the Germans.

The dangerous presence of British and German ships in Norwegian waters led to the Altmark Affair, which changed the entire course of the war for Norway. On February 16, 1940, the British navy attacked the *Altmark*, a German merchant ship that had taken refuge in a Norwegian fjord called Jøssingfjord near Egersund in southern Norway. For weeks the British navy had been trying to locate the *Altmark*, which had made a long voyage from the South Atlantic carrying three hundred British prisoners. The British boarded the *Altmark*, some Germans were killed, and all of the British prisoners were freed. There were two small Norwegian torpedo boats in the fjord, but they did not intervene or try to stop the attack. Germany protested Norway's failure to act, and Norway sent a protest note to Britain for taking military action in a neutral country.

The Altmark Affair completely altered Hitler's attitude and plans in regard to Norway. He was incensed, and he came to the realization that Norway would not defend its own neutrality and that Britain might be emboldened to occupy Norway or at least Narvik. Therefore, he immediately ordered the German military to prepare for an invasion and occupation of Norway – and also Denmark for good measure. The planned German operation against the two Scandinavian countries was named *Weserübung*, meaning exercise on the Weser River, which is the place in Germany where part of the invasion force would be assembled and trained. So Norway and Denmark moved ahead of France on the German invasion schedule.

One of Hitler's generals suggested that Hitler interview General Nikolaus von Falkenhorst as a candidate to lead the operation in Norway because he was one of the few German senior officers who had any experience in Scandinavia. In actuality, Falkenhorst had only served as a junior officer in Finland in 1918, and he did not know the first thing about Norway. Nevertheless, Hitler was duly impressed the first time he met with Falkenhorst on February 20, 1940. He asked Falkenhorst to quickly come up with a plan for the invasion of Norway and to come back and present the plan later the same day.

Falkenhorst immediately went to a local bookstore and purchased a Baedekers Norway travel guide to learn something about Norway and its geography. Then he formulated an invasion plan, returned to meet Hitler, presented his plan, and was appointed commander of Weserübung right on the spot.

The plan did not include Quisling's proposed coup, but it did provide for a peaceful occupation of Norway, with any resistance to be crushed by overwhelming military force. Falkenhorst promptly gathered his forces, and by early March there were already large numbers of German ships arriving at Germany's ports on the Baltic and North Seas, where they would subsequently pick up the troops for transport to Norway.

The British and French governments continued to develop plans for Norway, but they were not implementing those plans. Churchill came up with a plan called Operation Wilfred to lay mines in Norwegian waters. The British cabinet first approved the plan and then thought better of it and suspended its approval. On March 1 Britain and France asked Sweden and Norway for permission to send military units through the two countries to assist the Finns in the Winter War. They also secretly wanted to occupy Narvik and the Swedish iron mines. Three days later Norway refused to give its consent because it did not want to be drawn into the war. However, the British and the French decided not to take no for an answer, and they were ready to send troops to Narvik anyway when the Winter War suddenly ended and the Soviets and the Finns signed a peace treaty on March 13. At that point, Britain and France could no longer use the Winter War as an excuse to occupy Narvik and the Swedish mines. Instead, Britain reassigned its troops to France.

Operation Weserübung was originally planned for March 15, 1940, but Hitler postponed the date in order to reappraise the situation when the Winter War ended. However, at a military conference on April 2, Hitler gave Falkenhorst the final go-ahead by setting April 9 as the date for the invasion of Norway and Denmark.

The ambitious plan called for a large-scale combined air, sea and ground operation to invade Norway simultaneously at several different locations from Oslo to Narvik. The invasion force would include almost the entire German navy, and the *Luftwaffe* [German air force] would provide 220 bombers, over 100 fighters and reconnaissance planes, and many transports. The army troops, including ordinary soldiers as well as paratroopers, would be transported to Norway by air and sea. In early April, the Germans met with Quisling in Copenhagen, and he gave them information on Norwegian defenses.

The German ships promptly left their ports and sailed toward Norway. At this point Norway and the Western Allies were aware of the large buildup of German troops along the Baltic Sea, and they anticipated a German invasion somewhere. But they did not yet know where the Germans were headed, although much of the conjecture centered on the Netherlands as a possible invasion site. However, on April 3 and 4, Danish and Dutch military attachés, respectively, told Norwegian diplomats in Berlin that the German forces were going to invade Norway on April 9.

The plot thickened on April 5 when the British and French governments and the Norwegian embassy in Berlin notified the Norwegian government that Norway might be the destination of the German invasion forces. As a precaution, Britain sent part of its navy toward Norway, and assembled troops in Scotland for possible embarkation to Norway if that turned out to be the German target. But the Norwegian Labor government did absolutely nothing to protect Norway from an increasingly likely German attack. In fact, in an April 6 speech to the Storting, Foreign Minister Koht only raised concerns about the plans of the Western Allies in Norway! So the Norwegian government was complaining about the British and French, who they expected to protect them from the Germans, just a few days before Norway was about to face a forewarned massive invasion by Nazi Germany.

On April 7, a Norwegian newspaper informed Norway's naval staff of German plans to occupy southern Norway, but the

Norwegian naval commander disregarded the warning. On the same day, British bomber aircraft spotted and bombed part of the German invasion fleet that was en route to Norway. The following day the British navy laid a minefield on the sea approach to Narvik, and Britain informed Norway's government that a German fleet was sailing north toward Narvik. But the Norwegian government still could not fathom the fact that the Germans were about to invade Norway. Koht thought that the Western Allies were making the whole thing up in order to pressure Norway into entering the war against Germany. Instead of cooperating with the Allies or doing anything to defend the country from the imminent German attack, he sent off a sharp protest note to Britain and France about the mining operation in Norwegian waters.

In the late morning of April 8, a Polish submarine attached to the British fleet sank the German transport ship *Rio de Janeiro* just off the southern Norwegian coast near Lillesand. Norwegian naval ships and fishing boats picked up the survivors, who said they were on their way to Bergen to protect the city from a British invasion. By the afternoon, the incident and the Germans' planned destination were reported on the front page of Norwegian newspapers.

The same afternoon and evening, the Storting and the Norwegian cabinet met to discuss the situation. But they only debated the British mining operation, and they were still seemingly blind to the German invasion. Koht was sure that a German warning or ultimatum would precede any possible invasion of Norway. He remained suspicious of the Allies' motives and he refused to believe their warnings, even in the face of so much evidence of German intentions and actions.

The weather off the Norwegian coast had now turned stormy and foggy, and the British navy was unable to locate and attack the German invasion fleet. Meanwhile, on the streets of Oslo, the NS was setting up posters encouraging Norwegians to support an immediate NS takeover of the government. That night a meeting of the Norwegian government was postponed until the next day. Norwegian military officers who for days had been asking the Norwegian government for an order to mobilize the military were left waiting for a response and told to go to bed.

Invasion

On the following day, the 9th of April 1940, in a massive coordinated air, sea and land attack at several locations, Nazi Germany invaded Norway. It was an unprovoked attack on a defenseless neutral country. The immediate German targets of the simultaneous attacks were Oslo and the Oslofjord, Kristiansand and Arendal, Egersund and Stavanger, Bergen, Trondheim, and Narvik. In all of those places, an almost totally unprepared Norwegian military was taken by surprise and defeated.

Already at 11:00 p.m. on April 8, a German naval fleet entered the Oslofjord and was confronted by a small Norwegian observation ship called *Pol III*. After the Norwegian ship fired a few warning shots and flares, the Germans asked the Norwegians to surrender. When they courageously refused to do so, the Germans opened fire and put *Pol III* out of action. The ship's captain was killed and became the first Norwegian casualty of the invasion. The German ships continued north up the Oslofjord covered by fog. At about the same time, a Norwegian warship identified another German fleet sailing into Korsfjorden and heading towards Bergen. The Norwegians ordered the Germans to stop, but the Germans just sailed right by them and no shots were fired.

Shortly after midnight on April 9, the ministers of the Norwegian government met in Koht's office in Oslo and received reports of German ships approaching the Oslofjord, Bergen, and Stavanger. It finally occurred to them that Germany was invading their country, and the shocked ministers decided to mobilize the Norwegian military and request British assistance to defend the country.

Defense Minister Birger Ljungberg tried to reach General Kristian Laake, the commander in chief of the Norwegian military. Laake was an old officer who had been chosen as commander to carry out reductions in the defense budget and not because of his military qualifications. The old general thought it was just a false alarm, and he did not want to leave his vacation home. But he reluctantly went to his headquarters at Akershus Fortress and called Ljungberg, who ordered Laake to mobilize the military.

Unfortunately, both Ljungberg and Laake were confused and did not know which part of the military to call up. Ljungberg went to Akershus to discuss the matter with Laake. At their meeting they could not decide what to do, so Ljungberg went back to Koht's office to obtain clarification of the order to mobilize. The whole process took hours, and the issue never was clarified. Laake's staff appealed to him to immediately order a mobilization of the entire Norwegian military by an announcement on the radio. But instead, as the Germans were invading Norway, Laake decided to send out the mobilization order by mail and not to make it effective until April 11! This incomprehensible confusion and decision-making caused a serious delay in the mobilization of Norwegian troops and allowed the Germans to easily waltz into the country in several places. Unfortunately, others in the Norwegian government and military were just as confused.

Prime Minister Johan Nygaardsvold called King Haakon and informed him that Norway was at war. The dazed and sleepy king asked, "With whom?" He was told that it was the Germans.

In the early morning hours of April 9, there was a naval battle between Norwegian and German ships in the Oslofjord. Near the Horten naval base, the headquarters of the Norwegian navy in the Oslo region, two German ships were sunk, and sixty German survivors made it to shore without their senior officers. Originally they were supposed to attack the town of Horten and the naval base, but now there were clearly not enough survivors to accomplish that mission. So at that point, the two junior German officers who found themselves in charge decided to attempt the ultimate bluff.

They walked up to a road, carjacked the car of the local police chief, and forced him to drive them to the naval base with a white handkerchief hanging out the window. Once they arrived at the base, the Germans walked right into the office of the Norwegian commander, Admiral Smith-Johannsen. They bluntly informed the admiral that the Germans had already taken the town of Horten with a superior force, and they threatened to bombard the town by air and sea unless the admiral signed a surrender within fifteen minutes. Without checking the facts or calling the bluff, Smith-Johannsen called naval headquarters in Oslo, which told him to use his own discretion. Incredibly, the admiral then signed and handed over a document which, to the utter amazement of the young German officers, contained a surrender of not just Horten but the entire Oslo naval district!

Another German fleet sailed into the Trondheimsfjord, where a Norwegian patrol boat ordered the Germans to halt. They sailed right past the hapless defenders. A Norwegian coastal battery guarding the fjord tried to fire on the German ships, but the guns did not work. Two other gun batteries were not manned until the German fleet had already passed them by. The Norwegian commander in Trondheim decided not to fight and surrendered, and the Germans quickly occupied the city without taking any casualties.

Similar events played out in other parts of the country. In Bergen, Norwegian coastal batteries fired at the approaching German fleet, but the Germans occupied the city by 6:20 a.m. after German merchant ships already in the harbor unloaded hundreds of troops. All of the Norwegian forts around the city were in the hands of the Germans by 9:30 a.m. because the Norwegian commander surrendered when the Germans threatened a massive bombardment. Troops from another German fleet quickly occupied Egersund. Germans paratroopers stormed and conquered the Sola airfield near Stavanger despite strong Norwegian resistance.

The invaders had more problems at Kristiansand where the German fleet could not make it into the harbor because of heavy shelling from Norwegian coastal batteries. But then the lead German warship raised what looked like a French flag. The Norwegians stopped firing because they thought the French navy had arrived to save them. The German ships sailed into the harbor and unloaded their troops, and the city was taken by noon. Nearby Arendal was occupied by the Germans without incident.

Farther north the Germans were concerned about Norwegian artillery protecting the approaches to Narvik. But it turned out that some of the guns had been sent to Bergen and the rest were still in storage in Narvik, so the Germans sailed right to the town where two Norwegian warships refused to surrender and were about ready to fire. The Germans sank both ships, and 276 Norwegian sailors were killed. The German forces landed in Narvik at about 4:00 a.m., and German General Dietl met the Norwegian commander Colonel Sundlo and demanded that the Norwegians surrender to avoid further bloodshed. Sundlo was a member of Quisling's NS and a German sympathizer. He had been ordered to fortify and defend Narvik, but did virtually nothing. After delaying his answer while German troops occupied the town, Sundlo surrendered.

At 6:30 a.m. about two hundred Norwegian troops were stranded in the Narvik school surrounded by Germans. The telephone rang in the school, and at the other end of the line was General Carl Gustav Fleischer, the commander of the Norwegian army's Sixth Division. A Norwegian major explained to him what had happened, and Fleischer ordered the major to attack the Germans and arrest Sundlo. Since that was impossible, the major ordered his troops to do the next best thing. They all picked up their weapons and ammunition and calmly walked out of the school toward the edge of town. When they got there, a young German sentry tried to stop them, but the Norwegian major smiled and wished the sentry a good morning in German. Then the Norwegians marched right past the bewildered sentry and out of town, where they joined other units of Norwegian soldiers and blocked the railroad line to Sweden for several days. However, the Germans were now in control of Narvik.

Meanwhile the main German fleet continued up the Oslofjord towards Oslo. Before reaching the city, the German ships had to pass through a narrow strait between the eastern shore and the Oscarsborg Fortress. Norwegian soldiers at the fortress manned two of their three ancient heavy guns named Moses, Aaron, and Joshua, fired two large shells, and scored direct hits on the German cruiser *Blücher*, which was then also struck by Norwegian torpedoes from another battery. The ship quickly sank at 6:22 a.m. along with about one thousand dead Germans, including all of the civil administrators who were on their way to Oslo to take over and run the Norwegian government. Some German survivors made it to shore singing *"Deutschland über alles"*. The rest of the German fleet turned around and unloaded their troops along the fjord far south of Oslo.

7.1 The *Blücher* sinks into the Oslofjord on April 9, 1940.

The sinking of the *Blücher* gave the king and the Norwegian government time to escape Oslo before the Germans got there, and it ruined Hitler's plan to take over and operate the Norwegian government. The Germans had planned to quickly overrun Oslo, capture the king and the Norwegian ministers, and have them continue to govern Norway under German supervision. That is exactly what happened in Denmark, which surrendered to the

German invaders on the first day of the invasion. But now the German plans for governing Norway would have to be changed because the king and the ministers were not captured and the German administrators who were supposed to supervise the Norwegian government were dead at the bottom of the fjord.

At 4:00 a.m. Dr. Curt Bräuer, the German envoy in Norway, showed up at Koht's office, where the Norwegian ministers were still assembled. Bräuer and Koht met in candlelight with air raid sirens blaring in the background, and Bräuer read the German demands – the Norwegian government must instruct all Norwegians not to oppose the Germans; the Germans must be permitted to take over all military installations and communications and all newspapers, radio stations, and mail service; and no Norwegian ships should be allowed to leave Norway. So Bräuer demanded an immediate surrender of Norway. Koht briefly consulted with the other Norwegian ministers in the next room and came back to tell Bräuer that the German demands were rejected and that Norway would defend its independence. Bräuer replied that then there would be war and nothing could save Norway, but Koht motioned to the sirens outside and pointed out that the battle was already under way.

The king and the government left for the railroad station to catch the first train north to Hamar. At the station, a reporter interviewed Koht, who disclosed that the king and the government were on their way to Hamar (!) and that general mobilization of the military was ordered. The interview was broadcast on Norwegian radio at 7:30 a.m., so unfortunately it told the Germans exactly where the king and government were going. But it also caused the Norwegian military throughout the country to promptly mobilize instead of having to wait for General Laake's mobilization letter by mail.

In any event, the king and the government made it to Hamar, where the Storting convened at 1:00 p.m. Bräuer left a message for Koht, once again requesting Norwegian compliance with the German demands.

At 7:00 a.m. eighty German aircraft, including bombers, fighters, and troop transports, approached Fornebu airport in Oslo. Seven Norwegian biplanes attacked them and managed to shoot down five German planes. The Norwegian antiaircraft fire from the ground was also deadly. The Germans had planned to have their paratroopers jump and take the airfield, allowing the planes to land safely. But low clouds prevented a parachute drop, and the German planes were running out of fuel. Some of the planes turned back, but the pilots of the other planes decided to land amid fierce ground fire. Three German planes were destroyed, five more were severely damaged, and many Germans were killed. But the Norwegians finally ran out of ammunition, and the Germans took control of the airport.

The German troops then marched to downtown Oslo without facing any more opposition because the Norwegian military decided not to defend the city! Instead the Norwegians tried to form a line of defense north of Oslo. Once the Germans reached the royal palace at about 3:00 p.m., six hundred German soldiers marched down Karl Johans gate (Oslo's main street) in a show of force, acting like they had already taken the entire city. A large crowd of stunned Norwegian civilians lined the street, including a young man named Gunnar Sønsteby, who later joined the Norwegian resistance and became one of the most highly decorated and renowned Norwegians of all time.

But the German plans to govern Norway were in a shambles because the king and the Norwegian government had escaped and the German administrators were dead. So at 9:00 a.m. Quisling suddenly reappeared, contacted Alfred Rosenberg's representative in Oslo, and offered to take over the Norwegian government. A reluctant Hitler agreed to this offer in the afternoon. At 7:32 p.m. Quisling made an announcement on Norwegian radio. He stated that he was now in charge, he named a new NS government, and he told the Norwegians that all opposition to the Germans must cease. However, he had not bothered to check with most of the chosen members of his new government before the radio announcement. Some of them refused to serve in a Quisling government, and two of them were out fighting the Germans. Moreover, Quisling still had virtually no support in Norway and was now widely viewed as a puppet of the German invaders. So Quisling's first attempt to govern the country was quickly turning into a fiasco.

In the meantime, German paratroopers were loaded onto trucks in Oslo and sent north to Hamar to capture the king and the real Norwegian government. The king and the government found out that the Germans were coming, and they fled to Elverum by train.

At 9:20 p.m. the Storting met at Elverum and unanimously approved the Elverum Mandate. It authorized the Norwegian government of ministers (now expanded to include three opposition leaders) to govern Norway on its own as long as the war lasted. Then the Storting sang Norway's national song "*Ja, vi elsker*" and adjourned its last session with the ministers for the next five years.

When the German paratroopers approached Elverum early on April 10, they were blocked and defeated at Midtskogen by a small band of Norwegians. The Germans got back in their trucks and returned to Oslo, and once again the king and the ministers were saved from capture.

Later on April 10 Bräuer met with the king, but this time under different circumstances because Hitler had already appointed Quisling as Norway's new leader. So Bräuer was no longer in a position to ask the ministers to govern the country under German supervision since the ministers were now excluded from the German plans. Instead he asked the king to surrender to the Germans and to accept Quisling as the new prime minister of Norway. To his credit, King Haakon refused and said he would rather abdicate than serve with Quisling. The king left it up to the ministers, who agreed with him. Having failed in their attempts to obtain the king's surrender and cooperation, the Germans then tried to kill the king by bombing the town of Nybergsund where he was staying. The king and the ministers survived the air raid by running into the forest for cover.

King Haakon and his son Crown Prince Olav decided to stay in Norway, but the crown prince's wife and children went across the border to Sweden. Later they were invited by President Roosevelt to the United States, where they lived for the rest of the war.

On April 10 a despondent General Laake wanted to surrender Norway to the Germans. At the government's request, he retired and Colonel Otto Ruge was promoted to major general and named the new commander in chief of the Norwegian military. Ruge promptly came up with a strategy to delay the German advance north of Oslo, and then in cooperation with the Allies to try to retake Trondheim from the Germans. That would prove to be wishful thinking, as the British promised the Norwegian government that they would send a large contingent of troops to Norway, but they did not say when or where they would arrive.

German advances throughout Norway

Having successfully landed their troops at several places along the Norwegian coast and after taking control of the major cities, the Germans resupplied their army, which then began to advance throughout the rest of Norway on April 14. The hastily formed units of the Norwegian army tried to hold off the invaders, but they were outnumbered and outgunned and therefore they had little success.

During the month of April 1940, the Germans' main force advanced north from Oslo through Gudbrandsdalen toward Otta and through the eastern valley called Østerdalen to Røros. On April 19 British troops landed at Namsos north of Trondheim and at Åndalsnes south of Trondheim. They intended to initiate a pincer movement around Trondheim and then retake the city from the Germans. However, those plans quickly evaporated when the British troops in Namsos were met by a German force advancing north from Trondheim and a fierce air attack. The Brits south of Trondheim were persuaded by General Ruge to join the beleaguered Norwegian troops that were desperately trying to stop the German advance through Gudbrandsdalen.

The major problem was that the British troops were not regular army soldiers. Rather they were mostly poorly-trained and inexperienced territorial militia who were no match for the Germans and of little assistance to the Norwegians. A Norwegian colonel described them as young lads from the slums of London, who took an interest in the pretty Norwegian women, engaged in wholesale looting of stores and homes, and ran like jackrabbits at the first sound of an aircraft engine. He also said the British officers acted like arrogant Prussians. More importantly, the Brits had no armor, no artillery, no maps, and no transportation, and their single squadron of obsolete planes was destroyed within twenty-four hours. After a few days some regular British troops arrived in Gudbrandsdalen, but the British and the Norwegians could not stop the German advance, and the British troops south of Trondheim were quickly withdrawn and shipped back to Britain.

By the first week of May, the German army was in control of almost all of southern and central Norway. The Germans continued their advance from Trondheim north towards Bodø. In the meantime, King Haakon, Crown Prince Olav, and the Norwegian ministers had fled through Gudbrandsdalen to Molde, where they boarded a British cruiser to Tromsø in northern Norway on May 1, all the time surviving German bombing raids that attempted to kill them. The city in the Far North became the temporary capital of Norway.

After the loss of southern and central Norway, the British government of Neville Chamberlain was replaced on May 10 by a new government led by Prime Minister Winston Churchill. On the same day, the German army, supported by the Luftwaffe, invaded the Netherlands, Belgium, and France and quickly broke through the French and British defenses. By May 27 the British and Norwegian troops trying to stem the Germans' steady northward advance from Trondheim had retreated all the way to Bodø, which was then destroyed in a savage bombing attack by the Luftwaffe.

The situation was different in Narvik where the British navy had sunk all of the German ships, and General Dietl's troops who occupied the town were almost surrounded by the British navy and Norwegian, French and Polish military units. The Germans' only supply route to Narvik ran through Sweden. The Swedes had been threatened by Hitler, and they were deathly afraid that they would be invaded by the Germans just like Denmark and Norway. So in violation of its duties as a neutral country, Sweden secretly allowed the Germans to ship troops and supplies through its territory to relieve the siege at Narvik. Nevertheless, Dietl and the Germans were in a desperate situation, and the Germans were obviously unable to ship any iron ore from Narvik to Germany for the time being.

On May 28, 1940, in the Battle of Narvik, the British navy and Norwegian and French troops attacked the Germans in Narvik and retook possession of the town. Many Germans were killed, some surrendered, and Dietl and other Germans escaped and fled eastward into the mountains near the Swedish border. The Battle of Narvik was the first major German defeat in World War II. The residents of Narvik were overjoyed as they welcomed Norwegian troops back into their town.

Unfortunately, the Norwegians' joy was short-lived. On May 30 Britain informed the Norwegian government that the Allies were leaving Norway. The British navy and the British, Polish and French troops were to be transferred to France to fight the German invasion of that country. The Norwegian government and military were surprised and bitter that they were being abandoned by their new allies. In fact, the British and French governments had made the decision to leave Norway before the Battle of Narvik because the German *blitzkrieg* was threatening to overrun Belgium and northern France. The Allied soldiers were quickly evacuated from Narvik by June 8 after they destroyed the port and the railroad to Sweden. The Germans reoccupied the town, promptly repaired the damage, and resumed shipments of iron ore to Germany.

On June 1 the Norwegian government made plans to evacuate the king and the ministers to London to continue the war as a government-in-exile. King Haakon wanted to stay in Norway and share the fate of his people, but he was finally persuaded to go. On June 7, 1940, the Norwegian ministers held their last meeting on Norwegian soil for the next five years, and they made the final decision to evacuate. Later the same day, the king, crown prince, ministers, other officials, and military staff left Norway on the British cruiser *Devonshire*. They avoided the Luftwaffe and made it to Britain.

General Ruge stayed behind in Norway to negotiate an armistice with the Germans and to demobilize the Norwegian army. The fighting between the Norwegian and German armies in Norway ended on June 10. Under the armistice agreement, the Norwegian soldiers had to give up their arms, but they were permitted to safely return to their homes. Norwegian officers were also allowed to return home if they signed a pledge not to fight against the Germans again. Many of them signed the pledge but later joined the Norwegian resistance, and some were subsequently imprisoned by the Germans and sent to concentration camps in Norway and Germany. General Ruge declined to sign the pledge. He became a prisoner of war in Germany and Poland, where he survived the war.

As they had done in Denmark, the Germans had hoped to peacefully and quickly occupy Norway. However, things did not go according to plan because the uncooperative Norwegians and their allies fought against the invasion and occupation of Norway. The Germans ultimately succeeded in occupying the entire country, but they suffered serious losses, including 5,296 dead, 242 planes, 3 navy cruisers, 10 destroyers, and 6 submarines. Other Germans were wounded, and several German ships were damaged. In fact, as a result of the action in Norway, most of the German navy was lost for the rest of the war.

German and NS administration of Norway

General Falkenhorst was in charge of the German military in Norway, but the Germans needed to replace the Norwegian government that had escaped and the German civil administrators that were lost on the *Blücher*. Within just a few days after April 9, it was readily apparent to Falkenhorst and Bräuer that Quisling had no support in Norway and could not handle the administration of the country. They felt that Quisling was actually hurting the German cause in Norway through his incompetence and unpopularity. Bräuer wanted to find a government that would be acceptable to the

Norwegians. So he discussed the matter with Paal Berg, the chief justice of the Norwegian Supreme Court, and other Norwegian leaders who had not fled Oslo.

On April 15, 1940, with Falkenhorst's and Berlin's consent, Bräuer approved an Administrative Council of Norwegians who were not NS members. The council was selected by the Norwegian Supreme Court. Its assigned task was to run the civil administration in areas occupied by the Germans. The new administrators refused to serve with Quisling, so he was dismissed by Bräuer. The administrators also insisted that they did not constitute a new government of Norway because they were still loyal to the duly elected Norwegian government that was on the run from the Germans.

When Hitler found out on April 19 that Bräuer had replaced Quisling with an administration that was not considered a full-fledged new government, he became extremely angry at Bräuer, whom he blamed for not persuading the king and the Norwegian ministers to stick around in the first place. So Hitler fired Bräuer, made him a common soldier in the army, and sent him off to fight on the Western Front. Bräuer was later transferred to the Russian Front, where he was captured and spent nine years in a Soviet prison camp. Hitler did not abolish the Administrative Council, but he felt that firm Nazi German civilian leadership was needed in Norway.

So on April 24 Hitler appointed a longtime Nazi named Josef Terboven as *Reichskommisar* for Norway and made him responsible for the civil administration of the country. Terboven became the dictator and Hitler's personal representative in Norway, and Falkenhorst remained in control of the military.

Terboven was a ruthless, fanatical Nazi from the Rhineland who rode around Oslo in his armor-plated Mercedes with a cannon on the roof, preceded and followed by cars full of Nazi thugs. His main goal was to maintain peace and security in Norway so that the country would be a good strategic base for the German navy and the Norwegian economy could be converted to provide products and resources to the German war industry.

Terboven kept the Administrative Council in place as a temporary measure, but it was clear that the council was now working for him and his Nazi underlings.

Over the next few months, Terboven tried to negotiate with the Storting to form a new Norwegian government called the Council of State (*Riksrådet*). In doing so, he applied strong pressure on the Storting, whose leaders even agreed at one point to suspend the monarchy and asked King Haakon to abdicate. On July 8, in a radio address from London on the BBC, the king answered the request by refusing to step down, and he mentioned the Elverum Mandate by which a free Storting had authorized his government. The king's speech was printed and distributed throughout Norway, and it became a rallying point for Norwegian resistance to the German occupation. It also stiffened the backbones of the Storting negotiators.

In September 1940 the talks between Terboven and the Storting broke down over the question of who should be appointed to the Council of State. At this point, Hitler's patience reached its breaking point, and he ordered Terboven to form his own Nazi government without any input from the Storting.

Consequently, on September 25, 1940, in an angry speech on Norwegian radio, Terboven announced the formation of a new Council of Commissioner Ministers to run the country in cooperation with his German staff. Ten of the thirteen appointed members of the new council were NS members, but Quisling was not among them because Terboven also had no respect for him. In addition, Terboven announced that the king and Norway's government in London were deposed, the Administrative Council was terminated, and all Norwegian political parties except the NS were dissolved.

At that point, the only functioning institution under the Norwegian Constitution that still existed in Norway was the court system. But the Supreme Court resigned en masse on December 23, 1940, after Terboven's justice minister started firing judges and replacing them with Nazis, and after Terboven ruled that the courts could not review or overturn any of his orders. So by the end of 1940 the Norwegian government in Norway and the courts were fully controlled by the Nazis.

Quisling remained out of favor for months, but over time he was rehabilitated over the objections of Terboven and Falkenhorst after he appealed to Rosenberg and his other Nazi friends in Berlin. At a ceremony attended by Terboven in Oslo on February 1, 1942, Quisling declared himself to be the minister president and leader of Norway, and he appointed his own set of NS ministers to his new government. So Norway ended up with two Nazi civil administrations – one led by Terboven and the other by Quisling, although it was always clear that the Germans were supreme. Quisling and his NS men were given primary responsibility for certain activities, such as trying to Nazify the country.

Police state

Terboven's regime established a police state of brutal terror to maintain order and security in the country. Over the course of the war, over thirty thousand Norwegians were imprisoned, and many were tortured and executed. The Nazis established several concentration camps in Norway, including Grini, a former women's prison in Oslo. Thousands of Norwegians, including members of the resistance and leaders of the political parties, were sent to concentration camps in Germany, France, and Poland. Most of the men ended up in Sachsenhausen near Berlin, and women were sent to Ravensbrück not far away.

The Nazis took control of the Norwegian radio stations, the press, and the publishing houses, and there was strict censorship throughout the country. By August 1941 only Nazis were permitted to have radios. The Germans and the NS spread Nazi propaganda in Norway. The Germans also took control of the Norwegian economy and exploited Norway's industry and resources to serve German industry and the war machine. In fact, approximately 40 percent of the Norwegian economy was diverted to support the German war industry. Gasoline was sold only to Nazis, and ordinary Norwegians had to convert their cars, trucks, and buses to run on methane from wood-fired cookers mounted on the vehicles. Food was also rationed or unavailable. Meanwhile, the NS attempted to Nazify the country by turning all public and private institutions into Nazi organizations.

There was almost unanimous opposition to the regime's formation of new Nazi fishing, farmers, professional and sports organizations. On May 5, 1941, the regime received letters of protest signed by forty-three different organizations. In July of the same year, the leaders of those organizations were arrested, and their associations were dissolved by the regime. As a result, most of the organizations went underground and continued to operate secretly for the rest of the war, and there was very little participation in the Nazi associations. In fact, these events led to the creation of the civilian resistance organization called the Coordination Committee.

Initially Terboven did not interfere with the labor unions because he did not want to disrupt the Norwegian economy that was supporting the German war effort. So at first he opposed Quisling's idea to form Nazi labor unions. However, on September 9, 1941, there was a massive strike by about thirty thousand union workers in Oslo after the regime stopped deliveries of milk to the workplaces. The very next day, Terboven declared a state of emergency, arrested fourteen labor leaders, and executed two of them. He also arrested the chief of police, the rector and several leading professors at the University of Oslo, and many editors and journalists. He even banned the Boy Scouts. German police and the SS were stationed throughout the city. A new decree made the disturbance of economic life or work conditions punishable by imprisonment or death. Prominent leaders of the Labor Party were arrested and shipped to Sachsenhausen, while others escaped to Sweden. The German response to the Milk Strike marked the end of legal rights in Norway.

Shortly after Quisling named himself minister president in February 1942, his regime demanded that each teacher in Norway join a new Nazi teachers' organization and promote the students' understanding of Nazi ideology and society. Virtually all of the teachers refused to do so, and instead they provided form letters that objected to the practices of the regime. Quisling and the NS then arrested over 1,300 teachers and sent approximately 650 of them to hard labor camps in Finnmark. Most of the schools could no longer operate, and eventually the regime had to give in and drop the Nazification project in order to reopen the schools.

After the NS installed new Nazi leadership at the University of Oslo and terminated the student council in 1941, there was a series of student strikes, and secret committees of professors and students were established. In the fall of 1943 the Nazis issued new regulations that gave preference to NS members in admission to various departments of the university including the medical school. The professors and students objected, but their negotiations with the Nazi leaders went nowhere.

On October 15, 1943, ten professors and sixty-three students were arrested, causing widespread protests throughout the university. Then on November 28, 1943, members of the Norwegian resistance set the Great Hall of the university on fire. Two days later, Terboven sent in the army, the Gestapo, and the SS to arrest many professors and about 1,200 students. Other professors and students were forewarned and escaped. About 700 students were sent to retraining camps in Germany and France. The Nazis attempted to train a few hundred students to be SS soldiers, but that effort was a complete failure because the students were totally uncooperative.

Fortunately, almost all of the students in the camps survived the war. Terboven closed down all instruction at the university for the balance of the war, but Hitler was angry at Terboven's handling of the affair because of how it looked to the rest of the world.

The NS also tried to Nazify the churches. On February 14, 1942, all of the Norwegian bishops resigned in protest over the violations of the rights of the church. A few weeks later all pastors in Norway read a statement in their churches supporting the bishops. When the NS then arrested several church leaders, almost all of the pastors resigned. The NS formed a new church with Nazi pastors, but their churches were almost empty as most Norwegians worshipped at underground churches that held services throughout the rest of the war.

The Germans and the NS persecuted the Jewish people in Norway. There were 2,173 Jews in Norway in 1942, and most of them lived in Oslo and Trondheim. The regime first collected their names, registered their property, stamped the letter J on their identification cards, generally harassed them, and occupied their synagogues. Then they started arresting some of the Jews and seizing their property.

On October 24, 1942, an order was issued to arrest all Jewish males over the age of fifteen and to confiscate their property. The Norwegian resistance alerted the Jews. Unfortunately, some of the Jews refused to believe what was about to happen, but about 850 escaped to Sweden and Britain and some others went into hiding in Norway. On October 26 the remaining Jewish men were rounded up and sent to jails and concentration camps. A month later all Jewish women and children in Norway were arrested. On the same day, hundreds of Jewish men, women, and children were assembled on the Oslo pier, where they boarded the SS *Donau* for a journey to Stettin, Germany. From there they were transported by trains to the death camps at Auschwitz and Birkenau. Many more Jews in Norway were sent to Auschwitz on February 24, 1943. Of the 767 Norwegian Jews sent to concentration camps, only 26 survived the war.

When the Jews who had escaped to Britain and Sweden returned to Norway after the war, they found that their property had been confiscated. It was not until 1999 that the Storting granted $58 million in restitution to the Norwegian Jews. The former Quisling mansion at Bygdøy in Oslo is now the Norwegian holocaust museum.

Quisling tried to recruit Norwegians to fight in the German army, and it was his dream to create a fully Norwegian SS division, although he could never find enough volunteers. Most of the recruits ended up on the dreaded Russian Front. In 1944 Quisling came up with a new idea to draft Norwegian men into the German army, but about 75,000 Norwegians fled to the woods where they were cared for and fed by the Norwegian resistance. Thousands of them joined the resistance or went to Sweden, where many of them as well as university students became members of the new Norwegian police force that was being trained by the Norwegian government-in-exile.

Finally, Quisling tried to form a new Norwegian parliament called the *Riksting*, but the project went nowhere. He also repeatedly contacted Hitler and asked for a peace treaty between his Norwegian regime and Germany. Hitler consistently put off his requests. Eventually Hitler lost patience with Quisling, as civilians throughout Norway were literally in revolt against the NS regime and its clumsy Nazification efforts. So Hitler decided to place Terboven in sole control of the Norwegian government, and any further communications from Quisling to Hitler had to be directed through Terboven.

Even though Quisling and the NS were unsuccessful in their efforts to Nazify the country, the membership in the NS grew substantially to about 43,400 by November 1943, and then declined slightly until the end of the war. Most were inactive members, and some had to join the party to keep their jobs.

In addition to the Coordination Committee, various other civilian resistance organizations were formed in Norway, including the Circle (later called the Home Front Command) led by Paal Berg, and the Communists. They organized peaceful resistance against the regime, and hundreds of underground newspapers were published in Norway during the war.

Norway's government-in-exile

After fleeing Norway in June 1940, the king and his government ministers set up a Norwegian government-in-exile with offices in London. They had been given sweeping powers in the Elverum Mandate, and they were recognized as the sole legitimate Norwegian government by the Western Allies and many neutral countries and subsequently by the Soviet Union. Unlike various other governments-in-exile in London at the time, the Norwegians had the advantage of being able to financially support themselves from their gold reserves and merchant marine.

While the Germans were invading Norway on April 9, 1940, fifty tons of Norwegian government gold were removed from the national treasury in Oslo and shipped on trucks to Lillehammer just before the Germans entered Oslo. From there the gold was transported by train to Åndalsnes, by trucks to Molde, and then by ships and boats to Tromsø, always one step ahead of the Germans. Eventually the gold made it to Britain where it was stored in the vault of the Bank of England in London until it was shipped in installments across the Atlantic Ocean to North America. All but 297 gold coins made it from Oslo to the final destination. So the Norwegian gold was smuggled out of Norway, and it was gradually sold by the Norwegian government-in-exile to finance its operations during the war.

On April 10, 1940, Quisling instructed the captains of all Norwegian ships to proceed to Norwegian, German or neutral ports and await instructions. Not a single captain complied, and over 80 percent of the Norwegian merchant fleet wound up under the control of the government-in-exile. In April and May of 1940, Norwegian shipowners, in cooperation with the government, organized Nortraship, the largest shipping company in the world. Nortraship merchant ships carried cargo for the Allies and other countries throughout the war, and the substantial freight income helped to finance the government-in-exile. Unfortunately, almost half of the total tonnage of the Norwegian ships was sunk by the Germans during the war, and many Norwegian sailors lost their lives.

The foreign policy of the government-in-exile, as announced by new Foreign Minister Trygve Lie in December 1940, was to maintain close ties to the Western Allies and other seafaring nations, with the ultimate goal being the liberation of Norway. On January 1, 1942, in the Declaration of the United Nations, Norway and twenty-six other countries pledged all of their military and economic resources to defeat their common enemy. Thus, Norway became an ally in the war against Germany. Subsequently, Norway signed on as a charter member of the United Nations in 1945, and Trygve Lie was named the first secretary-general of that organization.

The government-in-exile also maintained ties to the people of occupied Norway. There were periodic BBC radio broadcasts in Norwegian by the king and various ministers, and the government cooperated with the civilian and military resistance in Norway.

The government-in-exile built up its armed forces to fight with the Allies against Germany. When the government arrived in Britain in June 1940, it only controlled twelve ships and about four hundred men in the Norwegian navy and only a few men in the Norwegian army and air force. But the armed forces gradually attracted more young men as recruits after they escaped from Norway to Sweden or Britain. Eventually the government-in-exile had a navy of 118 vessels that were all commanded by Norwegian officers but as part of the British navy.

The Norwegian air force established a flight training school at Little Norway near Toronto, Canada, and Norwegian air squadrons flew over the Atlantic, Britain, the English Channel, and Norway. In fact, in 1943 a Norwegian fighter squadron led the Allies in the number of enemy planes destroyed.

The Norwegian army in Britain served mostly in Scotland as part of the British home defenses or in Scotland and Norway as special operations commandos. The government-in-exile paid all of the expenses of its armed forces, as well as the Norwegian police force that trained in Sweden in preparation for the liberation of Norway.

Norwegian military resistance

Apart from the civilian resistance, there were several Norwegian military resistance organizations in Norway and elsewhere during the war.

The Special Operations Executive (SOE) was a multinational force under British command that was set up by Churchill in July 1940 "to set Europe ablaze." SOE trained young men from Norway and other occupied countries as commandos and then sent them back to their native lands to conduct military operations against the Germans. The Norwegians were trained near Inverness, Scotland, where they learned sabotage, fighting, weapons, explosives, radio operations, and parachute jumping. Then they were periodically sent or dropped into Norway where they conducted operations and training along with British commandos and the local Norwegian resistance.

The Norwegian commando unit in SOE was formally called Norwegian Independent Company No. 1, but it was commonly known as *Kompani Linge* after Captain Martin Linge, a Norwegian officer who was killed early in the war in a raid along the Norwegian coast. A total of 530 Norwegians served in Kompani Linge, and 55 of them were killed during the war.

SOE also established a fleet of Norwegian fishing boats called the Shetland Bus, which secretly ferried men, women, radios, and supplies between the British-controlled Shetland Islands and the west coast of Norway. Later in the war, the fishing boats were replaced by faster submarine chasers that were provided by the US Navy but manned by Norwegian crews.

7.2 Shetland Bus fishing boat *Heland*

The major Norwegian military resistance organization in Norway was *Milorg* (short for military organization), which was eventually made a part of the Norwegian armed forces and led by a young Oslo lawyer named Jens Christian Hauge. Milorg had resistance cells throughout Norway that engaged in some sabotage operations, often in cooperation with Kompani Linge. But they primarily trained men and women and gathered supplies and weapons to fight alongside the Allies in any future invasion of Norway or to disarm the Germans and keep the peace after the country was liberated. By 1944 there were about thirty-five thousand Norwegian men and women in Milorg.

The British Secret Intelligence Service (SIS) and the Norwegian XU had intelligence agents in Norway, Germany, and other countries that collected information on the German administration, military, communications, and industry. They sent the intelligence to Britain, usually by using hidden radio transmitters. For example, the German battleships *Tirpitz* and *Scharnhorst* were sunk by the British air force and navy, respectively, based in part on such intelligence from Norway.

While the foregoing resistance organizations operated in conjunction with the British and Norwegian governments, the Communists had their own organizations of saboteurs and assassins that operated independently in Norway. The Communist Osvald Gang led by Asbjørn Sunde began sabotage operations in and around Oslo shortly after Germany invaded the Soviet Union in June 1941. Some of their most significant operations included the destruction of ammunition transports and fifty thousand tons of shipping, attacking the State Police Office, and assassinating Germans and Norwegian collaborators. The Norwegian Communist Party leader Peder Furubotn (nicknamed *Gubben*) had his own sabotage organization that he directed from his mountain hideout, where he was almost captured by the Germans in 1942. There were many other Communist military units in the rest of the country. During the war, the Communists became popular among the Norwegian people for their fearless attacks against the Germans and the NS.

The men and women who served in these and other resistance organizations were very courageous. It was extremely dangerous duty, and many of them were killed or caught, tortured, and executed by the Nazis. Others were captured and sent to concentration camps. Moreover, in response to sabotage, assassination, and other resistance operations, Terboven and his Nazi henchmen frequently executed prisoners and even innocent Norwegian civilians in reprisal. Some of the most significant resistance actions and Nazi reprisals were the following.

Austvågøy

Operation Claymore was a raid by British and Norwegian commandos and the British navy at Austvågøy in the Lofoten Islands on March 4, 1941. The commandos destroyed fish oil factories and 3,600 tons of fish oil, kerosene, and paraffin that were used by the Germans to extract glycerin and manufacture high explosives in the war industry. The raiders sank 10 German ships, captured 228 Germans and 12 NS members, and left the scene with 314 additional Norwegians who volunteered to go to Britain to join the Norwegian military. The local Norwegians on the island thought it was the beginning of the British invasion and liberation of Norway, so they set up Norwegian and British flags and sang "Ja, vi elsker". In a sinking German trawler, the commandos found code books and rotor wheels for the Germans' Enigma cipher machine, and this discovery subsequently allowed the Brits to secretly decipher the German naval codes for several months.

Hitler was furious. At first he ordered everything on the Lofoten Islands to be destroyed, but the Germans needed fish and fish oil. So instead the Germans destroyed many houses, murdered some Norwegians, and sent one hundred Norwegians to Grini concentration camp.

As a result of the Austvågøy raid and several others, Hitler ordered that from now on all captured commandos would be handed over to the Gestapo for execution, even if they were in uniform. This was a clear violation of the Geneva Convention. Hitler also decided to drastically increase the size of the German military in Norway to 430,000 troops, and he built fortifications and artillery installations along the Norwegian coast. So he turned the country into Fortress Norway to try to prevent further commando raids and a British invasion of Norway. In fact, Churchill had planned another operation called Jupiter as an Allied invasion of Norway, but the operation was replaced by Operation Torch, the Allied invasion of North Africa.

In accordance with the plans of Admirals Raeder and Dönitz, the German navy built several bases along the Norwegian coast for surface ships and submarines that operated in the North Atlantic. For example, wolfpacks of German subs sank hundreds of Allied ships carrying military supplies and equipment to Britain and northern Russia over the course of the war.

However, other than manning coastal defenses against an Allied invasion that never materialized, guarding the short Norwegian border with Russia, helping the Gestapo track down Norwegian resistance members, and keeping watch over Russian and Serbian prisoners in northern Norway, the hundreds of thousands of German army soldiers in Norway had literally nothing to do for most of the war. Hitler's angry obsession with Norway and his massive concentration of forces in that country led to a huge waste of military manpower and resources that could have been put to much better use in the Germans' desperate battle on the Russian Front.

Telavåg

Telavåg was a fishing village southwest of Bergen on the west coast of Norway. It was also one of the many landing places for the Shetland Bus. Fishing boats armed with machine guns and carrying commandos and supplies arrived and left Telavåg at night. This operation was run by local fishermen Lauritz and Lars Telle.

To keep the local Norwegians satisfied and quiet, the Telles and their passengers would often give them various goodies from Britain. In the spring of 1942, a local woman became angry and jealous because she did not receive her share of coffee and other things. So she told the local Norwegian Nazi sheriff about the operation, and he reported it to the Gestapo in Bergen. On April 23 a Gestapo agent disguised as a Bible salesman arrived at Telavåg and started poking around. On the following day another Gestapo agent showed up and told the Telles that he wanted to go on a "fishing trip", meaning he wanted to escape to Shetland. The Telles agreed to take him there.

Then on April 26 four Gestapo agents burst into the Telle farmhouse in the middle of the night when two commandos from Kompani Linge were hiding and sleeping there. One Linge man and two Gestapo agents were killed in a shootout, and the other Linge man was shot, arrested, and later executed.

Terboven arrived on the scene the very next day. He decided to wipe Telavåg off the map. All Telavåg men between the ages of sixteen and sixty-five were sent to Sachsenhausen or Grini, and all women, children, and elderly men were shipped to a prison camp in Bergen. Eighteen unrelated Norwegian prisoners in Ålesund were executed. Telavåg was totally destroyed, all boats were sunk or confiscated, all livestock was taken or killed, and the name of the town was removed from all maps in Norway. There were also additional German reprisals in western Norway as a result of the Telavåg incident.

These and many other German reprisals led the Norwegian government-in-exile to demand a reduction in sabotage raids in Norway, and Milorg was ordered to stop any further sabotage activity. But raids by SOE and the Communists continued. Telavåg was rebuilt after the war, and it remains a fishing village to the present day.

Heavy water sabotage

German scientists were the first to discover atomic fission in 1938. During World War II, both the Allies and the Germans attempted to use this discovery to make an atomic bomb, a weapon so powerful and destructive that it could determine the outcome of the war. In their project to develop an atomic bomb, the Germans used deuterium oxide, more commonly known as heavy water, as a braking substance to keep the atomic reaction under control. The only source of heavy water in Europe was the Norsk Hydro hydrogen plant at Vemork near Rjukan, Norway, where heavy water was produced as a byproduct of chemical fertilizer. Once the Germans occupied Norway, this source of heavy water was readily available to them. They needed five tons of heavy water, and so it was shipped periodically from Norway to the atomic scientists in Germany.

However, by the summer of 1942, Hitler and his armaments minister Albert Speer had lost confidence in the German atomic bomb project, which was proceeding too slowly for their taste. Therefore, they reduced the funding for the project, and they transferred several scientists to other projects. As a result, the Germans were still far from a breakthrough, and their atomic bomb project was clearly on the backburner. All of this information was reported to the Allies by a young Norwegian XU intelligence agent in Germany named Sverre Bergh. But the British and American governments did not want to take any chances that Hitler might still get his hands on an atomic bomb. So they made destruction of the Vemork heavy water production facility a top priority, and the mission was assigned to SOE which formulated plans for destruction of the plant.

On October 18, 1942, four Linge men (code named Grouse) and their supplies parachuted into the Hardanger mountain plateau above Rjukan. They were the advance party for a sabotage action called Operation Freshman against the Vemork plant to be carried out by British commandos. It was an ill-advised plan because the area was covered with snow, the Brits could not ski, and they never would have made it to the plant. But the plan was not carried out because on November 19 the two gliders carrying the British commandos could not land due to low clouds, and then the gliders crashed near Stavanger on their way back to Britain. Most of the commandos were killed in the crashes, and the rest were captured and executed by the Germans, who recovered all of the plans for the attack. So the plan and the landing area near Rjukan had to be changed.

The Grouse commandos hid deep in the mountains over an extremely harsh winter, and SOE changed their code name to Swallow. On February 17, 1943, six more Linge men (now called Operation Gunnerside) parachuted into the mountains, and they joined up with Swallow on February 23. So now they were all Norwegian commandos who could ski and accomplish the mission. On February 27, 1943, nine of them skied down to Vemork, crossed an icy river and climbed a steep embankment, avoided the German guards, sneaked into the plant, placed explosive charges in the basement where the heavy water was produced and stored, and escaped without being detected by the Germans. There was a muffled explosion, and the heavy water production and storage facility was destroyed.

Later that same night the Germans discovered the damage. Falkenhorst inspected the scene and called it the greatest coup he had ever seen. Terboven wanted Falkenhorst to order reprisals against Norwegians in Rjukan, but the general refused because he thought that the damage was the work of British commandos and not Norwegians. In fact, the Linge men had left bits and pieces of British uniforms and other British items behind to fool the Germans and hopefully avoid any reprisals against Norwegians.

In the meantime, the Norwegian commandos vanished into thin air. Some of them skied all the way to safety in Sweden. A few of them stayed high in the Norwegian mountains where they could not be found.

The other commando, Claus Helberg, decided to take off on his own. He made it to Oslo, where he was hidden by the resistance. A few weeks later he heard that the coast was clear back on the Hardanger plateau, so he returned to the commandos' hideout near Rjukan to recover some equipment. After he reached the cabin he was suddenly ambushed by a German ski patrol. Helberg outskied all of the Germans except one who he shot in a gunfight in the mountains. Then he skied off a small cliff in the dark and broke his shoulder. He struggled into the next town, where he convinced the Germans that he was working for them. They took him to their doctor to treat his shoulder and then transported him to a hotel in Dalen. Helberg checked in, washed up, and went down to the dining room for dinner, extremely relieved to have escaped again.

But then Josef Terboven and his police chief Wilhelm Rediess walked into the dining room surrounded by German guards and sat down at a table close to Helberg! What terrible misfortune, after everything he had endured, to be sitting near the Nazi dictator of Norway. At that point, Terboven propositioned a pretty Norwegian woman, who not only rejected his advances but also informed the Nazi that her father was a colonel in the Norwegian army and that she was proud of it. Terboven got mad and ordered all of the Norwegians in the hotel to be sent to Grini concentration camp. Helberg soon found himself on a German prison bus headed to Grini. He knew he would be executed there. So near Drammen he jumped through the door of the bus, broke the same shoulder, was hit in the back by a German grenade that did not explode, and ran safely into the woods. This time he went to Sweden, and he survived the war and lived to a ripe old age.

Back at Vemork, the Germans managed to rebuild the plant and resume production of heavy water within just five months. On November 16, 1943, the US Air Force tried to bomb the heavy water facility. They missed the target, but other parts of the Vemork plant and several other factories were damaged and twenty-one Norwegians were killed. The Norwegian government-in-exile strongly protested this action.

The Germans also had enough and decided to move their heavy water production equipment and their inventory of heavy water from Vemork to Germany. On February 20, 1944, on the way to Oslo, all of the barrels of heavy water were sunk on a ferry that exploded in the deep water of Lake Tinn. This action, which unfortunately killed twenty-six Norwegian passengers on the ferry, was carried out by Norwegian saboteurs.

Thus ended the German production of heavy water in Norway. A German scientist later confirmed that the heavy water sabotage in Norway was the principal reason that the Germans could not build an atomic reactor before the end of the war. Unlike the Germans, the Americans were able to develop an atomic bomb in their Manhattan Project. The Americans subsequently dropped two atomic bombs on Japan in 1945 to end the war in the Pacific.

The Oslo Gang

By 1944 Milorg was successful in persuading the Norwegian government-in-exile to allow a resumption of sabotage and assassinations in Norway despite the continued possibility of severe German reprisals. As a result, with the cooperation of the Norwegian government and Milorg, the Oslo Gang of twelve Linge men led by Gunnar Sønsteby carried out repeated sabotage raids in and around Oslo in 1944 and 1945.

They bombed the Labor Office that was going to be used by the NS to call up Norwegians to join the German military. They also destroyed 25 Messerschmidt fighters and 150 airplane engines, weapons factories, several ships in Oslo harbor including the SS *Donau* that had transported Norwegian Jews to Germany, sulfuric acid factories, ball bearings, and oil storage facilities. They even commandeered a truckload of ration cards that the Nazis were withholding from Norwegians.

On February 8, 1945, acting on orders of the Norwegian government-in-exile, the Oslo Gang ambushed and killed Karl Marthinsen, the notorious Norwegian commander of the state police. Marthinsen was planning to organize armed NS resistance to the liberation of Norway if the Germans surrendered. In response to the assassination, Terboven had twenty-nine Norwegians executed, including four prominent Norwegians who were pulled from their homes.

Near the end of the war in March 1945, the Allies became concerned that the Germans would transfer thousands of their troops from Fortress Norway to fight in Germany and prolong the war. In order to prevent this from happening, on March 14, 1945, over a thousand Milorg and Linge men carried out Operation Cement Mixer by blowing up railroad lines in over a hundred places throughout Norway. As part of this operation, the Oslo Gang destroyed the railroad headquarters in Oslo. The entire operation was a huge success and an impressive show of force by the Norwegian resistance.

Scorched earth

By the fall of 1944, the Allies were clearly winning the war in Europe, as their forces approached Germany from east and west. Meanwhile, in October the Soviet Red Army came across the border and invaded northern Norway. A small Norwegian army unit was embedded in the Russian advance. The Germans were forced to retreat and give up Norwegian territory for the first time since 1940. In fact, they decided to withdraw all the way back to the more defensible Lyngen Line near Tromsø.

Terboven was worried that a Norwegian government might be established on the Norwegian territory liberated by the Russians. So he persuaded Hitler to order the German army to remove the Norwegian people from the area to be abandoned to the Russians, if possible. But as far as the German commander in northern Norway was concerned, an evacuation of Norwegians was not possible. He was busy with the battle against the Soviets and the survival of his army, and he did not have the time, the inclination, or the transportation to pick up a bunch of Norwegians.

Terboven sent his NS police chief Jonas Lie to Finnmark to oversee the evacuation of the Norwegians. Since the German army was uncooperative and no transport was available, he could do nothing more than encourage Norwegians to voluntarily leave the area on foot. The only Norwegians who volunteered to leave were NS members who wanted to get as far away from the Russians and certain death as possible. So the voluntary evacuation turned into a fiasco.

On October 26, 1944, Terboven arrived in northern Norway and promptly sent a telegram to Berlin demanding a forced evacuation. That did the trick, and on October 28, 1944, Hitler ordered that everything was to be destroyed and all Norwegians were to be evacuated by the retreating German army.

The message got through, and the German soldiers destroyed towns, buildings, bridges, roads, ports, boats, farms, crops, livestock, businesses, and factories as they retreated. For example, the towns of Hammerfest and Kirkenes were leveled to the ground in November. About fifty thousand Norwegians were forcibly evacuated and thrown out of their homes without notice. They were loaded onto ships with unsanitary conditions for transport south. It was utter chaos.

However, approximately twenty-five thousand Norwegians avoided evacuation, either because they were already behind Soviet lines or because they hid from the Germans. After the Germans left and the Soviet advance halted, thousands of Norwegians lived in a no man's land between the two armies. They lived in caves, huts, basements of burned-out homes, overturned boats, and tunnels, and they somehow survived the winter which fortunately was not too severe. Many fishermen sank their boats and buried or hid their equipment, which they retrieved after the Germans left.

Despite urgent requests by the Norwegian army units in Finnmark, the Norwegian and British governments did virtually nothing to rescue or assist the survivors. By the spring of 1945, the Norwegian army was able to provide some food, and fishing and other activities resumed in the burned-out areas.

White buses

Over the course of the war, about eight thousand Norwegian and Danish prisoners were sent to concentrations camps at Sachsenhausen, Ravensbrück, and other places in Germany, Poland, and France. The conditions were terrible, and many of the prisoners died. Niels Christian Ditleff was a former Norwegian diplomat who escaped to Sweden and worked diligently with the Swedish Foreign Ministry and the Swedish Red Cross to provide assistance to Norwegian prisoners in Europe. The Norwegian government-in-exile initially refused to support Ditleff or the Swedes in this effort because the Norwegian ministers still resented the fact that Sweden allowed Germany to transport soldiers, weapons, and equipment through its territory to the German occupiers in Norway for most of the war.

As the war was winding down in late 1944, it was the policy of the Allies that all prisoners in Germany should stay where they were until they were rescued by the Allied armies. However, Ditleff and others strongly disagreed with this policy. They were justifiably concerned that the Nazis would kill all the prisoners before surrendering at the end of the war. Therefore, on November 30, 1944, Ditleff proposed a plan to save the Norwegian prisoners. He wanted the Swedish Red Cross to contact and meet with the Germans and ask them to free the Norwegian prisoners or to deliver them to Sweden and Denmark where they would stay until the end of the war.

Count Folke Bernadotte, the vice president of the Swedish Red Cross and a member of the Swedish royal family, thought it was a great idea, and he also wanted to rescue all Danish prisoners. He worked with Ditleff and the Swedish government to carry out the plan.

At the time there were many leading Nazis who knew that the war was lost and were looking to make deals with the Allies to save their skins. One of them was Heinrich Himmler, the leader of the SS and the second most powerful person in Germany. Himmler wanted to go behind Hitler's back and negotiate a peace treaty between Germany and the Western Allies. The Swedes indirectly contacted Himmler through his masseur named Felix Kersten, who happened to live in Stockholm. As a result of those efforts, some Scandinavian prisoners were secretly released in December 1944, but the vast majority remained in several different concentration camps.

In February 1945 Bernadotte traveled to Berlin and met with Himmler and other Nazi leaders. He asked Himmler if the Norwegian and Danish prisoners could be transferred to Sweden, and Himmler said no. But at Bernadotte's request Himmler agreed that all the prisoners could be transported by the Swedish Red Cross to a single camp where they would be under the supervision of the Swedish Red Cross.

So that is what happened. In mid-March, thirty-six white buses from the Swedish Red Cross began to pick up Norwegian and Danish prisoners all over Germany and transport them to Neuengamme concentration camp near Hamburg. The Swedish government paid all the expenses. The buses were painted white with Swedish flags and Red Cross markings to hopefully avoid air and ground attacks by the military forces that were still at war.

Bernadotte kept pressing Himmler, and on April 9, 1945, Swedish and Danish white buses started transporting the Norwegian and Danish prisoners through Denmark to ferries that took them to safety in Sweden. All prisoners were evacuated from Neuengamme by April 21, 1945.

Prisoners who were near death just days before could not believe their eyes when their buses were greeted by cheering crowds of Danes who threw flowers at them. A total of 4,255 Norwegian and Danish prisoners were rescued by the white buses. They included several future leaders of Norway.

7.3 A white bus transports concentration camp prisoners through Denmark in 1945.

Liberation

By May 1945 Hitler was dead, the Russians were in Berlin, and the Allied forces had divided Germany in two at the Elbe River. The next step was a final German surrender to end the war in Europe. However, there were still 360,000 well-armed Germans who were in firm control of Fortress Norway, which had not been invaded by the Allies. Almost forty thousand Milorg men and women and thirteen thousand Norwegian police were standing by and ready to take over the country when it was liberated. But no one knew if the Germans in Norway would surrender peacefully or would stay and fight it out until the country was conquered by the Allies. By April 1945 the Norwegian resistance ended its sabotage operations so as not to provoke the Germans to make a last stand in Norway.

The uncertainty was resolved on May 7. On that date the Germans unconditionally surrendered all of their forces to the Allies in a meeting at US General Eisenhower's headquarters in France. Later that same day, Hitler's successor Admiral Dönitz ordered all Germans in Norway to surrender at midnight on May 9. He also fired Terboven and handed his duties to General Böhme, the German military commander in Norway. The Norwegian resistance had bravely done its job, but Norway was to be liberated because the Allies defeated Germany and won the war in Europe.

On the evening of May 7, Milorg leader Jens Christian Hauge negotiated with Böhme to arrange a peaceful transition. They agreed that Milorg and the Norwegian police could appear on the streets of Norway on May 8 to maintain order, and that uncensored newspapers could be published on that date. However, Böhme insisted on waiting until May 9 to surrender his forces to British officers who were due to arrive in Oslo on May 8. After negotiating with Hauge, Böhme announced on Oslo radio that he would comply with the order to surrender.

As May 8 dawned, it was clearly a new day in Norway. Church bells rang and people filled the streets to celebrate and sing "Ja, vi elsker". Milorg and the police also appeared in uniform on the streets to guard buildings, and the police began mass arrests of NS members.

Everyone was eagerly awaiting the arrival of the British military commission to accept the German surrender. So at 2:00 p.m., when a British air force general and other officers landed at Fornebu airport, they were greeted by jubilant crowds as their motorcade made its way to the Grand Hotel in downtown Oslo. Unfortunately, it was not the British military commission, but rather a group of British officers who took a joy ride from Copenhagen to Oslo to see what was going on. The Brits were promptly driven back to the airport and took off in their airplane.

The scene was replayed a couple of hours later when the official British military commission, consisting of British and Norwegian officers led by Brigadier Richard Hilton, stepped off their plane at Fornebu. They were cheered all the way downtown to the Hotel Bristol, where they arrived at 6:00 p.m. covered with flags, flowers, and confetti. After a brief meeting with the resistance, the commission traveled to German army headquarters in Lillehammer and signed the capitulation agreement with General Böhme. Command of all German forces in Norway was transferred to Hilton and the British at midnight. The Germans in Norway peacefully surrendered, the war was over, and Norway was liberated after more than five long, hard years of Nazi occupation.

Terboven and many Nazi and NS leaders killed themselves. Others changed uniforms and tried to hide. The notorious Gestapo chief Siegfried Fehmer changed into a Luftwaffe uniform, but Milorg tracked him down in late May by listening to a telephone conversation when Fehmer called his Norwegian mistress to check on his dog.

At 7:00 a.m. on May 9, Quisling and six other NS ministers arrived at Oslo police headquarters to be arrested. Two hours later, Norwegians listened to the first free Norwegian radio broadcast in five years. Norwegian political prisoners were freed, and the Germans were disarmed by the British.

Over the next month there were almost daily celebrations in Oslo and other cities. On May 13 Crown Prince Olav and some of the government ministers returned to a throng of people and a parade in Oslo, and King Haakon received the same welcome when he arrived in Oslo on June 7, five years to the day after he left Norway for exile in Britain and also the fortieth anniversary of Norwegian independence in 1905. During the celebrations, the Oslo Gang was responsible for protecting the royal family.

In trials held after the war, Quisling and twenty-four other Norwegian collaborators were condemned to death and executed, and twelve Germans were shot as war criminals. Over ninety thousand Norwegians were investigated, and approximately fifty-three thousand of them were convicted of treason, more than in any other European country. About twenty-three thousand Norwegians were sentenced to prison and others were fined, but all of the convicted Norwegians and their families were marked for life and faced decades of abuse and discrimination. Thousands were convicted just for being members of the NS without proof of other wrongdoing. Those convictions were arguably questionable under the Norwegian Constitution because they were based on a criminal law that was enacted by the government-in-exile after most of them became NS members. Furthermore, many other Norwegians were never prosecuted or punished even though they had cooperated with the Germans and profited from the occupation.

Unfortunately, tens of thousands of *tyskerjenter*, Norwegian women who had relations with Germans during the war, were treated very badly. Many were publicly humiliated, had their hair shaved, and suffered beatings, and some were imprisoned. Those who had married Germans were shipped off to Germany. Others were permanently treated as second class citizens in Norway, and even their children were considered outcasts.

The Norwegian government-in-exile resigned on June 12, 1945, and was replaced by a new coalition government led by Einar Gerhardsen, who had been the Labor Party mayor of Oslo before the war and a prisoner of the Nazis at Sachsenhausen and Grini. A Storting election in October gave the Labor Party a majority, and successive Labor Party governments ruled Norway for the next twenty years.

In World War II the Norwegian death toll exceeded 10,000, including approximately 4,000 sailors, 2,000 members of the armed forces, and 2,000 resistance fighters. There were also 1,340 Norwegians killed in concentration camps, of which more than half were Norwegian Jews. So the Norwegians definitely suffered from the Nazi invasion and occupation, although the number of deaths paled in comparison with the millions of Russians and Chinese who were killed in the war.

CHAPTER EIGHT:

To the Present Day

Norway had to be rebuilt after the Second World War, but turned into a very wealthy country with a high standard of living and a nation that is well respected around the world. This final chapter concentrates on the important themes of the Norwegian economy, immigration, the Sami, and foreign and defense policy from the end of the war to the present day.

Norway's economy

The top priority of the Norwegian government and people right after World War II was reconstruction of the country. New housing was built in the devastated areas of the Far North, and numerous houses and high rise apartments were constructed in the cities throughout the late 1940s and the 1950s.

Norway also wanted to rebuild its industry, which had been converted during the war to serve the German war machine, but little money was available for that purpose. However, on June 5, 1947, US Secretary of State George C. Marshall announced the Marshall Plan to provide billions of dollars to rebuild the European economy. Some members of Norway's governing Labor Party had reservations about accepting funds from a capitalist country and complying with certain Marshall Plan requirements. Nevertheless, Norway eventually participated in the Marshall Plan and received $425 million from the United States to rebuild and modernize its economy. Among other things, Norway used the funds to build hydroelectric plants, communications facilities, and various industries.

The Norwegian government imposed rationing and price and wage controls for several years after the war. For example, sugar and coffee were rationed until 1952, and cars were not generally available before 1960. Despite these and other restrictions on economic life, the Norwegian economy experienced strong and stable growth for many years after 1945.

The Labor government expanded the welfare state by providing benefits to all Norwegians and not just the poor. For the first time there were subsidies for families with children, disability benefits, pensions for everyone, and universal health insurance and a government-financed public health system. Many hospitals and nursing homes were built, more doctors were trained, and medical services were improved and made more accessible for everyone. A system of child care was introduced as more women entered the workforce. There were also expanded vacations and free education for all Norwegians. These benefits were financed by higher taxes and contributions from employers.

Most of the country's political leaders were strongly in favor of Norwegian membership in the European Community (EC), later called the European Union (EU). But a majority of Norwegian voters twice rejected such membership in referenda in 1972 and 1994 because of widespread concern over possible European control of the Norwegian economy, society, and resources, including oil and gas. While a majority of city dwellers voted in favor of EC or EU membership, a larger majority of farmers, fishermen, and others outside the cities were opposed. However, in 1994 Norway signed the European Economic Area Agreement with the EU, so Norway has free access to European markets while protecting its own oil, gas, agricultural and fishing industries. Norway's participation comes at a high price because Norway must pay huge sums of money to the EU each year to be used primarily for development of poorer EU member countries. In addition, as a non-member, Norway has no vote in the EU, but it is essentially required to adopt EU regulations. The net effect is that Norway participates in the EU, but not as a voting member.

Phillips Petroleum discovered oil in the Norwegian sector of the North Sea in 1969, and production of Norwegian oil began two years later. The national oil company called Statoil was founded in 1972 and received preferential treatment in developing the country's oil and gas resources. Over time, Statoil became an integrated oil and gas company with operations throughout the world. Oil and gas gave an enormous boost to the Norwegian economy and made Norway a very wealthy country. In fact, Norway became one of the five largest exporters of oil and gas in the world. While Norwegian oil production has been decreasing, the production of natural gas continues to increase.

In 1990 the Norwegian government established the State Petroleum Fund, now officially called the Government Pension Fund Global and more popularly known as the oil fund. The government's profits from oil and gas are deposited in the oil fund, where they are invested primarily in American and European stocks and bonds to build financial wealth for future generations in Norway. Currently there is approximately one trillion dollars in the oil fund, and each year the yield from the fund is returned to the government to finance the state budget. There is an ongoing debate among Norwegian politicians on the question of whether more money from the oil fund should be allocated to the annual government budget.

Norway and Russia signed the Barents Sea Treaty in 2010. This agreement settled their longstanding border dispute in the Barents Sea and the Arctic Ocean. The area is believed to contain rich deposits of oil and gas on the continental shelf, which can now be developed by the two countries. This development has been controversial, as environmental groups have objected and pointed out the potential danger to the ecosystem in the Far North. The treaty also provides for joint Norwegian and Russian regulation of fishing resources in the same region.

Immigration

In contrast to the hundreds of thousands of Norwegians who emigrated from Norway to America in the last half of the nineteenth century, over the past fifty years hundreds of thousands of people have immigrated to Norway from all over the world. The first and second generations of immigrants now make up about 14 percent of Norway's population. In Oslo, the figure is approximately 30 percent.

Norway had a very liberal immigration policy that allowed all kinds of people into the country in the 1950s and 1960s. The immigrants first came primarily from the United States, Britain, and other countries in Scandinavia. By the late 1960s immigration greatly increased as more and more people arrived from countries such as Morocco, Turkey, Yugoslavia, and especially Pakistan. Many of those immigrants were employed as drivers or as unskilled workers in hotels and restaurants.

The increased wave of immigration began to cause problems, particularly in the cities. There were housing issues, and exploitation of immigrant workers was a common occurrence. The discrimination against immigrants and their generally poor language skills and high crime rate threatened to create a permanent underclass of people. There was also a growing burden on the welfare system. As a result, the labor movement became opposed to unregulated immigration, and the government was persuaded to impose some restrictions over time. By 1975 the Storting suspended most immigration, but provided exceptions for family members and people with certain occupations.

The next wave of immigration began in the mid-1980s when refugees and asylum seekers from Vietnam, Latin America, Iran, Iraq, Sri Lanka, Africa, and Yugoslavia entered the country. These were people who were not safe in their own countries as a result of war, insurrection, or political persecution. In 1993 the Norwegian government came up with new restrictions to reduce the flow of people seeking asylum in Norway.

The elimination of most border controls under the Schengen Agreement in the 1990s and the subsequent eastward expansion of the EU resulted in a large increase in immigration from eastern European countries such as Poland and Lithuania.

In 2004 the Storting passed a law that provides for a mandatory introduction program for all immigrants on public assistance. For each immigrant there is a written plan that includes language training and assistance in finding employment. Despite this program and the generally favorable Norwegian economy, there is still a high unemployment rate among immigrants who do not come from western countries. Immigration continues to be a political issue, and Norway's Progress Party has made immigration reform part of its platform.

Norway also has its share of extremists who warn of a Muslim takeover of the country. On July 22, 2011, a Norwegian extremist named Anders Breivik set off a car bomb in Oslo that killed eight people, and then he massacred sixty-nine young people at a Labor Party summer camp on Utøya Island. He was convicted and sent to prison in August 2012. Norwegians were shocked by this incident, and many criticized the police for failing to respond promptly. In fact, the slow response also resulted in serious criticism of the government led by the Labor Party and played a major role in the defeat of that government in the 2013 election.

Sami rights

Hundreds of years of Norwegian discrimination against the Sami began to subside in the last twenty-five years of the twentieth century. The turning point came in the 1970s when the Norwegian government decided to build the Alta Dam Project, which involved construction of a hydroelectric power station and dam on the Alta River in Finnmark. The project flooded the river valley and destroyed Sami villages, reindeer grazing land, plant and animal life, and salmon fishing.

The Sami and their allies in the environmental movement strongly objected to the project. There were repeated demonstrations at the construction site and a hunger strike in front of the Storting building in Oslo, and many people were arrested. Opponents of the project started a lawsuit to stop the construction, but the Storting decided to proceed with the project, and in 1982 the Norwegian Supreme Court ruled in favor of the Storting. So the project was completed, although the prime minister and a government commission later admitted that the project was a mistake and was not needed.

The opposition to the Alta Dam Project significantly increased the public's awareness of the Sami and their rights as indigenous people, and this resulted in changes to the government's policy regarding the Sami. In 1987 the Storting passed the Sami Act that created a Sami Parliament called the *Sameting* elected by the Sami. The Sameting meets in Karasjok, advises the Storting on laws affecting the Sami, and makes decisions on Sami education, language, culture, and nutrition.

There was additional progress in the following year when the Norwegian Constitution was amended to recognize the Sami as indigenous people who are entitled to special protections and rights. The amendment made the government responsible to ensure that the Sami language, culture, and way of life are preserved and developed. Also in 1988, Sami children were given access to the Sami language in their schools. A new Sami school curriculum was implemented in 1997. Under a 1990 language law, the Sami language was given equal status with the Norwegian language in parts of northern Norway. Reindeer husbandry is now legally protected as an exclusive livelihood of the Sami. At the Sameting in 1997, King Harald apologized to the Sami people for the government's former Norwegianization policy. Finally, in 2005 the Finnmark Act was enacted to authorize the Sameting to elect half the members of the Finnmark Estate, which controls 95 percent of the land in Finnmark.

Since 1980, Sami culture, including literature and music, has flourished in Norway. The Sami language can be read or heard in Norwegian newspapers, radio and television broadcasts, and films. The Sami even have their own flag, which was created in 1986. It is based on a shaman's drum and an epic poem, and it features a red sun and a blue moon surrounded by colors of red, blue, green, and yellow, representing the Sami as sons and daughters of the sun.

Foreign and defense policy

Even though the Western Allies provided substantial support to Norway during and after World War II, and the Allies' victory in Europe led to the liberation of Norway in 1945, the postwar Norwegian government initially decided to avoid military alliances, return to neutrality, and concentrate on reconstruction of the country. Norway also saw itself as a bridge builder to facilitate and improve the relations between the Western Powers and the Soviet Union.

However, in the late 1940s the Norwegian government became increasingly concerned about Communist expansion in Europe at the beginning of the Cold War. The Labor Party mistrusted the Norwegian Communists, who were called supporters of terror and dictatorship by Prime Minister Einar Gerhardsen. The turning point for Norwegian foreign policy occurred in 1948, when the Communists engineered a coup and took over the government in Czechoslovakia and the Soviets blockaded Berlin. Having just experienced five years of Nazi occupation, the Norwegians feared that they could be occupied once again – this time by the Russians.

So Norway entered into discussions with Sweden and Denmark about a possible Nordic neutral defense alliance. Ultimately, both Norway and Denmark decided that neutral status and a Scandinavian alliance would not adequately protect them or give them access to American weapons and assistance. Therefore, despite Soviet objections, Norway abandoned its neutrality and joined the North Atlantic Treaty Organization (NATO) in 1949. This was the first peacetime defense alliance in Norwegian history.

However, in order to maintain some control over their own affairs and to avoid unduly antagonizing the Russians, the Norwegians placed some restrictions on their NATO membership. They did not permit any foreign bases or atomic weapons on Norwegian territory in peacetime, and they did not permit any NATO exercises in Finnmark – the province on the border with Russia. But Norway's enforcement of those restrictions was called into question in the U2 incident in May 1960. The Russians shot down a high altitude US spy plane that was flying over their territory on its route from Pakistan to Bodø, Norway. The Russians sent a protest note to Norway and questioned why Norway was allowing the Americans to use a Norwegian airport as a base for spy planes.

During the first few decades of the NATO alliance, northern Norway was a listening and radar post used by NATO to listen to and track Soviet communications and troop movements on the other side of the border. There were also NATO reconnaissance flights near the Soviet border, and Norwegian spies occasionally slipped across the border to spy on the Soviet military in northern Russia.

More recently, Norway has maintained a strong military and has been an active member of the alliance. The Norwegian air force participated in the NATO bombing of Serbia and NATO airstrikes in Libya, and Norway maintained ground forces in northern Afghanistan for many years. The Norwegian government tried to portray its military presence in Afghanistan as some kind of humanitarian mission for the purpose of education and rural development, but Norwegian journalists and authors disclosed that

Norwegian troops were also actively fighting the Taliban. In any event, Norway continues to be a close ally of the United States, and the two countries regularly share their military intelligence with each other. In 2014 Jens Stoltenberg, the former Norwegian prime minister and leader of the Labor Party, became NATO's secretary general.

Apart from the military alliance, Norway's foreign policy has emphasized humanitarian assistance to underdeveloped countries, promotion of human rights, and protection of the environment around the world. The Norwegians have strongly supported the United Nations and have participated in UN peacekeeping forces in Kashmir, Suez, Lebanon, and Congo, as well as NATO peacekeeping missions in Bosnia and Kosovo. Finally, Norway has served as a mediator in several foreign disputes in Palestine (including the 1993 Oslo Accords), Guatemala, Sri Lanka, and Colombia.

8.1 A Royal Norwegian Air Force F-16A over the Balkans in 1999

Norway began as a poor country divided into many kingdoms that were finally united, and subsequently survived the Black Death, centuries of foreign domination, and five years of wartime occupation to become a very wealthy country that is active and influential throughout the world.

BIBLIOGRAPHY

Abell, Arthur M. *Talks with Great Composers*. Germany: Schroeder, 1964.

Alnæs, Karsten. *Historien om Norge*. Oslo: Gyldendal, 1996-2000.

———. *Historien om Norge i bilder og fortellinger*. Oslo: Gyldendal, 2001.

Andenæs, Johs., Olav Riste, and Magne Skodvin. *Norway and the Second World War*. Norway: Tanum-Norli, 1966.

Andenæs, Tønnes, ed. *The Constitution of Norway*. Oslo: Oslo University Press, 1960.

Andersen, Per Sveaas. *Vikings of the West*. Oslo: Tanum, 1971.

Asbjørnsen, Peter Christen, and Jørgen Møe. *Norwegian Folk Tales*. Translated by Pat Shaw and Carl Norman. New York: Pantheon, 1982.

Askedal, John Ole, and Ann-Berit Aarnes Breder, eds. *Ivar Aasen – vandreren og veiviseren*. Oslo: Emilia, 2002.

Bagge, Sverre. *Cross & Scepter*. Princeton, NJ: Princeton, 2014.

———. *From Viking Stronghold to Christian Kingdom*. Copenhagen: Museum Tusculanum Press, 2010.

———, ed. *Statsutvikling i Skandinavia i Middelalderen*. Oslo: Dreyers, 2012.

———, and Knut Mykland. *Norge i dansketiden*. Copenhagen: Politikens, 1987.

Barton, H. Arnold. *Sweden and Visions of Norway*. Carbondale, IL: Southern Illinois University Press, 2003.

Bately, Janet, and Anton Englert, eds. *Ohthere's Voyages*. Roskilde: Viking Ship Museum, 2007.

Benedictow, Ole J. *The Black Death 1346-1353*. Rochester, NY: Boydell, 2004.

Benestad, Finn, and Dag Schjelderup-Ebbe. *Edvard Grieg: The Man and the Artist*. Translated by William H. Halverson and Leland B. Sateren. Lincoln, NE: University of Nebraska Press, 1988.

Berend, Nora, ed. *Christianization and the Rise of Christian Monarchy.* Cambridge: Cambridge University Press, 2007.

Berg, Paal, Frede Castberg, and Sverre Steen. *Arven fra Eidsvoll.* Oslo: Sverdrup Dahls, 1945.

Bergh, Sverre, and Svein Sæter. *Spion i Hitlers rike.* Norway: Damm, 2006.

Bergh, Trond. *Norsk historie 1860-1914.* Oslo: Det Norske Samlaget, 1999.

Bjørgo, Narvo, Øystein Rian, and Alf Kaartvedt. *Selvstendighet og union.* Oslo: Universitetsforlaget, 1995.

Bjørnskau, Erik. *Carl XIV Johan.* Oslo: Cappelen, 1999.

Bomann-Larsen, Tor. *Folket.* Oslo: Cappelen, 2004.

———. *Vintertronen.* Oslo: Cappelen Damm, 2008.

Brækstad, H.L. *The Constitution of the Kingdom of Norway.* London: David Nutt, 1905.

Brochmann, Grete, and Knut Kjeldstadli. *A History of Immigration.* Oslo: Universitetsforlaget, 2008.

Brøgger, A.W., and Haakon Shetelig. *The Viking Ships.* Translated by Katherine John. Oslo: Dreyer, 1951.

Byock, Jesse. *Viking Age Iceland.* London: Penguin, 2001.

Cavill, Paul. *Vikings: Fear and Faith.* Grand Rapids, MI: Zondervan, 2001.

Chartrand, R., K. Durham, M. Harrison, and I. Heath. *The Vikings: Voyagers of Discovery and Plunder.* Oxford: Osprey, 2006.

Clarke, E.D. *Travels in Various Countries, Vol. X.* London: Cadell, 1824.

Clements, Jonathan. *A Brief History of the Vikings.* Philadelphia: Running Press, 2005.

Collett, John, and Bård Frydenlund, eds. *Christianias handelspatrisiat.* Oslo: Andresen, 2008.

Crouch, David. *The Normans: The History of a Dynasty.* London: Hambledon, 2002.

Cunliffe, Barry. *Britain Begins.* Oxford: Oxford University Press, 2013.

Danielsen, Rolf, Ståle Dyrvik, Tore Gronlie, Knut Helle, and Edgar Hovland. *Norway: A History from the Vikings to Our Own Times.* Translated by Michael Drake. Oslo: Scandinavian University Press, 1995.

Derry, T.K. *Short History of Norway.* London: Allen, 1957.

DeVries, Kelly. *The Norwegian Invasion of England in 1066.* Rochester, NY: Boydell, 1999.

Dyrvik, Ståle. *Norsk historie 1625-1814.* Oslo: Det Norske Samlaget, 1999.

Eidum, Espen. *Blodsporet.* Harstad: Kristiansen, 2012.

Emberland, Terje, and Matthew Kott. *Himmlers Norge.* Oslo: Aschehoug, 2012.

Erlandsen, Hans Christian. *Kalde kyster ukjent land.* Bergen: Vigmostad, 2009.

Ersland, Geir Atle, and Hilde Sandvik. *Norsk historie 1300-1625.* Oslo: Det Norske Samlaget, 1999.

Etting, Vivian. *Queen Margrete I and the Founding of the Nordic Union.* Boston: Brill, 2004.

Feldbæk, Ole. *Danmark-Norge 1380-1814, Bind IV.* Oslo: Universitetsforlaget, 1998.

Ferguson, Robert. *The Vikings: A History.* New York: Penguin, 2009.

Fitzhugh, William W., and Elisabeth I. Ward, eds. *Vikings: The North Atlantic Saga.* Washington: Smithsonian, 2000.

Frydenlund, Bård. *Stormannen Peder Anker.* Oslo: Aschehoug, 2009.

Fure, Jorunn Sem, ed. *Studenter under hakekorset.* Oslo: Forum for Universitetshistorie, 2004.

Fure, Odd-Bjørn. *Mellomkrigstid.* Oslo: Universitetsforlaget, 1996.

Furre, Berge. *Norsk historie 1914-2000.* Oslo: Det Norske Samlaget, 1999.

Gade, John Allyne. *The Hanseatic Control of Norwegian Commerce.* Leiden: Brill, 1951.

Gallagher, Thomas. *Assault in Norway.* New York: Harcourt, 1975.

Gaski, Harald, ed. *Sami Culture in a New Era.* Norway: Davvi Girji, 1997.

Gathorne-Hardy, G.M. *A Royal Impostor: King Sverre of Norway.* London: Oxford University Press, 1956.

Gervin, Karl. *Det store bruddet: Reformasjonen i Norge.* Norway: Andresen, 1999.

Gjelsvik, Tore. *Norwegian Resistance 1940-1945.* Translated by Thomas Kingston Derry. Montreal: McGill, 1979.

Gran, Gunnar. *Til kjølen skilte oss ad.* Kristiansand: I.J., 2005.

Gravett, Christopher, and David Nicolle. *The Normans.* New York: Osprey, 2006.

Grimley, Daniel M. *Grieg: Music, Landscape and Norwegian Identity.* Woodbridge, UK: Boydell, 2006.

Hammer, Anders Sømme. *Drømmekrigen.* Oslo: Aschehoug, 2011.

Haugland, Knut, and Svein Sæter. *Operatøren.* Oslo: Cappelen Damm, 2009.

Heidar, Knut. *Norway: Elites on Trial.* Boulder, CO: Westview, 2001.

Helland, Amund. *Nordlands Amt, Vol. 18.* Kristiania: Aschehoug, 1908.

Helle, Knut. *The Cambridge History of Scandinavia, Vol. 1.* Cambridge: Cambridge University Press, 2003.

———. *Norge blir en stat.* Kristiansand: Universitetsforlaget, 1964.

Hjardar, Kim, and Vegard Vike. *Vikinger i krig.* Oslo: Spartacus, 2012.

Høidal, Oddvar. *Trotsky in Norway.* DeKalb, IL: NIU Press, 2013.

Holmsen, Andreas. *Norges historie fra de eldste tider til 1660.* Oslo: Universitetsforlaget, 1977.

Hovland, Torkel. *General Carl Gustav Fleischer.* Oslo: Forum-Aschehoug, 2000.

Howarth, David. *1066 The Year of the Conquest.* London: Collins, 1977.

———. *The Shetland Bus.* Guilford, CT: Lyons, 1951.

Hudson, Benjamin. *Viking Pirates and Christian Princes.* New York: Oxford University Press, 2005.

Huntford, Roland. *The Amundsen Photographs.* New York: Atlantic Monthly, 1987.

———. *Fridtjof Nansen.* Translated by Jan Christensen. Oslo: Aschehoug, 2003.

Hustvedt, I.D. "Nogle Erindringer om Lars Nelsen Nesheim." *Vossingen,* April 1924.

Ibsen, Bergliot. *The Three Ibsens.* Translated by Gerik Schjelderup. London: Hutchinson, 1951.

Ingstad, Benedicte. *Oppdagelsen.* Oslo: Gyldendal, 2010.

Jacobsen, Alf R. *Blücher.* Oslo: Vega, 2010.

———. *Scharnhorst.* Oslo: Aschehoug, 2003.

———. *Til siste slutt.* Oslo: Aschehoug, 2004.

Jaklin, Asbjørn. *Historien om Nord Norge.* Oslo: Gyldendal, 2004.

———. *Isfront.* Oslo: Gyldendal, 2009.

Jones, Gwyn. *A History of the Vikings.* Oxford: Oxford University Press, 1984.

Kent, Neil. *The Sámi Peoples of the North.* London: Hurst, 2014.

Kersaudy, Francois. *Norway 1940.* London: Collins, 1990.

Kittelsen, Th. *Svartedauen.* Kristiania: Stenersen, 1900.

Koht, Halvdan. *Norway: Neutral and Invaded.* New York: Macmillan, 1941.

Krag, Claus. *Norges historie fram til 1319.* Oslo: Universitetsforlaget, 2000.

Kurzman, Dan. *Blood and Water: Sabotaging Hitlers Bomb.* New York: Holt, 1997.

Kvandal, Lilleba Lund. *Norske folkeviser gjennom tusen år.* Oslo: Cappelen, 2000.

Laing, Samuel. *Journal of a Residence in Norway.* London: Longman, 1836.

———. *A Tour in Sweden in 1838.* London: Longman, 1839.

Larsen, Karen. *A History of Norway.* Princeton, NJ: Princeton, 1948.

Larson, James L. *Reforming the North.* New York: Cambridge University Press, 2010.

Lehtola, Vel-Pekka. *The Sami People.* Fairbanks: University of Alaska Press, 2004.

Libæk, Ivar, and Øivind Stenersen. *History of Norway from the Ice Age to the Oil Age.* Translated by Joan Fuglesang and Virginia Siger. Oslo: Grøndahl Dreyer, 1992.

Lorenz, Einhart. *Samefolket i historien.* Oslo: Pax, 1981.

Lovoll, Odd S. *The Promise of America.* Minneapolis: University of Minnesota Press, 1999.

Luihn, Hans. *Den frie hemmelige pressen.* Oslo: Nasjonalbiblioteket Oslo, 1999.

Lunde, Henrik O. *Hitler's Preemptive War.* Philadelphia: Casemate, 2009.

Magnusson, Magnus, and Hermann Pálsson, eds. *King Harald's Saga.* Baltimore: Penguin, 1966.

———, eds. *The Vinland Sagas.* New York: Penguin, 1965.

Mann, Chris, and Christer Jörgenson. *Hitler's Arctic War.* New York: St. Martin's, 2002.

Manus, Max. *9 Lives Before Thirty.* Garden City, NJ: Doubleday, 1947.

Midgaard, John. *A Brief History of Norway.* Oslo: Tano, 1986.

Mørkhagen, Sverre. *Kristins verden.* Oslo: Cappelen, 1995.

Morris, Marc. *The Norman Conquest.* New York: Pegasus, 2012.

Mykland, Knut, ed. *Omkring 1814.* Oslo: Gyldendal, 1967.

Nansen, Odd. *From day to day.* Translated by Katherine John. New York: Putnam, 1949.

Nerbøvik, Jostein. *Norsk historie 1860-1914.* Oslo: Det Norske Samlaget, 1999.

Nissen, Bernt. *1905.* Oslo: Olaf Norlis, 1930.

———. *1814.* Oslo: Sverdrup Dahls, 1945.

Njølstad, Olav. *Jens Chr. Hauge.* Oslo: Aschehoug, 2008.

Nordstrom, Byron J. *Scandinavia Since 1500.* Minneapolis: University of Minnesota Press, 2000.

Ødegaard, Sverre, and Jiri Havran. *Bergstaden Røros.* Oslo: ARCO, 1997.

O'Leary, Margaret Hayford. *Culture and Customs of Norway.* Santa Barbara, CA: Greenwood, 2010.

Oliver, Neil. *The Vikings.* New York: Pegasus, 2013.

Ottosen, Kristian. *I slik en natt.* Oslo: Aschehoug, 1994.

———. *Redningen.* Oslo: Aschehoug, 1998.

Page, R.I. *Norse Myths.* Austin: University of Texas Press, 1990.

Paulson, Trond S. *Iskald krig.* Oslo: Aschehoug, 2008.

Petrow, Richard. *The Bitter Years.* New York: Morrow, 1974.

Pharo, Helge Ø., and Patrick Salmon, eds. *Britain and Norway.* Oslo: Akademika, 2012.

Pryser, Tore. *Norsk historie 1814-1860.* Oslo: Det Norske Samlaget, 1999.

Ravnåsen, Sigbjørn. *Ånd og hånd.* Oslo: Luther, 2002.

Riesto, Harald. *Den lille byen og krigen: Vadsø 1940-1945.* Norway: Orkana, 2000.

Riste, Olav. *Norway's Foreign Relations – A History.* Oslo: Universitetsforlaget, 2001.

———, and Berit Nökleby. *Norway 1940-1945: The Resistance Movement.* Oslo: Tanum, 1970.

Roesdahl, Else. *The Vikings.* Translated by Susan M. Margeson and Kirsten Williams. London: Penguin, 1998.

Rørosboka. Røros: Globus, 1942.

Rusten, Grete, Kerstin Potthoff, and Linda Sangolt, eds. *Norway: Nature, Industry and Society.* Bergen: Fagbokforlaget, 2013.

Sawyer, Birgit, and Peter Sawyer. *Medieval Scandinavia.* Minneapolis: University of Minnesota Press, 1993.

Sawyer, Peter, ed. *The Oxford Illustrated History of the Vikings.* New York: Oxford University Press, 1997.

Schreiner, Johan. *Olav den hellige og Norges samling.* Oslo: Steenske, 1929.

Sebag-Montefiore, Hugh. *Enigma: The Battle for the Code.* London: Wiley, 2000.

Sejerstad, Francis. *The Age of Social Democracy.* Princeton, NJ: Princeton, 2011.

Semmingsen, Ingrid. *Norway to America.* Translated by Einar Haugen. Minneapolis: University of Minnesota Press, 1978.

Sigurdsson, Jon Vidar. *Norsk historie 800-1300.* Oslo: Det Norske Samlaget, 1999.

Skartveit, Andreas, ed. *Vi valgte det vi ikke kjente.* Oslo: Forum, 1995.

Skeie, Tore. *Jomfruen fra Norge.* Oslo: Spartacus, 2012.

Skre, Dagfinn, and Frans-Arne Stylegar. *Kaupang: The Viking Town.* Oslo: University of Oslo, 2004.

Solberg, Bergljot. *Jernalderen i Norge.* Oslo: Cappelen Akademisk, 2000.

Sønsteby, Gunnar. *Report from No. 24.* Translated by Maurice Michael. Fort Lee, NJ: Barricade, 1999.

Stenersen, Øivind, and Ivar Libæk. *The History of Norway from the Ice Age until Today.* Translated by James Anderson and Marthe Burgess. Norway: Dinamo, 2007.

Sturluson, Snorri. *Heimskringla.* Austin: University of Texas Press, 1967.

Sverres saga. Translated by Anne Holtsmark. Oslo: Aschehoug, 1986.

Tamelander, Michael, and Niklas Zetterling. *Niende april.* Translated by Bertil Knudsen. Oslo: Spartacus, 2001.

Terjesen, Bjørn. *Vi skiltes i fred.* Oslo: Universitetsforlaget, 2001.

Tharaldsen, Knut. *Den norsk-russiske grensen.* Oslo: Kolofon, 2010.

Thompson, John M., ed. *The Medieval World: An Illustrated Atlas.* Washington: National Geographic, 2009.

Ulateig, Egil. *Den lange reisen hjem.* Oslo: Vega, 2011.

Ustvedt, Yngvar. *Svartedauen.* Oslo: Gyldendal, 1985.

Vetlesen, Vesla. *Kommunist og sabotør.* Oslo: Aschehoug, 2008.

Wasberg, Gunnar Christie. *Historien om 1814.* Oslo: Dreyers, 1964.

Westlie, Bjørn. *Fars krig.* Oslo: Aschehoug, 2009.

Whitelock, Dorothy, ed. *The Anglo-Saxon Chronicle.* Westport, CT: Greenwood, 1961.

Wisting, Alexander. *Hjalmar Johansen: Seierens pris.* Oslo: Kagge, 2012.

Yttrehus, Ståle. *Fred og fare.* Norway: Font, 2013.

LIST OF ILLUSTRATIONS

Front cover: Old town of Røros, *Etter snestorm, Lillegaten Røros* by Harald Sohlberg (1903)

1.1 Reindeer rock art in Alta, *Helleristninger i Alta*, photo by Ahnjo (2012), Creative Commons Attribution – ShareAlike 3.0 Unported license at: creativecommons.org/licenses/by-sa/3.0/legalcode

1.2 Reconstructed long house in the Vikingmuseum in Borg, Vestvågøy/Lofoten, Norway, photo by Jörg Hempel (2008), Creative Commons Attribution – ShareAlike 2.0 Germany license at: creativecommons.org/licenses/by-sa/2.0/de/legalcode

2.1 Viking helmet, *Hjelm av jern fra vikingtid fra Gjermundbu, Ringerike, Buskerud*, photo by NTNU Vitenskapsmuseet (2010), Creative Commons Attribution 2.0 Generic license at: creativecommons.org/licenses/by/2.0/legalcode

2.2 *Oseberg* Viking ship, *Osebergskipet, Vikingskipmuseet, Oslo*, photo by Karamell (2005), Creative Commons Attribution – ShareAlike 2.5 Generic license at: creativecommons.org/licenses/by-sa/2.5/legalcode

2.3 Statue of Rollo the Viking, photo by SinSpinadas (2008)

3.1 Hopperstad stave church, photo by Jean-Louis Malpertu (2006)

3.2 Birchlegs and the prince, *Birkebeinerne* by Knud Bergslien (1869)

4.1 Drawing of the Black Death, *Mor, der kommer en kjærring* by Theodor Kittelsen (1900)

4.2 A small farm and a fishing boat on a fjord in the mountains of western Norway, *Munken gård i Esefjorden* by Adelsteen Normann

5.1 Prayer meeting of friends society established by Hans Nielsen Hauge, *Haugianerne* by Adolph Tidemand (1848)

5.2 Portrait of Christian Frederik by J.L. Lund (1813)

5.3 Eidsvoll assembly in 1814, *Riksforsamlingen på Eidsvoll 1814* by Oscar Wergeland (1885)

6.1 A husmann's cottage from Skarderud, Ringsaker, photo by Mahlum (2006)

6.2 A Sami family in Vesterålen in the 1890s

7.1 The *Blücher* sinks into the Oslofjord on April 9, 1940.

7.2 Shetland Bus fishing boat *Heland*, photo by Andrva (2010), Creative Commons Attribution – ShareAlike 3.0 Unported license at: creativecommons.org/licenses/by-sa/3.0/legalcode

7.3 A white bus transports concentration camp prisoners through Denmark in 1945.

8.1 Norwegian F-16A over the Balkans in 1999

Back cover: Map of Norway by Peter Fitzgerald, Creative Commons Attribution – ShareAlike 3.0 Unported license at: creativecommons.org/licenses/by-sa/3.0/legalcode

INDEX

Aasen, Ivar, 157-58
absolute monarchy, 99, 112-14, 131-32, 137
Act of Union, 146, 182
Administrative Council, 215-16
Age of Greatness, 74-78
Age of Migration, 13-14
Alfred the Great, 25, 31, 34
alodial inheritance, 11
Alta, 8-9, 246
Altmark Affair, 199
amtmenn, 99
Amundsen, Roald, 171, 175-76
Anker, Bernt, 115
Anker, Peder, 115-16, 119, 124, 131, 136, 145
art, 83-84, 154, 156
Asbjørnsen, Peter Christen, 156-57
Aud the Deep Minded, 39
August War – see War of the Cats
Austvågøy, 226

Baglers, 72-73
Barents Sea Treaty, 244
Battle of Fimreite, 71
Battle of Hafrsfjord, 47
Battle of Kalvskinnet, 69
Battle of Kringen, 97
Battle of Stamford Bridge, 61-63
Battle of Stiklestad, 56, 58
Bergen, 65, 70, 77-78, 80-81, 85-88, 90, 103, 108-9, 143-44, 154, 156, 161, 202-3, 205
Birkebeinere (Birchlegs), 68-73
Bjarne Herjolfsson, 41
Black Death, 80-84, 96, 103-4
Blücher, 206-7, 214
blue men, 23
Bodø Affair, 148-50, 176

bonde, 10-11
Borg, 15-16
Boström, Erik, 179-80
Bräuer, Curt, 208, 210, 214-15
Breivik, Anders, 245
Bull, Ole, 155

Charlemagne, 21, 27
chieftains, 11-12, 15-16, 27, 33-35, 39, 46-48, 51, 55-56, 59, 75
Christian 2, 93
Christian 3, 93-96
Christian 4, 96-99
Christian 7, 112-13
Christian August, 118, 121
Christian Frederik, 125, 129-37, 139-43, 148
Christian of Oldenburg, 91
Christiania – see Oslo
Christie, W.F.K., 136, 144-45
church, 54-55, 66-67, 71-74, 76-78, 80, 82, 89, 91-96, 102-3, 106, 109-11, 138-39, 163, 166, 219
Churchill, Winston, 196-97, 200, 212, 223, 227
civil wars, 63-73
Communists, 188-89, 221, 225, 228, 247
concentration camps, 217, 226, 234-36, 240
Concession Laws, 184-5
constitution, 132-51, 167-70, 180, 216, 239, 246
Continental System, 116-17, 121
Council of Commissioner Ministers, 216
Council of State, 74, 89-96, 216

Danelaw, 25
Ditleff, Niels Christian, 234-35
Doggerland, 4, 5
Dönitz, Karl, 197, 227, 237

Eidsvoll assembly, 134-38, 143
Eidsvoll meetings, 131-32
Eirik Bloodaxe, 48-49
Eirik Ivarsson, 72
Eirik the Red, 39-42
Elverum Mandate, 210, 216, 221
emigration from Norway to America,
162-66
Erik of Pomerania, 90-91
Erling Skakke, 66-67, 69, 72, 74
European Economic Area Agreement,
243
European Union (EU), 243, 245

Falkenhorst, Nikolaus von, 199-201,
214-15, 217, 230
Falsen, Christian Magnus, 135-36
farming, 5-6, 10-11, 29, 32, 76, 81,
102, 104-5, 117, 120, 158-61, 164-66,
243
Finnmark Act, 247
fishing, 77, 85, 87-88, 104-5, 120,
146, 161, 243-44
flags, 184, 247
Fleischer, Carl Gustav, 206
folk tales, 156-57
foreign and consular affairs, 132, 137,
145-46, 148-50, 170, 176-82, 184,
222, 247-49
Fortress Norway, 227, 232, 237
Fox River Valley, Illinois, 164
Frederik 1, 92-94
Frederik 6, 113, 117-19, 123-31, 140,
147

Gerhardsen, Einar, 239, 247
gold, 221-22
government commission, 118-19
government-in-exile, 221-23, 239

governor, 96, 99, 130, 133, 145, 150-
51, 167
Greenland, 39-42, 51, 74, 128-29,
172-73
Grieg, Edvard, 154-56
Guri, 97
Gustav, Crown Prince, 180
Gustav Adolf, King, 120-21, 123

Haakon 7, 182-83, 188, 204, 210-14,
216, 221-23, 239
Håkon Håkonsson, 73-74
Håkon the Good, 48-49
Hanseatic merchants, 77, 84-87, 89,
92
Harald 5, 91, 247
Harald Fairhair, 31, 35-36, 39, 46-49
Harald Gilchrist, 64-67
Harald Hardråde, 57-63
Harold Godwinson, 60-63
Hasting, 23-24
Hauge, Hans Nielsen, 109-11
Hauge, Jens Christian, 225, 237
heavy water sabotage, 228-32
Helberg, Claus, 230-31
Hitler, Adolf, 193, 195-201, 209-10,
215, 221, 226-27, 229, 233, 237
hoards, 28-29
Horten, 204-5
husmenn, 104, 110, 138, 159, 161,
165

Ibsen, Henrik, 154, 156, 176
Ibsen, Sigurd, 176, 178-79
Ice Age, 4-5
Iceland, 16, 38-41, 48, 51, 74, 128-29
immigration to Norway, 244-45
independence in 1905, 151, 176-83
Ingolf Arnarson, 38-39
Ingstad, Helge and Anne Stine, 42
Integrity Treaty, 184
invasion of Norway in 1945, 199-211
Irgens, Joachim, 100-2

jarls of Lade, 46, 49-53, 55-56
Jews, 138-39, 220, 232, 240
Jordanes, 11

Kalmar Union, 90
Karl, King, 121-22, 128, 144-45, 148
Karl Johan, 122-25, 127-30, 139-51, 167
Karlstad Convention, 182
Kaupang (Skiringssal), 33-35
Kellogg-Briand Pact, 192-94
Kittelsen, Theodor, 82-83, 157
knarr, 31
Knut the Great, 25, 55-58
Koht, Halvdan, 189, 195-96, 201-2, 208
Kompani Linge, 223-33
Kristiania – see Oslo
Kvalsund ship, 14

Laake, Kristian, 203-4, 208, 211
Labor Party, 187-89, 192-94, 218, 239, 242, 245, 247
lagmenn, 71, 74
lagting, 48, 63-64
L'Anse aux Meadows, 42-43
League of Nations, 192-94
leidang, 48-49, 51, 76
Leiv Eiriksson, 41-43
lendmenn, 53-54, 59, 70-71, 74-75
lensmenn, 74-75, 99
liberation in 1945, 237-39
licensed trade, 119-20
Lie, Trygve, 222
Lindisfarne, 18-19
literature, 96, 154, 156-57
Ljungberg, Birger, 203-4
Lofthuus, Christian Jensen, 109
longhouse, 14-16
longports, 20-21
longship, 31
lumber, 84, 104, 115-17, 119, 146
Luna, Italy, 23-24
Lunge, Vincens, 93-94

Magnus Erlingsson, 67-72
Magnus Olavsson, 57-60
Magnus the Blind, 65-66
Magnus the Lawmender, 74
map of Norway, back cover
Margrete, Queen, 88-91
Marshall Plan, 242
Marthinsen, Karl, 232
Michelsen, Christian, 180-81
Midtskogen, 210
military, 48-49, 96, 98, 101, 104, 141-42, 145, 178, 192-94, 196, 223-26, 248-49
Milk Strike, 218
Milorg, 225, 228, 232, 237-38
Moe, Jørgen, 156-57
Moors, 22-24, 27, 29, 31
Mörner, Carl Otto, 122
Moss Convention, 142-44

Nadd-Odd, 38
Nansen, Fridtjof, 171-75
Napoleonic Wars, 114-46
Narvik, 195-203, 206, 212-13
Nasjonal Samling (NS), 197-98, 202-3, 206, 216-21, 225, 232-33, 237-39
NATO, 248-49
Nesheim, Lars Nilsson, 160
Nidaros – see Trondheim
Normandy, 35-38, 53
North America, 41-43
North Pole, 173-75
Norwegian language, 6, 96-97, 101, 108, 146, 156-58, 247
nybrottsmenn, 160

oil and gas, 243-44
Olav, Crown Prince (later King), 183, 210-13, 238
Olav Engelbrektsson, 92-95
Olav Haraldsson (St. Olav), 52-56, 59, 61, 95
Olav Kyrre (the Peacemaker), 63, 77
Olav Nilsson, 86

Olav the White, 20-21, 39
Olav Tryggvason, 49-54, 59
Old Norse, 12, 37, 157
Olsen, Ole, 161
Operation Cement Mixer, 232-33
Oscar 2, 167-70, 177-83
Oseberg ship, 31-32
Oslo (Christiania), 59, 78, 80, 84, 88, 96, 103, 115-16, 131, 150, 154, 162, 167, 173, 201-3, 207, 209, 245-6
Oslo Gang, 232-33, 239
Ottar, 34-35
Øverland, Arnulf, 193

parliamentary democracy, 167-70, 177
Pathfinder, The, 75-76
Pesta, 82-83
Pol III, 203
polar explorers, 171-76
Portland, 18
Proto-Norse, 10-12
Pytheas, 7

Querini, Pietro, 87-88
Quisling, Vidkun, 197-98, 200-1, 209-10, 214, 216-22, 238-39

Raeder, Erich, 197-98, 227
Ragnar Lodbrok, 22
Reformation, 91-96, 118
resistance in World War II, 214, 218, 220-21, 223-33, 237-38
Restauration, 163
Rjukan, 229-31
rock art, 5, 8-9
Rollo, 35-38
Roosevelt, Franklin Delano, 195, 211
Røros, front cover, 99-103
Rosenberg, Alfred, 198, 217
Ruge, Otto, 193, 211, 214
runes, 12

St. Olav – see Olav Haraldsson
Sameting, 246-47
Sami, 5, 7-9, 35, 75-76, 105-6, 161, 170-72, 246-47
Schengen Agreement, 245
scorched earth, 233-34
Scott, Robert Falcon, 175-76
Secret Intelligence Service (SIS), 225
Shetland Bus, 224, 227-28
ships and shipping, 14, 16, 29-32, 47-49, 70-71, 84, 105, 108, 115-17, 119, 161, 173, 176, 186-87, 221-22
Sigurd Slembe, 65-66
Sigurd the Crusader, 64-65, 67
Skiringssal – see Kaupang
Slaalien, Gjendine, 156
Smith-Johannsen, Admiral, 204-5
Sønsteby, Gunnar, 209, 232-33
sorenskrivere, 99
South Pole, 175-76
Special Operations Executive (SOE), 223, 228-29
Spell-Ola, 101-2
Spitzbergen – see Svalbard
Steinvikholm, 92
Stone Age, 4-6
Stril War, 108-9
Struensee, Johann, 112-13
Supreme Court, 138, 169, 215-17, 246
Svalbard (Spitzbergen), 174, 187
Svein Forkbeard, 49-53
Sverdrup, Georg, 132, 137
Sverdrup, Johan, 167-70
Sverre Sigurdsson, 66-74
Swedish wars, 97-99, 141-42
sysselmenn, 71, 74
syttende mai, 137, 150-51, 165

Tacitus, Cornelius, 8
Telavåg, 227-28
Terboven, Josef, 215-21, 226, 228, 230-33, 237-38
Thrane, Marcus, 162

ting, 12, 39, 48, 63-64, 74
Tostig, 60-62
Treaty of Kiel, 128-32, 139, 141, 147
Treaty of Versailles, 192
trials after World War II, 239
Trondheim (Nidaros), 46, 51, 56, 69-70, 72, 78, 94-95, 98, 100, 102-3, 125, 127, 147, 150, 197, 203, 205, 211
Turgeis, 20
tyskerjenter, 239

U2 incident, 248
United Nations (UN), 192, 222, 249
University of Oslo, 113, 120, 218-19
Utøya, 245-46

Varangian Guard, 25-26, 58
Vikings, 12, 16-43, 46, 48, 50, 52, 58, 60-63, 77

War of the Cats (August War), 141-42
Wedel Jarlsberg, Count Herman, 119-20, 124, 129, 135-36, 138, 143-45, 151
welfare state, 189, 242
Weserübung, 199-211
Westen, Thomas von, 106
white buses, 234-36
William the Conqueror, 38, 60-63
Winter War, 196-97, 200-1
World War I, 184-87
World War II, 194-238, 240

XU, 225, 229

Yngling family, 13, 20, 31, 33-34, 46, 49

Printed in Great Britain
by Amazon

10957503R00155